GW01018187

# AS and A2 Psychology

# Revision Guide

# for the

# Edexcel Specification

Faye Carlisle

Text Copyright @ 2014 Faye C Carlisle

All Right Reserved

## Introduction

### About this guide

This revision guide covers Units 1,2,3 and 4. It includes descriptions of key studies, theories, treatments, example practicals and research methods. It also uses a clear system of evaluation throughout, which makes it easier to evaluate in the exam.

### Edexcel Examination Structure

Unit 1 examines your knowledge of two approaches: the Cognitive Approach and the Social Approach. Unit 1 is worth 40% of the marks at AS (20% of the whole A-level) and is assessed in an 80 minute exam.

Note: The unit 1 exam has 60 marks available so you have 1 minute 20 seconds for each mark. Therefore, you should spend 16 minutes on the 12 mark essay. Make sure you leave enough time to do the essays. The essays are marked with an asterisk and this means that your essay will be marked on spelling, grammar and structure as well as content.

Unit 2 examines your knowledge of three approaches: the Biological Approach, the Learning Approach and the Psychodynamic Approach. Unit 2 is worth 60% of the marks at AS (30% of the whole A-level) and is assessed in a 100 minute exam.

Note: The Unit 2 exam has 80 marks available so you have 1 minute 15 seconds for each mark. Therefore, you should spend 15 minutes on the 12 mark essay.

Unit 3 examines your knowledge of two applications of psychology. This revision guide looks at the most popular applications at A2: Criminological Psychology and Child Psychology. Unit 3 is worth 40% of the marks at A2 (20% of the whole A-level) and is assessed in a 90 minute exam.

Note: The unit 3 exam has 60 marks available so you have 1 minute and a half for each mark. Therefore, you should spend 18 minutes on the 12 mark essays. Make sure you leave enough time to do the essays. The essays are marked with an asterisk and this means that your essay will be marked on spelling, grammar and structure as well as content.

Unit 4 examines your knowledge of Clinical Psychology and Issues and Debates. The Clinical Psychology chapter looks at the mental disorders: Schizophrenia and anorexia nervosa. Unit 4 is worth 60% of the marks at A2 (30% of the whole A-level) and is assessed in a 2 hour exam.

Note: The Unit 4 exam has 90 marks available so you have 1 minute and a third for each mark. Therefore, you should spend 24 minutes on an 18 mark essay.

## Exam Tips

Describe means explain the characteristics of something. When describing a study, remember to give the aim, procedure, results and conclusion unless the question specifies that you only describe the procedure or findings.

Describe the methodology of a study means that you should only describe the aim and procedure of the study.

Outline means explain the characteristics of something briefly.

Evaluate means that you have to discuss the strengths and weaknesses of something.

Assess means evaluate.

Discuss means describe and evaluate.

Discuss research means describe the findings of studies and evaluate the studies. Compare means that you have to discuss similarities and differences. For example, you might be asked to compare two explanations. Make sure you don't just describe each explanation in turn. Start your sentences with 'They are similar because....', 'They both say....' or 'X says ..... whereas Y says....' to ensure you are making comparisons.

## Revision strategies

Do at least 5 past exam papers for each unit. Look at the mark schemes and examiners reports to see what the examiner wants.

Focus on what you find difficult to understand and get to grips with it.

Revise in 25 minutes chunks, with 5 minute breaks in the middle to keep your mind alert.

Do not just read this revision guide. Active revision is more effective: Make notes, draw mind maps, record audio clips and write revision cards.

Remember to revise methodology i.e. research methods, types of design, levels of data, inferential tests and any practicals you carried out. 30% of the Unit 1, 2 and 3 papers is methodology. 23% of the Unit 4 paper is methodology.

# Chapter 1-The Cognitive Approach

## You need to be able to describe what the cognitive approach is about

The cognitive approach studies how we process information. One of the assumptions of the cognitive approach is that the human mind can be seen as a system for handling information. Information from the environment is interpreted to make sense of it. Thinking, perceiving, using language and memorising are all ways of processing information.

The computer analogy- Psychologists use a computer metaphor to describe how the brain processes information. Like a computer, the mind has an input in the form of senses, a store in the form of memory and an output in the form of behaviour. Cognitive processes are like computer software.

## You need to be able to describe the following key terms

**Information processing** occurs when information is taken in by the senses (input) and processed by the brain. Once the brain has processed the information, there is an output in some form.

**Cognition** refers to the mental processes needed to make sense of the world such as perception, attention, language, thinking, problem solving and memory.

**Memory** is the encoding, storage and retrieval of information. Encoding refers to taking in information either in a visual, auditory or semantic form. **Storage** refers to retaining the information we have learned. **Retrieval** is the process of locating and extracting stored memory.

**Forgetting** refers to the inability to recall or recognise something which has been learned. Forgetting could be due to a problem with accessibility (cue-dependent forgetting) or a problem of availability (trace dependent forgetting).

## You need to be able to describe and evaluate the levels of processing theory of memory

Craik and Lockhart (1972) explained that memories are formed as a result of the way we process information. They proposed that the more deeply we process information, the more likely we are to be able to retrieve it later. Elaborative rehearsal (really thinking about/elaborating on information) leads to more durable memories whereas maintenance rehearsal (not thinking about the information for longer than needed) leads to less durable memories. Semantic processing (processing information by meaning) requires more elaborative rehearsal. An example of semantic processing is when we have to consider whether an object belongs to a certain category i.e. if we are asked to think about whether a dog is a type of animal. Categorising objects leads to deeper processing and longer lasting memories. In contrast, phonetic processing and structural processing lead to shallower processing and less durable memories. Phonetic processing is processing information by how it sounds e.g. does it rhyme with dog. Structural processing is processing information by the way it looks e.g. considering whether a word has the letter t in it. Craik and Lockhart said that semantic processing was the deepest level of processing and structural processing the shallowest.

**How to evaluate a theory:**

You can use SEA to help you evaluate a theory.

Studies-Describe the findings of any studies that support or contradict the theory. You can make one evaluative point per study used. However, your evaluation should be focused on evaluating the theory rather than any study used to support or contradict it.

Explanation-Discuss limitations of the explanation. Compare the theory with alternative theories.

Application to real life-Discuss how the theory can be applied to real life events or situations.

**Evaluation:**

Studies-Craik and Tulving's (1975) study supports the levels of processing theory of memory. They found that participants had better recognition for words they had processed semantically than words they had processed phonetically or structurally.
Hyde and Jenkins (1973) found that when participants were asked to judge the pleasantness of words, they recalled them better. This supports the idea that processing words semantically improves recall and the levels of processing theory.
Bower and Karlin (1974) asked participants to judge whether faces were male or female (shallow processing) or to judge whether they were honest (deeper processing). They found that the deeper processing condition resulted in better recognition.
However, Morris et al. (1977) found that participants recalled more words processed phonetically rather than semantically. This contradicts the levels of processing theory.
Reber et al. (1994)'s study also contradicts levels of processing theory. They presented participants with words high or low in emotional content and asked them to process the words in either a deep or shallow way. Words with emotional significance were recalled well whether or not they were processed in a deep or shallow way. This suggests that the emotional content of words affects recall more than depth of processing.

Explanation-The levels of processing theory explains why we remember some things better than others. However, the theory has been criticised for not explaining how memory works as it just says that we remember information well if we process it deeply and poorly if we process it at a shallow level. This is more a description of memory than an explanation.

Application to real life-The levels of processing theory can be applied to real life in terms of learning and revision. It suggests that we will remember information better if we process it by meaning and elaborate on the information.

**You need to be able to describe one theory of memory other than levels of processing: The multi-store model of memory**

Atkinson and Shiffrin (1968, 1971) described memory as having separate stores. These are referred to as sensory memory, STM and LTM. For information to go from your sensory memory to your STM, attention is needed. Information in the STM that is sufficiently rehearsed is coded into LTM. Information that is stored in the sensory memory is only stored for a fraction of a second. The STM holds plus or minus seven items or chunks of information and can last between 18 and 30 seconds. The capacity of LTM is unlimited and information can last a lifetime. LTM is a single store which means that everything is stored together and items are stored in the order in which they have been learnt. In STM, information is held in acoustic form while in LTM it is held in semantic form.

**Evaluation:**

Studies-Glanzer and Cunitz (1966) presented participants with a list of words and found that people remembered more words from the beginning (primacy effect) and the end of the list (recency effect) and the fewest words from the middle. This primacy and recency effect support the idea of a separate STM and LTM. Participants remember more words from the beginning of the word list because they have had time to rehearse them and put them into LTM and they remember more words from the end of the word list because they are still in STM. The words in the middle of the list are forgotten because they have not been rehearsed and they are no longer in STM.
Other evidence for the existence of a separate STM and LTM comes from case studies of brain damaged patients. One example is the case of HM who had difficulty forming new long term memories but whose short term memory was relatively normal.

Explanation-The multi-store model of memory is too simplistic. It is now widely believed that both STM and LTM have several separate storage systems. Seitz and Schumann-Hengsteler found that a visual-spatial task would not interfere with someone's ability to do sums. This suggests that there are separate short-term memory systems to handle visual and verbal information. HM could remember new motor skills and past information, suggesting that there are separate stores for LTM e.g. there may be different stores for facts, events and skills.

Application to real life-The concept of a separate STM and LTM is useful in helping psychologists think about memory. The multi-store model of memory helps to explain some of the memory problems with anterograde amnesia as people with this type of amnesia cannot form new long-term memories although they still have old memories and their STM is intact e.g. Clive Wearing.

**You need to be able to describe and evaluate cue-dependent forgetting (a theory of forgetting)**

Cue-dependent forgetting suggest that we forget information because we do not have the right cues to aid its retrieval. The information is stored in our memory but we temporarily cannot access it. According to Tulving (1974) when we learn information we also encode details about the environment in which we learned the information and our physical and emotional state. If we don't have the same cues at recall as we had at encoding, we are more likely to forget the information. There are two types of cues: contextual cues (cues relating to the environment) and state cues (cues relating to our emotional and physical state). Reinstating the context we were in when we learnt something can aid recall, for example, if we go back to the place we learnt something, we may be able to recall it. Going back to the same state we were in when we learnt something can also trigger recall of information, for example, we may learn something whilst being drunk and only recall it when we are drunk again.

## Evaluation:

Studies-Godden and Baddeley (1975) found that divers recall was better when they were in the same environment at learning and recall. However this study lacked experimental control as it was a field experiment and the task (learning words under water or on the beach) lacks ecological validity.
Duka et al.'s (2001) study also supports cue-dependent forgetting and in particular how state cues affect recall. Participants' recall was better when alcohol was drunk at both encoding and recall than when only drunk at encoding.
Smith and Vela (2001) carried out a meta-analysis of 75 experiments on context dependent forgetting and found that reinstatement of context such as being in the same place could improve recall.

Explanation-The theory has face validity because we have all experienced recalling a memory when we go back to a place from our childhood or when we smell a certain scent. However, cue-dependent forgetting does not explain why we remember emotional events really well even without cues or why we tend to recall happy memories over unhappy ones.

Application to real life-Cue-dependent forgetting can be applied to real life. The police use cues to aid witnesses' recall of incidents.

## You need to be able to describe and evaluate one theory of forgetting other than cue dependent forgetting: Repression

Repression is a defence mechanism used to protect the ego. It refers to the pushing of anxiety-provoking thoughts into the unconscious mind. Repression is sometimes described as motivated forgetting. Traumatic events such as military combat, rape, sexual abuse and witnessing a murder are forgotten because people do not want to remember such incidents. We can partially or completely repress entire events. Sometimes we can recall events but repress the emotions related to it. Repression can be used as a way of protecting ourselves from negative emotions. However, repressed events in our unconscious mind can affect our behaviour and can lead to mental health issues such as depression and anxiety.

## Evaluation:

Studies-Myers and Brewin's (1994) study supports the theory of repression. They found that participants classified as repressors (because they scored highly for defensiveness) had more difficulty recalling unhappy memories. Elliott found that 20% of people said they had forgotten traumatic events for a period of time.

Walker et al. (1997) had participants keep diaries of pleasant and unpleasant events for a few weeks. When tested later they showed good recall of pleasant events but poor recall of unpleasant events.

Explanation-The theory has face validity. There are many recorded cases of people forgetting traumatic events. However, repression cannot explain why we forget more as time goes by. It also cannot explain why some people who undergo traumatic experiences have difficulty forgetting them rather than remembering them. Furthermore, repression cannot explain how we can remember things if we have the right cues.

Application to real life-The concept of repression has been used by therapists to help patients deal with traumatic events in their lives.

**You need to be able to describe and evaluate Godden and Baddeley's (1975) study**

Aim: To see if context-dependent cues affect recall.

Procedure: 18 divers on a diving holiday were given word lists to learn either on the beach or 15ft under the sea. They were then asked to recall the words either in the same setting (for example, learning on land and recalling on land), or in a different setting (for example, learning on land and recalling underwater). There were four conditions altogether: learning on land/recalling under water, learning on land/recalling on land, learning under water/recalling under water and learning under water/recalling on land. The divers took part in all four conditions on different days. The locations changed each day. The words lists consisted of 36 unrelated words of two to three syllables. The divers listened to the word lists on a DUC device. After the divers had heard each word list twice, they had to remember and write down 15 numbers to prevent rehearsal of the word list.

Results: Recall was around 50% higher when it took place in the same environment as learning. The mean number of words recalled in the dry land learning and recall condition was 13.5 and 11.4 for underwater learning and recall. This contrasted with 8.4 mean recall in the underwater learning and dry land recall and 8.6 for dry land learning and underwater recall.

Conclusion: Environment can act as a contextual cue for recall.

**How to evaluate a study:**

You can use GRAVE to help you evaluate a study.

Generalisability-How generalisable is the study? Are the participants in the sample representative of the wider population?

Reliability-How easy is the study to replicate and get similar results? If a study have a standardised procedure and was done under controlled conditions, then it is easy to replicate. A study is reliable if it has been replicated and similar results have been found.

Application to real life-Can the study explain real life events or be applied to real life situations.

Validity-Does the study have ecological validity? If a study is done in participants' natural environment and involves a natural task that might be experienced in everyday life then it has ecological validity.

Does the study have experimental validity? If the participants believe the experimental situation is real and they don't change their behaviour to please the experimenter (demand characteristics), then the study has experimental validity.

Ethics-Does the study have any ethical issues? Were participants protected from physical and psychological harm? Were participants given the right to withdraw? Did the participants give fully informed consent or were they deceived about any aspect of the study? Were the participants debriefed? Was the anonymity of the participants protected? Was the researcher competent to carry out the research?

Note: GRAVE is just a trigger to jog your memory and to help you evaluate. You do not have to discuss all the elements of GRAVE in your evaluation. For example, if there are no ethical issues then you can leave them out.

**Evaluation:**

Generalisability-The participants were all research scientists and part of a university diving club so they might have processed the information in a different way than the general population. Therefore, the study lacks generalisability.

Reliability-It was a field experiment therefore there was less control over the extraneous variables (i.e. the breathing equipment, weather and sea life) this makes it more difficult to replicate.

Application to real life-The study showed that being in the same context at learning and retrieval, aids recall. This idea can be used in education to help students recall more information. For example, students are more likely to recall information if they are examined in the same room that they learnt it in.

The study can also be applied to interviewing witnesses of a crime incident. If witnesses are taken back to a crime scene, the context cues may aid their recall of the incident.

Validity-The study has good ecological validity as the participants were in a normal environment (for them). The task however was not ecologically valid (we don't try to learn and recall meaningless words in everyday life).
The study may have lacked experimental validity as the researchers did not see the participants during the learning and writing stage so cheating was possible. However, the participants were research scientists and tested in pairs so they were unlikely to have cheated.

Ethics-There are no major ethical issues with this study so in the exam, you can leave discussion of ethical issues out.

**You need to be able to describe and evaluate Craik and Tulving's (1975) study**

Aim: To see whether processing words semantically leads to better recognition than processing words phonetically or structurally.

Procedure: Participants (university students) were presented with lists of words via a tachistoscope, a device which presents items for a very brief period or time. After each word was presented the participants were to asked a question that involved processing the words semantically, phonetically or structurally. Participants had to respond 'yes' or 'no' to these questions. At this point they were not aware that they were going to be tested on their memory for the words. Later, however, they were given an unexpected recognition test. They were shown the words they had seen and answered questions on, mixed in with a number of new words. The participants' task was to identify the words they had seen before.

Results: The researchers found that participants recognised around 70% of the words processed semantically, around 35% of the words processed phonetically and around 15% of the words processed structurally.

Conclusion: Recognition is better for words processed at a semantic level as deeply processed material is better remembered.

**Evaluation:**

Generalisability-The participants were all students who are not representative of the wider population so the study lacks generalisability.

Reliability-The experiment had a standardised procedure and extraneous variables were controlled. The time the words were viewed for, the questions asked and even participant variables were controlled as it was a repeated measures design and so each participant took part in all conditions. The study has been replicated often and the findings have been similar.

Application to real life-The study can be applied to how students learn. If students process information deeply, elaborate on it and really try to understand it, then they are more likely to recall it later.

Ecological validity- The task and the environment were artificial, people are not usually asked questions about words and then asked to recognise them mixed together with new words. Therefore, the study lacks ecological validity. Furthermore, the task was a recognition task rather than pure recall (participants were shown the words they had seen, mixed in with new words and asked to identify the words they had seen before. This is not pure recall).

Experimental validity-Participants were not told that they would be asked to recognise the words later. Therefore, this stopped them focusing on the words in order to recall them, so the study has good experimental validity.

Ethics-There are no real ethical issues with this study so there is no need to discuss this.

You can also use other studies to support a study.

Bower and Karlin's (1974) study supports Craik and Tulving's study. They asked participants to judge whether faces were male or female (shallow processing) or to judge whether they were honest (deeper processing). They found that the deeper processing condition resulted in better recognition.

**You need to be able to discuss the key issue in the cognitive approach- the reliability of eyewitness testimony**

Eyewitness testimony refers to the recalled memory of a witness to a crime or incident. Innocent people have been convicted on the basis of eyewitness testimony alone and have later been found innocent using DNA evidence. Cases like this call into question the reliability of eyewitness testimony. There is also the issue that juries tend to trust eyewitness testimony too much.

Explaining why eyewitness testimony is unreliable gets you AO1 marks.
Explaining why eyewitness testimony is reliable gets you AO2 marks.

**Eyewitness Testimony is unreliable because:**

Leading questions can influence eyewitness memory and produce errors in recall. Loftus and Palmer (1974) found that they could affect participants' recall by changing the way a question is worded. Participants were asked how fast a car was going when it 'hit', 'smashed', 'collided' or 'bumped'. Participants gave a higher estimate of speed if the word was 'smashed' rather than 'collided', they were also more likely to report seeing broken glass in the 'smashed' condition when asked back a week later.

Weapon focus effect: Studies show that when a weapon is used by a criminal, witnesses focus on the weapon rather than the criminal's face or their environment, probably because a weapon is a major threat. Loftus et al. (1987) showed half their participants a film with a customer in a restaurant holding a cheque, and the other half were shown a film with a customer holding a gun. They found that participants had worse recall for a the customer's face when they were holding a weapon.

Yarmey's (2004) study supports the view that jurors should question the reliability of witness identification from line-ups. They found that when participants had actually spoken to a female target, only 49% of them could identify her in a photo line-up when she was present and when she was not present 38% of them identified someone in the photo line-up who was completely different.

Poor line-up procedures may lead to misidentification of a suspect. Simultaneous line-ups (where all the people are presented together in the line-up) may lead to witnesses using a relative judgement strategy (choosing a person who looks most like the perpetrator of the crime rather than really looking at the person's individual characteristics to see whether they match up).

Meissner and Brigham (2001) found that people are less able to recognise people from a different ethnic background to them so this can lead to problems in eyewitness identification.

Buckout (1974) highlighted that photo line-ups can be biased if the suspect's photo is physically different from the fillers.

Busey and Loftus (2006) pointed out that lack of double-blind procedures can mislead witnesses. They gave the example of a police officer who knew who the suspect was in a line-up and when a witness identified the suspect, the police officer said sign here as if to confirm their identification was correct.

Wells and Bradfield found that if a participant was given confirming feedback about an identification, they became more confident that their identification was correct. Therefore, by the time a case gets to court, a witness who has had their identification confirmed by a police officer, may be overly confident even if they are wrong.

If there is a long period of time between recall and the incident, people are likely to forget details.

Stereotypes can affect eyewitness memory. People's views on what type of person commits a crime can affect recall. People are less likely to believe that a man in a suit committed a crime compared to someone who is scruffily dressed.

The memory conformity effect can affect witnesses' memory for events. For example, if witnesses discuss a crime incident together, their memory for events becomes more similar. Wright et al. (2000) placed people in pairs to investigate the memory conformity effect under controlled conditions. One of the pair saw pictures of a man entering with the thief, the other saw pictures without the man. They were then asked to recount the story together but fill out questionnaires separately. About half of the participants who had not seen the picture with the man conformed to their partner's account.


**Eyewitness Testimony is reliable because:**

Yuille and Cutshall (1986) examined the recall of witnesses to a real life gun shooting in Canada. 21 witnesses saw a man try to rob a gun shop and then shoot the shop owner. The shop owner shot back and killed the thief. After the witnesses had been interviewed by police, the researcher used the opportunity to ask them whether they would like to take part in their research into eyewitness testimony. 13 of the 21 witnesses agreed to take part in their research 5 months later. They found that even 5 months after the incident, witnesses had good recall of events and were not affected by the leading questions asked.

This study suggests that eyewitness memory in real life is not as likely to be distorted as laboratory experiments suggest.

Rinolo et al. (2003) questioned 20 survivors of the shipwrecked Titanic shipwreck and found that 15 of the 20 witnesses were able to recall details accurately many years later despite inaccurate media coverage.

Cognitive interviews can improve eyewitness testimony: this involves getting the witness to freely describe events without the risk of leading questions. Eyewitnesses are asked to not leave out any detail even if they think it is unimportant and they may be asked to recall the incident in reverse order. Questions can be asked at the end in order for information to be un-altered.

Flashbulb memory may lead witnesses to recall crime incidents very clearly as they are likely to have strong emotions related to the incident and may replay events in their mind.

**Exam tip**: You may be asked to discuss problems of research into eyewitness testimony. You should then discuss problems with laboratory research and field research in relation to eyewitness testimony.

e.g. Laboratory experiments investigating eyewitness testimony can lack ecological validity as the participants do not experiences the same emotions as real witnesses and participants may feel correct recall is not as important compared witnesses of a real crime.

**You need to be able to describe and evaluate the laboratory, field and natural experiments**

**Laboratory Experiments** involve manipulating an independent variable to see the effects on a dependent variable. The dependent variable is measured. Extraneous variables are controlled so that a cause and effect relationship can be established.

**Evaluation:**

Laboratory experiments have standardised procedures and good controls. This makes them easily replicable and reliable. They can establish cause and effect. However, laboratory experiments lack ecological validity as they are carried out in artificial situations and often involve artificial tasks.

**Field experiments** looks at participants in their natural environment whilst manipulating the independent variable. The dependent variable is measured. As field experiments take place in a natural environment, extraneous variables are hard to control.

**Evaluation:**

Field experiments take place in the participants' natural environment. This means that not all the extraneous variables can be controlled and the findings might not be reliable. However, as field experiments have carefully controlled and planned procedures, they often give the same results when repeated. This means that they can be as reliable as laboratory experiments. Field experiments are carried out in the participants' natural environment so they have ecological validity in terms of setting. However, the independent variable(s) is still carefully manipulated to see the effect on the dependent variable, and therefore, the procedure may not be valid. On the other hand, researchers try to make the procedure as realistic as possible to enhance validity.

**Natural Experiments** are studies carried out in real-life setting where the independent variable occurs naturally. A dependent variable is still measured. Participants cannot be allocated to conditions so it is not a true experiment.

**Evaluation:**
Natural experiments have high ecological validity as they are carried out in participants' natural environments. However, it can be difficult to establish cause and effect as the extraneous variables are not controlled.

**You need to be able to discuss how quantitative data is obtained from experiments**

Experiments involve measuring a dependent variable such a number of words recalled, speed estimates and number of aggressive behaviours shown. This is quantitative data, which can be statistically analysed to see how significant the results are or whether they occurred due to chance. If quantitative research is repeated, often the same data will be found. This shows that quantitative data is reliable. However, the careful operationalising of variables in quantitative research means that real life events and interactions are not being measured so there can be a problem with validity.

**You need to understand and be able to write one-tailed, two-tailed and null hypotheses**

An experimental hypothesis predicts what change(s) will take place in the dependent variable when the independent variable is manipulated.

A two-tailed (non-directional) hypothesis predicts that there will be a change in the DV when the IV is manipulated.
e.g. There will be a difference in the number of words recalled when words are processed semantically compared to when they are processed phonetically.

A one-tailed (directional) hypothesis predicts in which direction the change will take place.
e.g. There will be more words recalled when they are processed semantically compared to when they are processed phonetically.

The null hypothesis states that there will be no changes due to the manipulation of the IV.
e.g.There will be no difference in the number of words recalled when processed semantically or phonetically.

Operationalisation: A hypothesis is operationalised when it is clear what is being manipulated and what is being measured. The dependent variable should refer to a numerical value. For example, if you are measuring recall, you might say number of words recalled.

**You need to be able to describe and evaluate different types of design**

**An independent groups** design involves testing separate groups of participants. Each group is tested in a different condition. For example, a researcher might ask one group to process words semantically and a second group to process words phonetically.

Advantages: An independent groups design avoids order effects. Each participant only takes part in one condition so they are less likely to become bored and tired (a fatigue effect) and less likely to become practiced at the task (a practice effect). There is also less likelihood of demand characteristics (where the participant guesses the aim of the study and changes their behaviour to please the experimenter) as they do only one condition.

Disadvantages: More people are needed than with the repeated measures design. Differences between participants in the groups may affect results, for example; variations in age, sex or social background. These differences are known as participant variables.

**A repeated measures design** involves testing the same group of people in different conditions. For example, the same group of people might be asked to process words semantically and phonetically.

Advantages: A repeated measures design avoids the problem of participant variables as the same participants do all conditions. Fewer people are needed.

Disadvantages: There are more likely to be demand characteristics as participants might guess the aim of the study as they take as they take part in more than one condition of the experiment. Order effects are more likely to occur. There are two types of order effects: practice effects and fatigue effects. Practice effects are when participants become better at a task such as learning a list of words in the second condition compared to the first condition. Fatigue effects are when participants might become bored or tired in the second condition.

**Counterbalancing** can overcome order effects in a repeated measured design. Counterbalancing is when the experimenter alters the order in which participants perform the different conditions of the experiment. For example, group 1 does condition A first then condition B, group 2 does condition B first then condition A.

**A matched pairs design** involves testing separate groups of people who are matched on certain characteristics. For example, each member of one group is the same age, gender, race and socioeconomic status as a member of the other group.

Advantages: A matched pairs design overcomes some of the problems of both an independent groups design and a repeated measures design. Firstly, matching the participants in the different conditions reduces the chance of participant variables affecting the results. Secondly, having different participants in each condition avoids the problem of order effects.

Disadvantages: A matched pairs design can be very time-consuming as the researcher need to find closely matched pairs of participants. It is also impossible to match people exactly.

**You need to be able to describe researcher effects**

Researchers can affect the behaviour of their participants and affect the results of the study. For example, the researcher might unwittingly communicate his expectations to the participants. Researchers can also interpret data in a biased way to match their expectations.

**You need to be able to to work out the mean, median, mode and range from a set of data.**

Note: The mean, median and mode are called measures of central tendency.

**The mean**

The mean is often referred to as the average of a set of numbers. You calculate the mean by adding up all the numbers and then dividing by the number of numbers.

Consider the following data set: 12, 17, 23, 27

Add the numbers together:  12+17+23+27=79
Divide 79 by 4:  79/4 =19.75

The 'Mean' (Average) is 19.75

**The median**

The median is the 'middle value' in a list of numbers. To find the median, your numbers have to be listed in numerical order. If you have an odd number of numbers, the median is the middle entry in the list. If you have an even number of numbers, the median is equal to the sum of the two middle numbers divided by two.

Consider the following data set: 13, 17, 21, 8

Sort the numbers into numerical order: 8, 13, 17, 21

There is not a single middle number in this data set as there is an even number of numbers. Therefore, add the two middle numbers, 13 and 17, and divide by two:

13+17=30
30/2=15

The median is 15

**The mode**

The mode is the number that occurs most frequently in a set of data. If no number is repeated, then there is no mode for the set of data.

**The range**

Note: The range is a measure of dispersion. It refers to how the data is spread out or 'dispersed'.

The range is the difference between the largest and smallest numbers.

Consider the following data set: 11, 15, 16, 21

Subtract the smallest number from the largest number: 21-11=10

The range is 10

**You need to be able to describe a practical in the cognitive approach. Example practical: Can context cues affect recall**

**Aim**: To find if music will act as cue for recall.

**One-tailed Hypothesis:** Participants will recall more words with the same music at recall (cue condition) compared to different music at recall (no cue condition).

**Null Hypothesis:** Having the same music as a cue at recall will not affect the number of words recalled. There will be no difference number of words recalled in cue or no cue condition. Any difference will be due to chance.

**Independent Variable:** Whether participants have the same music at recall or not

**Dependent Variable:** The number of words recalled

**Sampling Method:** Opportunity Sampling

**Design:** Independent Groups

**Procedure:**

Participants were recruited from the sixth form at our school and divided randomly into two groups by picking names out of a hat. One group received a cue (the same music at recall as at learning) and one group did not receive a cue (different music at learning and recall). In the cue condition, the music at learning and recall was 'Crying for no reason' by Katy B. In the no cue condition, the music at learning was 'Crying for no reason' and the music at recall was 'Hey Brother' by Avicii. Participants were briefed about the study and standardised instructions were read out to them as a group. Participants were told that that they have the right to withdraw from the study at any time. The experiment was carried out in groups in a silent school hall. The participants were given 2 minutes to learn a word list whilst listening to 'Crying for no reason'. There was a gap of one day before the participants were asked back to recall the words. Participants in the cue condition were played the same song again and given another 2 minutes to write down as many of the words as they could remember on a blank sheet of paper. Participants in the no cue condition, were played 'Hey Brother' and given 2 minutes to write down as many words as they could remember. A control was that the seats were in the same place at learning and recall. Another control was that all the words were the same length and nouns. Participants were debriefed at the end of the experiment.

Table to show the mean, median, mode and range for recall with a cue and without a cue:

|  | Cue condition (Same music at recall) | No cue condition (Different music at recall) |
|---|---|---|
| Mean | 12.4 | 9.9 |
| Median | 12 | 10.5 |
| Mode | 12 | 11 |
| Range | 6 | 5 |

**Results:**

Participants had a mean recall of 12.4 words in the cue condition compared to 9.9 words in the no cue condition.

**Conclusion:**

Music can act as a contextual cue, as those who listened to the same music during learning and recall, remembered more words.

**Evaluation:**

Generalisability: An opportunity sample of 16- to 17-year-olds in the sixth form at our school was used. Therefore, the sample is not representative of the wider population. However, as most people's cognitive abilities are similar, the results may be considered generalisable.

Reliability: The experiment is reliable because the extraneous variables were controlled and a standardised procedure was used. However, as the study used an opportunity sample, it might be hard for someone else to obtain the same sample and repeat the findings making the study less reliable.

Application to real life: Students might be able to use cues to aid their recall in an exam.

Validity: The experiment lacks ecological validity because learning and recalling a list of words is an artificial task. Music may act as interference rather than a cue, which can affect validity. Some participants may have liked the music, some may not have, which would affect concentration during the word task.

Ethics-The study has no ethical issues. Informed consent was obtained from the participants and they were given the right to withdraw.

**Exemplar exam question with student answer**

**Describe and evaluate one model of memory other than levels of processing.** (12 marks)

Student answer:

The multi-store model of memory suggests there are three stores of information in the brain. Information is taken in by the senses and held briefly in the sensory store. Information is then either retained in short-term memory (STM) or is forgotten. The STM can hold up to 7 chunks of information for a short amount of time. The information is encoded by the way it was processed in the sensory store i.e. if it was seen it will remain as visual information. In the STM, information can be encoded acoustically, visually or semantically. Information can then either be forgotten or retained in the long-term memory (LTM). In the LTM, the capacity is unlimited and the length of time it is held for is potentially unlimited also. The information can be encoded in any form. Information can be rehearsed by the rehearsal loop, which brings information into the STM from the LTM and back again.

Alternative theories such as the levels of processing theory of memory is not divided into stores and that it is the way in which you process something that leads to the accuracy of recall. However, the multi-store model was a breakthrough into memory theories and led to research and theories that are now accepted today. It can be applied to real life as it suggests that we can only attempt to remember 7 chunks of information for a short time. This has been supported by studies as 7 chunks of random trigrams could be remembered as 7 chunks but not all in one go. Peterson and Peterson showed that information is encoded by the senses. They used a table of letters and found that participants could not recall the letters after being briefly shown them. The multi-store model does not explain cases such as Clive Wearing who has brain damage and extreme memory loss but can still remember how to play the piano.

6/12 marks-level 2 answer

**Commentary:**

There is a reasonable description of the multi-store model of memory here. However, this student does not describe how information flows through the system. For information to go from sensory memory to STM, attention is needed. For information to go from STM to LTM, rehearsal is required. It can be helpful to draw a flow diagram in the exam. The description would also have benefited from a description of the capacity of each store. Information that is stored in the sensory memory is only stored for a fraction of a second whereas information in STM can last between 18 and 30 seconds. The capacity of LTM is unlimited and information can last a lifetime. There were a couple of errors in the description. The first error was that STM does not hold seven chunks of information but plus or minus 7 items or chunks. The second error was that STM encodes information acoustically not visually or semantically.

There was a good comparison with the levels of processing model of memory in the evaluation. However, the Peterson and Peterson study has been mixed up with a different study. Peterson and Peterson (1959) investigated the duration of short-term memory using 3 consonant trigrams (e.g. MCR). Participants were asked to recall the trigrams after 3, 6, 9, 12, 15 or 18 seconds. They found that after a 3 second delay, 80% of the trigrams could be recalled but after an 18 second delay, less that 10% of the trigrams could be recalled. This study provides support for the limited duration of STM. The case study of Clive Wearing is not well explained. Clive Wearing has difficulty forming new long term memories but his short term memory is relatively normal. Therefore, the study supports the existence of a separate STM and LTM. However, the case study also highlights problems with the multi-store model of memory. Although Clive Wearing cannot remember a conversation he had 30 seconds ago, he can form new procedural memories. Procedural memory refers to the memory for performing certain kinds of tasks such as tying shoe laces or riding a bike. Procedural memories are usually automatically accessed. The multi-store model is too simplistic because it does not take into account different types of LTM.

# Chapter 2-The Social Approach

## You need to be able to describe what the social approach is about

The social approach studies how our behaviour is affected by other people. At AS level, topics such as group behaviour, prejudice and obedience are covered. However, the social approach also covers topics such as bystander intervention, attraction and crowd behaviour.

## You need to be able to define the following key terms

**The agentic state** is when we obey others and put aside our personal beliefs and wishes to maintain a stable society.

**The autonomous state** is when our behaviour is controlled by our own free will. Agency theory refers to an agentic state.

**Moral strain** is the tension we feel when obeying orders that are against our own personal beliefs. Agency theory refers to an agentic state.

**In-group/out-group**-The group to which we belong is called the in-group and other groups are the out-group.

**Social categorisation** is when we categorise ourselves as being in a particular group often based on stereotypes. The group that we belong to is the in-group and any comparison group is the out-group. Social categorisation is the first stage in social identity theory.

**Social identification** is when we identify with a particular group and adopt the behaviours of that group. We may take on the group's values and norms. The way we view ourselves is affected by how well the group is doing relative to other groups. Social identification is the second stage in social identity theory.

**Social comparison** is when we compare our own group (the in-group) more favourably against other groups (out-groups) to boost our self-esteem. We may put down (denigrate) the out-group to make ourselves feel superior. In extreme cases, we may even dehumanise the out-group. Social comparison is the third stage in social identity theory.

## You need to be able to define obedience

Obedience is when we follow orders given by a person with authority over us. Social psychologists have studied obedience to understand what makes people obey and the circumstances under which people are more obedient.

## You need to be able to describe and evaluate Milgram's (1963) study of obedience

Aim: The aim of the experiment was to investigate what level of obedience would be shown when participants were told by an authority figure to administer electric shocks to another person.

Procedure: A volunteer sample of 40 males aged between 20 and 50 years of age, were recruited from a newspaper advertisement. Participants were told that the study was about the effects of punishment on learning and that they would be paid $4.50 for taking part. When participants arrived at Yale University, they were asked to draw lots for who would have the role of teacher or learner in the experiment. The draw was set up so that the participant was always the teacher and Mr. Wallace (the confederate) was always the learner. Participants were then shown an electric shock generator, which had 30 switches from 15V to 450V. They were then asked to give increasing levels of electric shocks to the learner if he got any words incorrect on a word pair task. Unbeknown to the participants the electric shocks were fake. At certain voltages, Mr. Wallace pretended to show signs of pain. At 315V, Mr. Wallace became silent. Whenever the participants said they wanted to stop giving the electric shocks, they were given verbal prods to continue.

Results: 100% (40/40) of the participants obeyed up to 300 volts and 65% (26/40) of the participants were fully obedient and gave all the shocks to 450V. During the study many participants showed distress at having to give the electric shocks.

Conclusion: People will obey authority figures even when it means causing harm to an innocent person. Milgram suggested the high levels of obedience in the study may have been due to the fact that the experiment took place at the prestigious Yale University. The participants may also have felt they should continue with the study because they had volunteered and were offered payment for their participation.

**How to evaluate a study:**

You can use GRAVE to evaluate a study.

Generalisability-How generalisable is the study? Are the participants in the sample representative of the wider population?

Reliability-How easy is the study to replicate and get similar results? If a study have a standardised procedure and was done under controlled conditions, then it is easy to replicate. A study is reliable if it has been replicated and similar results have been found.

Application to real life-Can the study explain real life events or be applied to real life situations.

Validity-Does the study have ecological validity? If a study is done in participants' natural environment and involves a natural task that might be experienced in everyday life then it has ecological validity.

Does the study have experimental validity? If the participants believe the experimental situation is real and they don't change their behaviour to please the experimenter (demand characteristics), then the study has experimental validity.

Ethics-Does the study have any ethical issues? Were participants protected from physical and psychological harm? Were participants given the right to withdraw? Did the participants give fully informed consent or were they deceived about any aspect of the study? Were the participants debriefed? Was the anonymity of the participants protected? Was the researcher competent to carry out the research?

You do not have to discuss all these points in your evaluation. For example, if there are no ethical issues then you don't need to discuss them. GRAVE is just a trigger to jog your memory and to help you evaluate.

**Evaluation:**

Generalisability- All the participants were volunteers who are likely to be more obedient than other participants so in the sample is not generalisable in this respect.
It could also be argued that Milgram's study is not generalisable as it was only carried out on American males who are not representative of the wider population. However, when Milgram tested females in exactly the same way, he found identical levels of obedience. Studies testing obedience across the world have found similar levels of obedience.

Reliability-Milgram's study was reliable because it had a standardised procedure, which makes it easy to repeat and get the same results. A script was followed and all participants heard the same recordings from Mr. Wallace. They were also give the same verbal prods such as 'You must continue' when they said they wanted to stop. This makes the study easily replicable.

Application to real life-The study can be applied to real life as it shows how under pressure people will obey an authority figure. The study has been used to explain why the Nazis were so obedient to Hitler even when it harmed innocent people. It can also explain why people are so obedient to their bosses at work even when it might cause harm to others such as firing colleagues.

Ecological validity-Some psychologists have suggested that Milgram's study lacks ecological validity or mundane realism as it involved an artificial situation. People are not usually asked to give electric shocks to another person for wrong answers on a word pair task. However, Milgram argued that the study does reflect how people behave in the real world as people do recognise authority figures and follow orders in the real world.

Experimental validity-The study has experimental validity as the participants believed the shocks were real. The fact that the participants showed signs of distress such as nervous laughter shows that their belief in the experimental situation was genuine. In fact, Milgram took great care to make sure his study had experimental validity so that the participants believed the situation was real:  He rigged a draw with the participant and Mr. Wallace so that participants thought they had randomly been allocated the role of teacher and he gave participants a sample 45V shock so that they believed the shocks were real.

Ethics-One of the main criticisms of Milgram's study was the effects it had on participants. Participants did not give informed consent and were deceived. They were told that the aim of the study was to investigate the effects of punishment on learning when it was actually about obedience. They also thought they were giving real electric shocks when they were fake. Furthermore, participants were not protected from psychological harm as many experienced distress and may have felt bad about themselves after the experiment for being so obedient. They were also given verbal prods to continue throughout the experiment. However, Milgram did give participants the right to withdraw at the beginning of the experiment. He also thoroughly debriefed his participants and they were followed up a year later by psychiatrists. 84% of participants said they were glad or very glad to have taken part in the experiment.

**You need to be able to describe and evaluate one variation of Milgram's study of obedience: Teacher forces learners hand onto shock plate. Touch Proximity Condition**

Aim: To see if level of obedience increased or decreased when the teacher and learner are in same room and the participant has to place the learner's hand on a shock plate.

Procedure: The experiment involved an electric shock generator as in the original experiment and participants were told to administer shocks to Mr. Wallace for wrong answers on a word pair task. Unbeknown to the participants, Mr. Wallace was a confederate of the experimenter and the shocks were fake. At each incorrect answer Mr.Wallace was shocked only when the teacher forced his hand on a shock plate. At 150 volts, the learner refused to place his hand on the plate, and the experimenter ordered the participant to hold the victim's hand on the plate.

Results: 30% (12/40) of the participants forcibly held the victim's hand in place and continued to administer shocks up to the maximum 450V.

Conclusion: Obedience decreased (in relation to the original experiment) as the subject came into close proximity with the victim and had to hold the learner's hand on a shock plate.

**Evaluation:**

The study was ethically more distressing for participants than the original experiment and other variations as they were in the same room as the learner and they had to place the learner's hand on the shock plate. As in the original experiment, participants were placed under pressure to continue due to the verbal prods and may have felt they didn't have the right to withdraw. All participants were thoroughly debriefed and the majority were glad to have taken part, so in this way the study was ethical. It could be argued that the study was less believable than other variations. However, many of the participants showed visible signs of mental anguish e.g. sweating and nervous laughter, which suggests that they did believe in the experimental situation. Therefore, the study has experimental validity.

**Note:** You can make many of the same evaluative points as you would for the original study.
e.g. The study was reliable because it had a standardised procedure, which makes it easy to repeat and get the same results. A script was followed and all participants heard the same comments from Mr. Wallace. They were also give the same verbal prods such as

'You must continue' when they said they wanted to stop. This makes the study easily replicable.

**Exam tip:** Remember don't just say a study is reliable because it is easy to repeat and has a standardised procedure as you can say this about most laboratory experiments. Explain why this particular study is easy to repeat and give details.

Don't just say a study lacks ecological validity because it was done in an artificial environment. Explain what aspects of this particular study were artificial.

**You need to be able to describe and evaluate Meeus and Raaijmakers (1986) study of obedience-the Dutch study**

Aims: To see how obedient participants are when they have to administer psychological harm to another person rather than physical harm (as in Milgram's study) in an everyday situation of a job interview. To compare obedience levels in a different culture (1980s Dutch culture versus 1960s American culture) when participants are fully aware they may be causing harm.

Procedure: 39 participants of both genders aged 18-55, were recruited from a newspaper advertisement. The experiment was conducted in a modern university building and the male researcher was friendly but stern. Participants were told that they had to interview a person who was applying for a job. They were told that the job required someone who could deal with stress so they would need to make the applicant stressed as part of the interview process. Participants were told privately that the 'job applicant's' ability to deal with stress would affect their job chances. However, participants heard the 'job applicant' being told that the test would not affect their job prospects. The 'job applicant', who was actually a confederate of the experimenter, followed a script and had to answer 32 oral multiple-choice questions to get the 'job'. There were 15 stressful remarks shown on a TV screen that participants were asked to give, ranging from mildly stressful remarks such as 'Your answer to question 9 was wrong' to very stressful remarks such as 'I think you are better suited to lower functions'. 24 participants were put in an experimental group and pressurised to give the stress remarks by verbal prods telling them to continue. The 15 participants placed in a control group were given the choice as to whether they wanted to give the stress remarks or not. The researcher also placed electrodes on the 'job applicant's' head and said that their stress level would show up on a sequence panel. As the participants gave increasingly stressful remarks to the 'job applicant', the sequence panel showed higher levels of stress. Unbeknown to the participants, the 'job applicant' was only pretending to show stress and the stress levels shown on the sequence panel were part of the set up.

Results: 92% of participants in the experimental group were fully obedient and gave all 15 stress remarks. However, they said afterwards that they intensely disliked giving the stress remarks. 96% believed the experimental situation was real. None of the control group gave the stress remarks.

Conclusion: Even in a more liberal Dutch culture, people will obey an authority figure even if it means causing harm to another. The higher levels of obedience in this study can be explained by psychological harm being easier to administer than physical harm.

**Variations:** When the experimenter was in a different room, obedience dropped to 36.4%. When two rebellious peers (actually confederates) suggested that they should stop giving the stress remarks, obedience reduced to 15.8%.

**Evaluation:**

Generalisability: The sample consisted of both genders and had a wide age range so in this way it could be said to be representative of the wider population. However, the participants were all volunteers so they may be more obedient than average.

Reliability: The study had a standardised procedure. The researcher followed the same script with each participant, they were asked to give the same 15 stress remarks and saw the same reactions from the 'job applicant'. The extraneous variables were also controlled. Therefore, the study is easy to replicate.

Application to real life: The study can explain why people are willing to psychologically harm colleagues or job applicants at work on the orders of their boss.

Ecological validity: The study lacks ecological validity as people are not normally asked to come to a university and give stressful remarks to a 'job applicant' as part of a psychological experiment on stress. However, it could be argued that the kind of psychological violence administered in the study reflects real life more than the electric shocks given in Milgram's study.

Experimental validity: 96% of participants believed the experimental situation was real, which suggests the study has experimental validity.

Ethics: The participants were deceived about the true aim of the study and so did not give informed consent. They all said they intensely disliked giving the stress remarks so they were not protected from psychological harm. However, they were debriefed and most of the participants showed no real opposition to the experimenter during the experiment.

**You need to be able to compare Milgram's study and Meeus and Raaijmakers' study drawing cross-cultural conclusions**

**Exam tip:** When asked to compare a study, think about how they are similar and how they are different.

Use terms such as 'They both …', 'They are different because…', 'One looked at…. whereas the other looked at….'

**Comparisons:**

Both studies had a similar aim as they were looking at how obedient people would be to an authority figure even if it meant causing harm to another. However, Milgram's study asked participants to administer physical punishment whereas Meeus and Raaijmaker's study asked participants to deliver a psychological punishment. The Dutch study found a much higher level of obedience (92%) than Milgram's study (65%). The researchers suggested that it is easier for people to give psychological rather than physical harm to another person. Both studies recruited volunteers through a newspaper advertisement and both studies took place in a university building. A difference between the studies is that Milgram's participants did not agree to cause physical harm to the victim: They were told by Milgram that no actual harm would come to the participants, which may have confused them. In contrast, in Meeus & Raaijmakers' study, participants did agree to cause psychological harm to the job applicant as they thought there was a real chance that their negative comments would affect the person's job prospects. Both studies support agency theory because in both cases the participants were unhappy about obeying the instructions to harm another. The participants showed moral strain in both studies. There were ethical issues with both studies as they deceived participants. For example, they both had a stooge (confederate) who pretended to be harmed by the participant and they were not told the true aim of the study. However, the participants were debriefed fully and followed up a year later in both studies. When two rebellious peers (confederates) stopped being obedient in the variation studies, obedience dropped. Milgram found 10% obeyed in this condition, compared with 16% in the Dutch study. When the experimenter was absent, both studies found a decrease in obedience: Milgram found 22.5% obedience and the Dutch study found 36.4%.

**You need to be able to describe and evaluate the Hofling et al. (1966) study**

Aim: To see whether nurses would obey a doctor when doing so would breach hospital regulations and endanger the lives of patients.

Procedure: It was a field study as it was conducted in three hospitals. Part of the procedure involved giving 12 graduate nurses and 21 student nurses in one hospital a questionnaire asking them what they would do if an unknown doctor called them on the telephone asking them to give an overdose of a drug Astroten to a patient. In another part of the procedure, 22 nurses from the other two hospitals were called by an unknown doctor when they were alone on a ward. The 'doctor', who was actually a researcher, asked the nurses to give a patient 20 mg of the drug Astroten without written authorisation. Hospital regulations stated that the nurses should wait for written authorisation before giving any medication to patients. Boxes of harmless capsules were placed in the wards prior to the nurses being called by the 'doctor'. The labels on the boxes said 'Astroten' and were marked with a maximum daily dose of 10mg.

Results: When the nurses were given the scenario of being asked by a doctor to give an overdose of a drug, most said they would not. 10 of the 12 graduate nurses and all 21 student nurses said they would not. However, when nurses were in the experimental situation and actually called by a 'doctor', 21 out of 22 nurses did obey the instructions. When debriefed afterwards, only 11 nurses were aware of the dosage limits of the Astroten and almost all of them said they knew that they should have waited for written authorisation to give the drug.

Conclusion: Although the nurses given the scenario believed that they would not obey a doctor unquestioningly, the nurses in the experimental situation did.

**Evaluation:**

Generalisability-The study may not be generalisable to the present day as it was conducted in 1966 when nurse-doctor relationships were different. Nurses nowadays may be less obedient.

Reliability-The study was repeated 22 times with a standardised procedure and there was control over many of the extraneous variables. The doctor followed a script with each nurse and all the nurses were approached when they were alone. Therefore, the study is reliable. However, some of the nurses may have been tired or busy, so they may have obeyed the doctor without thinking.

Application to real life- The study has important implications for the way nurses are trained. It suggests that nurses should be taught to question doctor's orders if they think there is a problem and to check with other professionals if necessary.

Validity- Nurses were approached at work doing their everyday job so the study has ecological validity. The study also has experimental validity as none of the nurses realised that they were part of an experiment and the 'doctor' was a researcher.

Ethics- The nurses were not protected from psychological harm. Many of the nurses felt ashamed and embarrassed after the experiment. Furthermore, the nurses did not know they were taking part in the study so they did not give informed consent and they were deceived. The nurses may also have been distracted by the doctor's instructions from attending to the patients. However, there was an observer on each ward who let the researcher know when it was the right time for the nurse to be called. The nurses were also fully debriefed after the study.

Studies that support/contradict this study-Raven and Haley's (1982) study supports Hofling et al.'s study as they found that 40% of nurses would obey an order to move an infectious patient out of isolation.

However, Krackow and Blass' (1995) study questions the findings of Hofling et al. They found that nurses would disagree with a doctor's order when they thought it might endanger the patient.

**You need to be able to describe and assess ethical issues arising from the obedience studies**

Milgram's (1963) study has been criticised for not protecting participants from harm. Participants were deceived about the aim of the experiment, put under extreme stress and prompted to continue even when they wanted to stop. However, Milgram fully debriefed his participants to make sure that they understood the research and to make sure there was no damage to their self-esteem. A follow-up opinion survey conducted a year later found that 84% of participants 'were glad to have been in the experiment.' 15% were neutral and only 1.3% were 'sorry or very sorry to have been in the experiment.' The participants were examined one year after the experiment by a psychiatrist who found no signs of harm. This study was ground-breaking because it suggested that everyone is capable of destructive obedience. In fact many Nazi war criminals claimed that they were 'just following orders.'

Hofling et al.'s (1966) study also has ethical issues. The nurses did not know they were taking part in the study so they did not give informed consent and they were deceived. Furthermore, the nurses may have been distracted by doctor's order and not attended to the patients. However, the study may have led to better training for nurses so that they question doctors when they have concerns.

Meeus and Raaijmakers (1985) study (unlike Milgram) was carried out with clear ethical guidelines in place. However, participants were still deceived and did not give informed consent for the study. If the participants refused to continue to make the stressful remarks they were pressurised to continue by the experimenter, which meant they may have felt they could not withdraw. The participants reported later that they 'intensely disliked' making the stress remarks. However, the study has helped us to understand that destructive obedience can be found in other cultures and that people will administer psychological harm to others on the orders of an authority figure.

When social psychologists carry out research they have two considerations in mind: the benefit to the society and the harm to the participants. This is called the ethical dilemma. Studies on obedience have been described as unethical but they have taught us about the dangers of blind obedience.

Ethical guidelines have also been developed as a result of the obedience studies.

**You need to be able to describe and evaluate agency theory**

This theory says that we obey others in order to maintain a stable society. Milgram said that in the **agentic state**, we put aside our own personal beliefs and wishes to obey an authority figure. Milgram believed that we acquire the agentic state in childhood as we become socialised at home and at school. Whilst in the agentic state we may experience **moral strain.** This is the sense that we are acting against our own beliefs. We might use a strategy called denial in order to cope. Milgram also identified an **autonomous state**, which is when we act according to own free will.

**How to evaluate a theory:**

You can use SEA to evaluate a theory.

Studies-Describe the findings of studies, which support/contradict the theory. You can make one evaluative point per study you use in your evaluation. Do not spend too long evaluating any studies as you have been asked to focus on evaluating the theory. Remember that a theory is someone's idea about how something works. Therefore, there is no point talking about generalisability as there is no sample of participants. There is no point talking about reliability as no study has been carried out that can be repeated.

Explanation-What are the problems/limitations of the theory? Are there alternative explanations?

Application to real life-How can the study be applied to real life situations or events?

**Evaluation:**

Studies-Milgram's study supports agency theory as it found that participants would obey an authority figure and give electric shocks to another person. Blass showed students an edited film of Milgram's study and questioned them about whether Milgram or his participants were more responsible for the shocks. Participants said Milgram was more responsible. This study provides support for agency theory. Meeus and Raaijmaker's study found that participants would obey an authority figure and give negative remarks to someone they thought was a job applicant. This study supports the notion that people can be agents of authority and act against their own conscience. Hofling et al.'s study found that nurses would follow the orders of a doctor even though they knew it was against hospital regulations, which supports the idea of an agentic state.

Explanation-The idea that obedience helps to maintain as stable society makes sense. Agency theory explains a range of real-life situations in which people obey orders. However, agency theory does not explain individual differences in obedience, for example why some people did not obey Milgram. 35% of participants did not give all the electric shocks. Furthermore, agency theory does not explain why some people are better leaders than others. The theory of charismatic leadership suggests that some people are particularly good at obtaining obedience from others because they exude charisma. Agency theory has been criticised for describing obedience rather than explaining it. The theory of social power explains obedience in more detail. It argues that we are more likely to obey those who have legitimate or expert power such as our boss or doctor respectively.

Application to real life-Agency theory can help to explain why the Nazis were so obedient to Hitler during the Holocaust. Eichmann said in his testimony that he was only following orders. It could also be used to explain why US soldiers tortured Iraqi prisoners in Abu Ghraib. Agency theory can also explain why people are willing to fire or reprimand their colleagues on the orders of their boss. The implications of agency theory are that training should be given to professionals such as nurses, police officers and the armed forces so that they don't obey authority figures without question.

**You need to be able to define prejudice and discrimination**

Prejudice: To form a judgement about a person before finding out anything about them as individuals. Prejudice is usually based on negative stereotypes about certain groups of people.

Discrimination: A behaviour towards another person based on prejudice.

**You need to be able to describe and evaluate social identity theory**

Social identity theory says that prejudice can arise from the mere existence of another group. Prejudice can be explained by our tendency to identify ourselves as part of a group and to classify other people as either within or outside that group. There are three stages to social identity theory: 1)Social Categorisation-This is when we categorise ourselves as being in a particular group often based on stereotypes. The group that we belong to is the in-group and any comparison group is the out-group. An example of social categorisation is when someone categorises themselves as a football supporter of a certain team and then views footballs supporters of other teams as the out-group.

2)Social Identification-This refers to when we identify with a particular group and adopt the behaviours of that group. We may also take on the group's values and norms. The way we view ourselves is affected by how well the group is doing relative to other groups. For example, a football supporter may adopt the behaviours of their club such as certain football chants and they may wear clothes that identify them as being part of the group such as wearing the club's scarf.

3)Social Comparison-Comparing our own group (the in-group) more favourably against other groups (out-groups) to boost our self-esteem. For example, football supporters may view their team as the best. This can lead to discrimination and sometimes even dehumanisation of the out-group. Football violence may be the unfortunate outcome of social comparison.

**Evaluation**:

Studies- Tajfel et al.'s (1971) minimal groups study found that boys overwhelmingly chose to allocate points to boys who has been identified as in the same group as themselves, which supports social identity theory.  Poppe and Linssen found that Eastern Europeans favour their own country over other Eastern Europeans, which supports the idea that people show in-group favouritism. Sherifs' Robbers Cave study provides further evidence for social identity theory in that the two groups of boys showed prejudice to the boys not in their group even before competition was introduced. Crocker and Luhtanen's (1990) study also supports social identity theory as it found that people tend to have high self-esteem if they think well of the group to which they belong. On the other hand, Dobbs and Crano's (2001) study contradicts social identity theory as it found that mere categorisation of people into groups is not always sufficient to create in group favouritism.

Explanation- Social identity theory does not explain individual differences in prejudice. Some people are much more prejudiced than others. Realistic conflict theory may be a better explanation of prejudice. It says that people become prejudiced when there is 'competition over scarce resources'. This theory can explain prejudice in competitive situations.

Application to real life- Social identity theory has face validity as it can explain behaviour real-life prejudice such as racism, snobbery and football violence.

**You need to be able to describe and evaluate Sherif (1961) 'Robbers Cave' experiment**

Aim: To see whether it is possible to create prejudice between two similar groups when they are put in competition with each other and to see if prejudice can be reduced through getting the groups to work together to achieve a superordinate goal (a goal that can only be achieved through cooperative working).

Procedure: Twenty-two eleven year-old boys were chosen to take part because they were well-adjusted. They were all from a similar background. Before the start of the experiment, the boys were randomly divided into two groups with eleven boys each.

The two groups of boys were taken to a summer camp in Robbers Cave State Park in Oklahoma. Initially, each group did not know the existence of the other group. In the first week the groups spent time bonding with each other while hiking in the park or swimming. Each group was asked to decide on a group name. One group chose the name Eagles and the other group chose the name Rattlers. The names were stencilled on to their flags and shirts to help build a sense of in-group identity.

During the second phase of the experiment, the two groups found out about each other's existence. A tournament with prizes was set up to create in-group favouritism. There was so much conflict between the two groups, phase two was cut short.

In phase three, the experimenters attempted to bring about cooperation between the two groups by getting them to work towards superordinate goals (tasks that can only be achieved by working together). For example, the two groups were told that they had to work together to restore the drinking water supply as it had been damaged by vandals.

Results: The boys developed a strong in-group preference and even before the tournament started, the groups were fighting each other and calling each other names. The competition increased the antagonism between the two groups. The group that lost the tournament even stole the prizes of the winning group.
After the groups had to cooperate with the each other in phase three, tension between the groups diminished.

Conclusion: Competition increased prejudice and led to conflict between the two groups. Cooperation reduced conflict between the two groups.

**Evaluation:**

Generalisability-The study lacks generalisability as the sample consisted of young boys who are not representative of the wider population. If the study was done with girls they may not have acted the same, as girls are often thought to be less competitive than boys.

Reliability-The study would be hard to replicate as it was a field study. Extraneous variables in the natural environment of the summer camp could have affected results. For example, if there had been a storm during the tournament it would have affected the boys' behaviour. However, some elements of the study are easy to replicate, for example, they carefully controlled how long the boys had to bond and when they introduced the competition element of the study.

Application to real life-The study can be applied to real life by helping reduce prejudice between groups in society through the use of superordinate goals.

Validity-This field study has high ecological validity as the boys were in a natural setting of a summer camp. The study also has experimental validity as the boys were unaware they were being observed and so would not have shown demand characteristics.

Note: Demand characteristics occur when participants guess the aim of the study and change their behaviour to please the researchers.

Ethics-There are ethical issues with Sherif's study. The researcher's deliberately created prejudice between the two groups of boys and this led to name-calling and even fighting between the boys. Therefore, the boys were not protected from psychological and physical harm. The boys did not know they were in the study and were not offered the right to withdraw. Although parents gave consent for the study, they did not know the full details of the study and probably would not have been happy at the idea of their boys being placed in situation where conflict was likely to occur.

**You need to be able to describe one key issue of relevance to today's society and apply concepts, theories and or/research from the social approach to explain the issue: Football Violence**

Trouble can flare up between rival sets of fans at football matches. This may take the form of actual fighting on the terraces, or a stand-off in the streets around the football stadium with two distinct groups shouting insults and throwing missiles at each other. The police become involved to keep the peace and may themselves become targets of this behaviour.

Social identity theory can be used to explain why football fans become violent to rival football fans. Fans may categorise themselves as belonging to an in-group (followers of a particular football team) and categorise fans of rival football teams as being the out-group. They identify strongly with their in-group by wearing scarves and strips that reflect their group membership. The fans compare themselves more favourably against rival football fans and deride the out-group in order to boost their self-esteem. Fans may focus on the fact the other team cheats more and this feeling of superiority allows them to dehumanise opposition fans. In some people, this may spill over into football violence/hooliganism.

Realistic conflict theory explains how competition over resources can lead to conflict between groups. This theory explain how football fans can become prejudiced towards each other when their football teams are competing for a football cup; only one team can win so there is competition over resources.
Football fans identify themselves as being in one group, the in-group. Other rival football teams/fans are the out-group. During a football match there is competition between groups and so hostility occurs.

The emergence of such prejudice was shown by Sherif et al. who produced prejudice between two groups of boys when they competed for prizes. However, Sherif et al.'s study only used boys so it may not explain the prejudice of female football supporters.

Levine et al. (2005) carried out an experiment on football supporters. Fans were invited to a secluded part of the university campus where they watched a stranger fall and apparently injure themselves. In one condition, the stranger wore their team colours whilst in another condition they wore neutral colours, or those of a rival football club. Football fans were much more likely to help someone wearing their team colours.

Agency theory can also explain football violence. Fans may be obeying orders from ring leaders whom they view as authority figures.

**You may need to describe how football violence can be reduced:**

One way that football violence can be reduced is by getting the fans from the different football teams to work towards a superordinate goal (a goal that can only be achieved by the teams working together). An example of this might be the fans cooperating to maintain peace when groups of school children attend a match. The theory is that when the fans work together it helps to breakdown in-group barriers.

Another way football violence could be reduced is for the police to target ringleaders who are instigating the violence. By removing troublemaker ringleaders there will not be an authority figure encouraging prejudice among the fans.

Introduction of role models who the fans can relate to and who show a lack of prejudice can help influence fans in a positive way.

**Note:** You may have to apply concepts, theories and/or research to a completely new issue/scenario in the exam that we have not studied so you need to know concepts and theories from the social approach well enough to do this.

**Your specification does not say that you need to know about reducing prejudice but as a past exam question has asked about it, here are some of the ways prejudice can be reduced:**

Intergroup Contact-This is the idea that regular contact in real-life situations between different groups can reduce prejudice.

Common in-group identity model-When different groups work together to achieve the same goals (superordinate goals), people begin to see themselves as one group.

Collective Action-When people see themselves as disadvantaged due to their membership of a particular group e.g. being female, gay or of a certain ethnic group then they may take action to improve the conditions for the whole group. This can take the form of marches and demonstrations.

Education-Teaching people about the causes and effects of discrimination in order to promote tolerance.

Social Policy-Introducing new legislation and practices can help deal with discrimination such as the age discrimination act.

**You need to be able to describe and evaluate surveys**

**Note:** Questionnaires and interviews are both types of survey.

**Questionnaires**

Questionnaires involve written questions to find out about people's views and opinions. They are able to collect data from lots of people as everyone is asked the same questions and can answer them in their own time. Questionnaires can be sent by post, filled in on the internet, given face-to-face or left in a public place for people to pick up. The questions can either be closed or open. Closed questions may involve a Likert type scale or yes/no questions. Open questions ask people to explain what they think about a certain topic in their own words. If closed questions are used then quantitative data can be obtained. If open questions are used then qualitative data can be obtained.

Advantages: Questionnaires allow data to be gathered from large samples without too much cost. If closed questions are used, the quantitative data can be statistically analysed. It is also easy to compare the data from closed questionnaires as everyone answers the same questions. Questionnaires with closed questions can be easy to replicate. Questionnaires with open questions can collect rich, qualitative data.
Disadvantages: A key problem with questionnaires is that people may give socially desirable answers because they want the researchers to think well of them. Participants may also misunderstand the questions and interpret the questions differently. Questions asked beforehand could affect later answers. Questionnaires with closed questions can limit participants' responses, which affects validity. Questionnaires with open questions are open to interpretation.

**Unstructured, structured and semi-structured interviews**

An interview involves asking participants questions verbally face-to face.

Structured interviews involve closed questions and produce quantitative data. Questions are decided upon in advance and all participants answer the questions in the same order. Unstructured interviews involve open questions and produce qualitative data. A couple of questions are decided on in advance but the researcher adapts their questions based on participants' responses. An unstructured interview often involves an in-depth discussion on a certain topic. Semi-structured interviews have prepared questions but allow participants to expand on some of their answers.

Advantages: Structured interviews allow quantitative data to be obtained, which can be statistically analysed. Unlike questionnaires, interviews allow the researcher to explain any questions that have been misunderstood. Unstructured interviews allow rich, detailed information to be obtained about people's opinions and views. Participants can expand on their answers and the researcher can follow up on any issues raised.

Disadvantages: Participants may give socially desirable answers to appear in a good light. Structured interviews can limit participants' responses. Unstructured interviews are open to interpretation and bias. Interviews can be time-consuming and expensive as they need to be delivered face-to-face.

**You need to be able to describe and evaluate quantitative and qualitative data**

Studies that focus on producing numerical results or data that can in some way be 'counted' (quantified) are described as quantitative research. Such studies tend to use large samples of people or animals so that results can be generalised to the wider population. Experiments, questionnaires and structured interviews are good sources of quantitative data. Quantitative data are measurable and firm conclusions can be drawn from the data. Statistical tests can be done to see how far the results are likely to be due to chance. In experiments, the independent variable is manipulated and the dependent variable is measured. Variables are also carefully operationalised and there are good controls. This makes the research more scientific. If quantitative research is repeated, often the same data will be found. This shows that quantitative data is reliable. However, the careful operationalising of variables in quantitative research means that real life events and interactions are not being measured (lack of validity).
In comparison, qualitative data can be gathered in more natural situations and reflects real life behaviour more so is more valid. Qualitative data can be gathered from case studies, unstructured interviews and observations in participants' natural environments. However, qualitative data is harder to replicate and can lack reliability.

**You need to be able to explain how different research methods produce qualitative and quantitative data**

Structured interviews and questionnaires give quantitative data because they involve set closed questions. The questions have yes/no answers or are rated on a scale such as the Likert scale (where participants can give answers from strongly agree to strongly disagree and these answers can be scored). This gives numerical data, which is quantitative.

Unstructured interviews and questionnaires use open questions and are good sources of qualitative data. For example, unstructured interviews may begin with a particular topic but then proceed like a conversation. They do not have set questions. The interviewer can explore areas that come up. No numerical data is obtained so the data is qualitative. An unstructured questionnaire would have open questions and then researchers would look for themes emerging from the participants' answers.

**You need to be able to describe and evaluate sampling techniques**

Random Sample-Each member of the population has an equal chance of being selected. For a small sample, you might draw names out of a hat/container. For a large sample, you might use birth records or the electoral role, allocate everyone a number and then get a random number generator to select certain people.

Self-Selected Sampling-You advertise for participants with specific characteristics e.g women over forty and the participants self-select themselves if they have those characteristics to take part in the study.

Opportunity Sample-This is when you select people based on who is available at a given time, often friends and family.

Stratified Sample-This is when certain people are selected to take part in a study to ensure a cross-section of the target population. For example, if you wanted to investigate the general population's attitude to childcare, you would select the right number of young females, young males, older males etc. that represents the proportion of them in the general population. Other criteria might include geographical locations and racial origins.

Volunteer Sample-This is when your sample consists of a group of participants who have chosen to take part.

**Evaluation:**

Random sample-Everyone in the chosen population has a chance of being in the sample. This is the best way of getting fair representation. However, if not everyone is in the sample, there is still a chance that it will be biased (e.g. regarding age).

Systematic Sample-This is a practical and manageable way of sampling. For example, if you choose every fifth person who comes along, the sample will not be biased by personal preferences. However, systematic sampling often involves selecting people who happen to be in a certain place at a certain time such as a train station on a Monday afternoon and this can cause bias.

Opportunity Sample-It is manageable and quick, as you can choose whoever is available. However, opportunity samples are often not representative of the wider population as they usually consist of family and friends.

Stratified Sample-This is less biased as there is usually a spread of different types of people in the sample. For example, there might be ten people in their twenties, ten people in their thirties and ten people in their forties. However, the individuals chosen may not be typical of the group they are meant to represent.

Volunteer Sample and Self-Selected Sample-This can be more ethical as the participants have chosen to take part. However, volunteers are not representative of the wider population as they tend to be people who have more time and who are more helpful.

**You need to be able to describe ethical guidelines for human participants**

**Informed consent**: Participants should be told about what the procedure entails and the aims of the study.

**Debriefing**: At the end of a study, participants should be told about any aspects of the study they were not informed about at the start. Participants should also be told about expected results and given the right to withdraw their data. The researchers should also check that the participants have not experienced any psychological harm.

**Right to withdraw**: Participants must be given the right to withdraw from the study at any time and given the option to withdraw their data at the end.

**Deception:** Participants should not be deceived about the aims of the study, what the procedure entails, the role of other participants or how their results will be used. Sometimes, it may be necessary to deceive participants about the aim of the study in order to investigate certain topics such as obedience. However, participants should only be deceived if they are not likely to come to any harm.

**Protection from harm**: Participants should be protected from physical and psychological harm. Psychological harm includes distress and damage to self-image. The risk of harm should be no more than participants might expect in everyday life.

**Confidentiality**: All data should be confidential and anonymous. When data is collected, participants' names should not be recorded and numbers or pseudonyms used instead to ensure anonymity.

**Competence**: Researchers should be qualified and have the experience necessary to carry out the research.

**You need to be able to describe a practical you conducted in the social approach: A questionnaire collecting both quantitative data and qualitative data on in-group/out-group attitudes based age**

Aim: To investigate in-group behaviour and whether participants show an in-group bias towards those of the same age as them.

Alternative directional hypothesis: Participants will have more positive attitudes towards people of the same age as them. People in a young age group (25 and under) will have more positive attitudes towards people in their own age group compared to people in an older age group (60+)

Null hypothesis: There will be no significant difference in the participants' attitudes towards people in a different age group to them. Participants who are 25 and under will not show an in-group preference for their own age group compared to the older age group (60+).

Sampling: An opportunity sample was used drawing on students from the sixth form. The sample size was 20 and they were all students between 16-17 years old.  9 males and 11 females were used.

Ethics: The participants were briefed before the questionnaire was administered and fully informed consent was obtained. They were given the right to withdraw during and after the questionnaire. They were also debriefed at the end of the questionnaire. Participants were assured that their responses would be kept anonymous and confidential as they were answering questions about their personal beliefs and attitudes.

Procedure: A questionnaire was designed to test participants' in-group attitudes towards people of the same age as them and out-group attitudes towards people of a different age to them. The questionnaire used a Likert scale to collect quantitative data about participants in-group/out-group attitudes and it also had four open questions to collect qualitative data. A pilot study was undertaken on three people to make sure the questions on the questionnaire were clear and unambiguous and to establish the reliability and validity of the questionnaire. 20 participants completed the questionnaire with the researcher present in small groups. Participants were briefed before the questionnaire and they completed it in silence so that they could not discuss answers. Participants were given the right to withdraw and debriefed at the end of the questionnaire. The quantitative part of the questionnaire was scored to measure attitudes to the in-group and attitudes to the out-group. The qualitative responses were analysed to look for dominant themes.

Results:

Quantitative research:

| Attitude Score | Positive attitude to in-group | Positive attitude to out-group |
|---|---|---|
| Mean | 3.4 | 2.4 |
| Median | 3.2 | 2.2 |
| Mode | 3.8 | 2.6 |
| Range | 1.4 | 1.2 |

Participants had a more positive attitude towards people of the same age as them. The mean score for positive attitude to the in-group was 3.4 compared to 2.4 for the out-group.

Qualitative research:

One theme was that younger people dress better.

Another theme was that younger people are more adaptable to change. For example, younger people are better with new technology.

Conclusion: The results suggest that younger people do favour those of the same age as them and have more negative attitudes towards people of a different age to them. Social identity theory suggests we prefer our in-group and devalue the out-group. Ageism is an example of this in-group preference.

Evaluation: Participants may have given socially desirable answers on the questionnaire so that they did not appear too prejudiced to the out-group even though they might have been privately. Participants may have been influenced by the age of the researcher carrying out the questionnaire. There can be problems with the Likert scale in collecting data on attitudes as participants can be inclined to give answers towards the middle of the scale rather than at the extremes, which could have affected overall scores. As an opportunity sample was used the sample may be unrepresentative of the wider population. There may also have been subjective interpretation of the qualitative data. Personal views and experience may have affected how the qualitative data was interpreted leading to a biased report being made.

**Exemplar exam questions with student answers**

**Compare Milgram's (1963) study of obedience with a study of obedience from a different country.** (6 marks)

Student answer:

Another study of obedience is Meeus and Raaijmaker's study. Unlike Milgram's study it was carried out in the Netherlands. Both of the studies used a volunteer sample and were carried out in places containing authority (a university and offices). A difference of Meeus and Raaijmaker's study is that they had a control group who did not have to give the stressful remarks, showing it was the authority figure that caused the participants to make the stressful remarks. Another difference is that Milgram's study made the participants believe that they were causing physical harm compared to psychological harm which is harder to do. Both studies deceived the participants, in Milgram's study they believed they were in an experiment for learning and in Meeus and Raaijmaker's study, they thought the study was about the effects of stress on performance. Both were laboratory studies. Meeus and Raaijmaker found higher levels of obedience with 92% giving all the stress remarks, whereas Milgram found that 65% of participants gave the full 450V. Both studies used a confederate who pretended to be the 'victim' but in neither study was actually harmed. Milgram's study was less generalisable as it only used males whereas Meeus and Raaijmaker's study used males and females.

6/6 marks

**Commentary:**

This student has made some good comparisons and gained the full 6 marks. Instead of just describing each study in turn, she has described similarities and differences between the studies.

**Apply concepts, theories and research in the social approach to the problem of terrorism.** (6 marks)

Student answer:

Terrorists may believe they are the in-group based on religion, race or political beliefs. Other people are in the out-group.

Social identity theory can be used to explain terrorism. Terrorists may categorise themselves as belonging to an in group based on religion, race or political beliefs and categorise people of other religions, race or political beliefs as being the out-group. They identify strongly with their in-group by taking on their values, beliefs and appearance. The terrorists may the compare themselves more favourably against the out-group in order to boost their self-esteem. Terrorists may focus on the fact people from other religions are more immoral or greedy and this feeling of superiority might lead them to dehumanise the out-group to the extent that So where quantitative data can have a lack of validity, qualitative data can be more valid.  that they are willing to kill them in an act of terrorism.

Realistic conflict theory explains how competition over resources can lead to conflict between groups. This theory explains terrorism as being related to competition over resources such as land. For example, the IRA wanted Northern Ireland to be governed by an Irish government not a British government. The IRA became so hostile towards the British government that they classed all British citizens as the out-group and bombed certain places in England.

Sherif's study showed how prejudice can occur between rival groups. Two groups of boys at a summer camp were put in competition with each other and prejudice quickly let to fighting and name-calling. This relates to how groups in competition with each other might commit terrorist acts against each other.

5/6 marks

**Commentary:**

This student applies their knowledge of social identity theory, realistic conflict theory and the Sherif study to terrorism well. One extra mark could have been gained by referring to agency theory. Agency theory might explain terrorism in terms of obedience to authority figures. People may commit acts of terrorism on the orders of their leader who they view as an authority figure. They may feel moral strain at committing the acts of terrorism.

# Chapter 3-The Biological Approach

## You need to be able to describe what the biological approach is about

The biological approach is about how our genes, hormones and nervous system affect our behaviour.

## You need to be able to describe the following key terms

**A Neuron:** is a nerve cell. They send electrical messages, called nerve impulses, along their length.

**The Central Nervous System (CNS):** consists of the brain and spinal cord. Sensory neurons are nerves that carry information from the sensory organs (such as our skin or ears) to the CNS. The brain processes this information and sends a message back to the motor neurons. These neurons then carry information to parts of our body to produce a response such as moving our leg.

**A Synapse:** is the tiny gap between two neurons. When a nerve impulse travels along a pre-synaptic neuron (a sending neuron), it triggers the nerve ending to release neurotransmitters across the synapse. The neurotransmitters diffuse across the synapse and bind with receptors on the post-synaptic neuron (the receiving neuron). This causes the post-synaptic neuron to transmit a nerve impulse.

**Neurotransmitters:** are chemical messengers that carry a signal across a synapse from one neuron to another. Examples of neurotransmitters are dopamine and serotonin.

**Receptors:** are sites on the post-synaptic neuron (the receiving neuron) that bind with neurotransmitters.

**Genes:** are units of information that pass on genetic traits such as personality and intelligence from parents to offspring. 50% of our genes come from our mother and 50% of our genes come from our father. Genes are found in our chromosomes. Chromosomes consist of long strands of DNA (deoxyribonucleic acid).

**Hormones:** are chemical substances that are produced by glands in the body. They travel in the blood to target organs. They are similar to neurotransmitters in terms of carrying messages but they move more slowly. For example, the adrenal glands produce the hormone adrenaline, which moves to target organs such as the heart. Heart rate increases to prepare the body for fight or flight. The testes produce the hormone testosterone, which moves to the male reproductive organs and causes changes at puberty in males.

**Brain lateralisation:** refers to how we use one side of our brain at a time. Males have greater brain lateralisation than females, because males use one side of their brain at a time, whereas females use both sides more equally.

**You need to be able to describe and evaluate twin and adoption studies**

**Adoption Studies:** Children who have been adopted are compared to their biological parents and adoptive parents for a certain characteristic. If there is greater similarity between the child and their biological parents, this suggests that genes are important for this characteristic. Heston found that 10% of adopted children whose biological mothers had schizophrenia went on to develop it themselves compared to none in the control group. Heston's study suggests a genetic basis for schizophrenia.

**Evaluation:**

A problem with adoption studies is that adoption agencies usually try to place children in families that are similar to the biological family. Therefore, it is difficult to separate out the influence of genes and the environment. Furthermore, most people are not adopted so it is hard to generalise findings from adoptees to the wider population.

**Twin studies:**

MZ twins are compared to each other to see whether they share the same characteristics. Concordance rates are used to see the similarity between the twins for a certain characteristic such as IQ, personality or mental disorder. For example, Gottesman (1991) found that if one MZ twin has schizophrenia, there is a 48% chance (0.48 concordance) that the other twin will have it too.

In a twin study, DZ twins are also compared to each other to see what the concordance rates are for certain characteristics in them. For example, Gottesman found that if one DZ twin has schizophrenia, there is a 17% chance (0.17 concordance) that the other one will have it too.

MZ twins share 100% of their genes whereas DZ twins only share 50% of their genes. Therefore, if MZ twins have a higher concordance rate than DZ twins for a certain characteristic such as schizophrenia, this suggests that genes are important in determining this characteristic.

**Evaluation:**

An assumption with twin studies is that MZ twins and DZ twins share similar environments and the only difference between MZ twins and DZ twins is that MZ twins share 100% of their genes whereas DZ twins share 50% of their genes. However, this assumption can be questioned. MZ twins are often treated more similarly than DZ twins, for example, they are often dressed the same and people may respond to them in similar ways because they look the same. Therefore, it may be the more similar experiences of MZ twins rather than genes, which leads to them having higher concordance rates for IQ, personality characteristics and mental disorders. Studying separated twins make it easier to assess the influence of genes versus environment. However, separated twins may still have shared the same environment for a certain amount of time before separation. Another problem with twin studies is that most people are not twins so it is hard to generalise from twins to the wider population.

**You need to be able to describe PET and MRI scans**

**Magnetic resonance imaging (MRI)** can be used to produce 3D static images of the brain using magnetic and radio waves. During an MRI scan, a person lies under a powerful magnet, which makes the atoms in the body line up in the same direction. Radio waves are then sent through the body, knocking the atoms out of alignment. When the radio waves are turned off the atoms realign and send out radio signals. The MRI scanner picks up the radio signals and combines them to create an image of the brain. The signals provide information about the location of certain structures in the brain and different types of tissue. MRI scans can be used to look for abnormal structures in the brain or for gender differences in brain structure.

**Positron emission tomography (PET)** can be used to produce 3D computer-generated images of the brain. A radioactive substance, called a tracer, is injected into the bloodstream and travels to the brain. As the tracer breaks down it releases energy waves called gamma rays, which are picked up by the PET scanner. More active areas of the brain break down the radioactive substance more quickly. Areas of high activity in the brain produce more gamma rays and this is shown up in red and yellow on the 3D computer image. Areas of low activity are shown in blue and darker colours on the 3D computer image. Psychologists can use PET scanning to find out which parts of the brain are active when performing certain tasks such as a language or spatial task. Raine et al. used PET scans to compare the brain activity of murderers and non-murderers.

**You need to be able to describe and evaluate the use of animals in psychological research**

Animal studies involve studying animal behaviour either in a laboratory or in the field. In an experiment, an independent variable is manipulated and a dependent variable is measured.

**Rechstaffen et al (1983)** aimed to see the effects of sleep deprivation on rats. In this laboratory experiment, researchers placed rats on a disc above a bucket of water. When the rats fell asleep the disc would rotate and in order to not fall into the water, the rats had to stay awake and walk on the disc. The rats eventually died after severe sleep deprivation. It is questionable whether there is any clear benefit to this research and it certainly caused the rats to suffer distress and die.

**Evaluation:**

Advantages: Animals are easier to use than humans because of ethical issues. For example, animals have been used to investigate how cutting and removing certain parts of the brain affects behaviour (lesion studies). Animals are also smaller on average, which makes certain experiments easier to run. Some animals such as rats breed quickly, which means that means that you can see how selective breeding affects behaviour. For example, if you breed rats that are good at finding their way around mazes together, then you can see whether their offspring are particularly good at mazes. Field studies on animals have ecological validity because they are done in the animals' natural setting.

Disadvantages: Humans are more complex than animals and so it is difficult to generalise results from animal studies to humans. The human brain functions in a different way to animals. There can be ethical issues with carrying out studies on animals.

**Ethical guidelines for non- human (animal) research**

**Caging and Stress:** Experimenters should avoid or minimise stress and suffering for all living animals. The cages the animals are kept in during the experiment should be large enough for the animals to be comfortable.

**Number or animals used:** Researchers should use as few animals as possible.

**Wild Animals:** Endangered species should not be used, unless the research has direct benefits for that species e.g. conservation.

**Qualified Experimenters:** The researchers conducting the experiment should have the necessary qualifications. They should also have a licence from the Home Office for that particular experiment.

**Look for alternatives:** Alternatives to using animals must always be sought, such as using humans or computers.

**You need to be able to describe the Bateson's cube**

Bateson's cube has 3 edges labelled; quality of research, animal suffering and certainty of medical benefit. These are on a scale high to low. When a research proposal falls into the opaque region, experiment should not be conducted i.e. when quality of research is low, animal suffering is high and certainty of benefit is low.

**You need to be able to describe how the central nervous system (CNS) affects behaviour and how neurotransmitters work in the brain**

The central nervous system (CNS) consists of the brain and spinal cord. Sensory neurons are nerves that carry information from the sensory organs (such as our skin or ears) to the central nervous system. The brain processes this information and sends a message back to the motor neurons. These neurons then carry information to parts of the body to produce a response such as moving our leg. For example, if we see that the TV remote control is on the other side of the room, sensory neurons send this information to the CNS. The brain processes where the TV remote control is in the room and it sends a message to the parts of the body involved in movement.

Messages travel along neurons via nerve impulses (electrical impulses). The tiny gap between two neurons is called a synapse. When a nerve impulse travels along a pre-synaptic neuron (a sending neuron), it triggers the nerve ending to release neurotransmitters across the synapse. Neurotransmitters are chemicals messengers that carry a signal across a synapse from one neuron to another. Examples of neurotransmitters are dopamine and serotonin. The neurotransmitters diffuse across the synapse and bind with receptors on the post-synaptic neuron (the receiving neuron). This causes the post-synaptic neuron to transmit the message onwards via a nerve impulse.

## You need to be able to describe what brain lateralisation means

The brain has two hemispheres. The left hemisphere is thought to be more involved in language and the right hemisphere is thought to be more involved in visuospatial abilities. Linking the two is the corpus callosum which is larger in females than males. Some research suggests that females use both hemispheres together when carrying out a task whereas males tend to use only one side of their brain or the other. This means that males have greater brain lateralisation. It has been suggested that males use the left hemisphere for language tasks whereas females use both.

## You need to be able to describe the role of hormones and how they affect behaviour

Hormones are chemical substances that are produced by glands in the body. They travel in the blood to target organs. They are similar to neurotransmitters in terms of carrying messages but they move more slowly. For example, the adrenal glands produce the hormone adrenaline, which moves to target organs such as the heart. Heart rate increases to prepare the body for fight or flight. The testes produce the hormone testosterone, which moves to the male reproductive organs and causes changes at puberty in males. The ovaries produce the hormone oestrogen, which causes changes at puberty in females.

## You need to be able to describe the role of genes in behaviour

Genes are units of information that pass on genetic traits such as personality and intelligence from parents to offspring. Genes are found in our chromosomes. Chromosomes consist of long strands of DNA (deoxyribonucleic acid). Humans have 46 chromosomes (23 pairs of chromosomes). One of the pairs of chromosomes relate to our gender. Females have XX chromosomes and males have XY chromosomes. These sex chromosomes determine which hormones are produced in the body and so affect gender behaviour.

## You need to understand that the biological approach mainly supports the nature side of the nature-nurture debate

The biological approach mainly supports the nature side of the debate. It says that we are born with certain genes and a nervous system that affect the way we think, feel and behave. However, the biological approach accepts that our environment, for example, our diet can affect our development.

**Note:** The learning approach mainly supports the nurture side of the nature-nurture debate. It says that most of our behaviour is learnt from our environment through operant conditioning, classical conditioning and social learning theory. However, it accepts that we are born with some natural behaviours such as automatic reflexes.

The psychodynamic approach supports the nature and nurture side of debate. It supports the nature side of the debate because it says we are born with certain drives and instincts.

On the other hand, it supports the nurture side of the debate because it says our experiences in childhood, our environment, affect us later in life.

**You need to be able to describe and evaluate Money's (1975) case study of David Reimer**

Aim: To see whether gender behavior can be changed through environment. Money believed that children are born gender neutral and that if a baby boy is brought up as a girl, then it will behave as a girl.

Background and Procedure: Bruce was one of two identical twins, whose penis was severely damaged by a mistake during a circumcision. Unsurprisingly, Bruce's parents were worried about how Bruce would deal with the absence of a penis when he reached puberty. They saw Money on a TV programme talking about gender reassignment and decided to contact him. Money believed that Bruce's gender could be reassigned and so Bruce's parents decided to follow Money's suggestions about how to do it. Bruce was given the new name 'Brenda' and was treated as a girl. At 12-years-old, Brenda was given oestrogen, a female hormone, to ensure feminine characteristics.

Money assessed Brenda's gender development at regular intervals and compared her development with her identical twin over a 9 year period. Brenda's mother also reported Brenda's behaviour to Money and was the main source of data.

Results: Brenda seemed to accept her female identity and displayed some feminine characteristics. For example, her mother reported that she liked to wear dresses and play with dolls and she wanted to be a teacher or doctor when she grew up, rather than a policeman or fireman like her brother. Brenda was tomboyish and boisterous but Money related this to her copying her brother's behaviour.

Conclusion: We are born gender neutral and our environment determines our gender behaviour. Gender identity is related to nurture (our environment and experiences) not nature (genes).

**Evaluation:**

Generalisability-It is hard to generalise from this study to the wider population as it involved only one person.

Reliability-It would be hard to test the reliability of this study as it was a unique case. The study also involved interviews and observations, which are hard to replicate.

Application to real life- Money's findings suggest that a person's gender can be reassigned and that children who are born intersex (with ambiguous outer genitalia) can be given sex assignment surgery and brought up according to the gender chosen during surgery. However, later evidence from David Reimer contradicts this finding and suggests that gender cannot be reassigned. David Reimer's case implies that intersex individuals should be allowed to find their own gender identity and that surgery should wait until adulthood. In 2013, the UN condemned surgery on intersex infants.

Validity- Money collected rich, detailed data about Brenda from interviews with her and reports from her parents. This should have given the data greater validity. However, David Reimer said that as soon as he found out he had been born male, everything made sense as he had never been happy as a girl. He asked to be called 'David' at 15-years-old and reverted to being male. He also had surgery to create a penis. In his 20s, he met a woman and later married her. This questions the validity of Money's findings.

Ethics- Money did not know the long-term effects of David's sex reassignment and did not protect David or his family from psychological harm. David's twin brother, Brian, killed himself in his late 30s. David blamed himself, became depressed and ended up separating from his wife. He later committed suicide at 38-years-old.

**You need to be able to describe and evaluate only one of the following studies: De Bellis et al., Raine et al. or Gottesman and Shields**

**De Bellis et al (2001) Boys' brains, girls' brains**

Aim: To see if there is a difference between the way boys' and girls' brains develop.

Procedure: 118 children between 6- and 17-years-old were recruited via an advertisement: 61 males and 57 females. Each participant was checked to make sure they were mentally healthy. They were also given tests to measure their cognitive abilities, IQ and whether they were right or left handed. Before the participants went ahead with the study, they were placed inside a machine, which was like an MRI scanner so they knew what to expect and to practice keeping their head still. Brain scans were then taken of each participant and a piece of computer software measured amounts of grey matter, white matter and the corpus callosum. The brain scans were also analysed by people who did not know whether they were from boys or girls.

Results: The older children had less grey matter than the younger children but more white matter and a more developed corpus callosum. The boys' brains changed faster than the females. Boys had a 19.1% reduction in grey matter between 6 and 17 years of age compared to 4.7% in girls. Boys had a 45.1% increase in white matter compared with a 17.1% increase in girls. Boys had a 58.5% increase in the corpus callosum compared with a 27.4% increase in girls.

Conclusion: The brain changes with age and changes occur faster in boys than girls.

**Evaluation:**

Generalisability: The children had higher than average IQs, which means they are not representative of the wider population.

Reliability-It was difficult to measure the grey and white matter and so if the study was repeated, different results might be obtained. However, there was good inter-rater reliability when measuring the grey and white matter and the corpus callosum. Giedd et al. (1999) found similar increases and decreases, which suggests the findings are reliable.

Application to real life-The study can help explain gender differences in cognitive abilities as boys' and girls' brains are different.

Validity- The boys and girls were matched for IQ, socioeconomic status and race, which makes the study more valid.

Ethics-Informed consent was obtained from the parents. The children were placed in a machine that was like an MRI scanner before the study started so they knew what to expect.

**You need to be able to describe and evaluate the biological explanations of gender behaviour:**

**The role of genes in gender development:**

Genetic sex is determined by chromosomes in the egg and in the sperm. The egg always has the X chromosome but the sperm can contain either an X chromosome or Y chromosome. Boys have XY chromosomes so if the sperm contains the Y chromosome, then a male foetus will develop. Girls have XX chromosomes so if the sperm contains the X chromosome, a female foetus will develop. The Y chromosome causes the male foetus to develop testes at around 7 weeks. In a female, other genes cause the foetus to develop ovaries.

**Evaluation:**

The case of David Reimer supports the theory that genes determine our gender behaviour. He was born with the male sex chromosomes XY but was brought up as a girl due to his penis being destroyed during a circumcision that went wrong. However, he was never happy as a girl and when he found out he was genetically male, reverted back to his male identity.

**The role of hormones in gender development:**

If a foetus is male, then H-Y hormone is released when the foetus is 6-weeks-old, which causes the testes to develop. The testes produce anti-Mullerian hormone, which stops the production of female sex hormones. The testes then produce androgens such as testosterone, which cause male sex organs to develop. If the foetus is female, no male hormones are released and female sex organs to develop. At puberty, the ovaries produce the hormone oestrogen in girls and the testes produce the hormone testosterone in boys. Oestrogen causes females to develop secondary sex characteristics such as enlarged breasts and wider hips. Testosterone causes male secondary sex characteristics such as a deeper voice and facial hair. Testosterone also stimulates the testes to produce sperm.

**Evaluation:**

Studies show that hormones affect gender behaviour. Female rats who were injected with testosterone behaved more like male rats. Female mice with a genetic trait that makes them unable to detect the hormone oestrogen, spend less time caring for their offspring. However, we may not be able to generalise the findings of animal studies to humans as we are more complex.

**Brain lateralisation and gender development:**

One biological explanation of gender differences is that males have greater brain lateralisation than females i.e. males tend to use only one side of their brain when carrying out a task. Another explanation for gender differences is that males tend to use the right side of their brain more than their left side.

**Evaluation:**

Men are on average better at visuospatial tasks than females but not so good at verbal tasks. Visuospatial tasks are controlled by the right side of the brain so this supports the idea that males use the right side of the brain more. Men who had decreased exposure to male hormones (androgens) in the womb tend to use both sides of the brain more. This suggests that 'normal' males who have higher levels of androgens than females have greater brain lateralisation. However, Sommer et al. (2004) found no differences between men and women in language lateralisation. Wallentin (2009) found no differences in the size of the corpus callosum between males and females.

**You need to be able to compare biological explanations of gender development with psychodynamic and learning explanations**

**Exam tip:** You can compare the different explanations in terms of nature/nurture, role of the parents and whether the approach considers gender development to be fixed or changing over time.

**Nature-nurture**
The biological approach believes that gender behaviour is affected by nature. It says that our genes, hormones and brain structure affect gender development.

The psychodynamic approach believes that gender behaviour is affected by both nature and nurture. It says that we are born with certain biological/anatomical differences (having or not having a penis) that combine with family dynamics to affect our gender behaviour. During the phallic stage, boys identify with their fathers to overcome their castration anxiety and girls identify with their mothers to overcome penis envy.

The learning approach believes that nurture leads to gender behaviour ie. That environmental influences only, such as parents, school, society, peers, TV and other models, lead to gender behaviour.

The biological and psychodynamic explanations are similar to each other in terms of the belief that biological differences lead to gender development. However, the biological approach believes gender identity is determined by our biological make-up whereas the psychodynamic approach believes family dynamics are also important. The biological approach is different from the learning approach because the biological approach believes that gender behaviour is determined by our biological make-up (nature) whereas the learning approach focuses on environmental influences (nurture).

## Role of the parents:

The biological approach says that the role of the parents in gender behaviour is limited to whether they donate X or Y sex chromosomes to their offspring. However, the psychodynamic and learning approaches believe parents have a more important role in the development of gender behaviour: The psychodynamic approach suggests that children learn gender-appropriate behaviour through identifying with the same sex parent; the learning approach argues that parents are important role models for gender behaviour and encourage gender-appropriate behaviour.

## Fixed or changing over time

The biological approach believes that gender is fixed from birth due to genes, although hormone changes particularly at puberty affect gender identity. In contrast, the learning approach believes that gender identity changes over time. For example, our gender identity can be affected by our life stage or our peer group. The psychodynamic approach believes that gender development occurs mainly during the phallic stage and is fixed after that.

## You need to be able to describe a key issue in the biological approach: Whether autism is an extreme male brain condition

Baron-Cohen et al. (2005) suggests that autism is an extreme male brain condition. He also linked the cause of autism with high levels of testosterone in the womb. Research supports the idea that autism is an extreme male brain condition. Male brains are heavier than female brains and those with autism have an even heavier brain than a normal male brain. Male brains also grow more quickly, as does the brain of someone with autism. On average males are better at spatial tasks such as map reading, mathematical reasoning and systemising and autistic children tend to focus on such skills. On average, females are better at language tasks and interpreting emotions, which autistic children have more difficulty with. Auyeung et al. (2009) found that pregnant women who had high levels of testosterone (a male hormone) in the amniotic fluid were more likely to have children who had autistic traits at age eight, such as a lack of sociability and poor verbal skills. Baron-Cohen et al. (2003) found that autistic children scored higher on systemising, a male trait, than the general population.

However, autistic people do not have greater brain lateralisation than normal people, which contradicts the idea of autistic people having an extreme male brain. Autism may have a genetic basis. Jorde et al. (1991) found that children who have a sibling with autism are 25 times more likely to develop it themselves than a child in the general population. Bailey et al. (1995) found a 60% concordance rate for autism in MZ twins compared to a 0% concordance for DZ twins. This suggests that there is a genetic basis for autism. DNA studies have been carried out to identify genes, which are related to autism. Schellenberg et al. (2006) found that chromosomes 4 and 7 are linked to autism. There may also be environmental causes of autism. Difficulties at birth and exposure to rubella in the womb have been linked to autism.

**You need to know why inferential tests are used**

**One problem with the mean is that it doesn't tell you whether the difference between two** conditions is significant or not. For example, you do an experiment to test whether cues affect recall and your results show that the mean number of words recalled with a cue is 11.2 and the mean number of words recalled without a cue is 12.3. These figures suggest that the participants can recall more words with a cue and so you might conclude that cues do aid recall. However, it is difficult to judge whether the difference in the number of words recalled with a cue or without a cue is big enough to be certain of this conclusion. Perhaps on a different day or with different participants, you might have found less of a difference between the two conditions. An inferential test is a statistical test that shows you whether the difference between the two conditions is significant or not.

You choose an inferential test based on the design of the experiment and the level of data you collected.

**You need to be able to recognise types of design**

An independent groups design involves testing separate groups of participants. Each group is tested in a different condition. For example, a researcher might ask one group to process words semantically and a second group to process words phonetically.

A repeated measures design involves testing the same group of people in different conditions. For example, the same group of people might be asked to process words semantically and phonetically.

A matched pairs design involves testing separate groups of people who are matched on certain characteristics. For example, each member of one group is the same age, gender, race and socioeconomic status as a member of the other group.

A correlational design is when two variables have been measured to see whether there is a relationship between them. For example, a researcher might look to see whether there is a relationship between number of hours of TV watched and level of aggression.

**You need to be able to recognise levels of data**

Nominal data is made up of discrete categories.  For example, you might categorise participants as either 'extroverts' or 'introverts'.

Ordinal data are ranked data.  For example, you might rank participants on how well they recognise emotional expressions. Helen came first, Alex came second and Philippa came third.

Interval data are measurements along a scale with no true zero.  For example, IQ can be measured along a scale but there is no true zero for IQ. Most people have an IQ between 70 and 130. For example, Helen has an IQ of 120, Alex has an IQ of 117 and Philippa has an IQ of 115.

Ratio data are measurements along a scale with a true zero. For example, time can be measured along a scale and there is a true zero. For example, Helen completed a spatial awareness task in 90s, Alex completed the task in 97s and Philippa completed the task in 105s.

**You need to know about level of significance**

In psychology, a significance level of $p \leq 0.05$ is chosen.

$p \leq 0.05$ means that there is an equal or less than 5% probability that the results could have occurred due to chance.

> $p$ = the probability of the results being due to chance

> $\leq$ = less than or equal to

> $0.05 = 1$ in $20 = 5\%$

Psychologists prefer to use the significance level: $p \leq 0.05$ to judge whether to accept a hypothesis or not. This means that there is an equal or less than 5% probability that the results are due to chance e.g. the group that received a cue recalled more words than the group that did not receive a cue and there is a less than 5% chance that the difference between the two groups could have been due to chance (random differences between the groups).

Sometimes researchers use the significance level: $p \leq 0.1$ to judge whether to accept a hypothesis or not. This means that there is an equal or less than 10% probability that the results are due to chance. You can see that this is less conservative than $p \leq 0.05$. It is easier for the hypothesis to be accepted even though the null hypothesis might be true. This leads to a type 1 error. Type 1 errors can lead to false positive results; accepting a hypothesis even though it is incorrect. This could lead to psychologists thinking that there is a significant difference between participant's recall when they are given a cue and not given a cue when there isn't a significant difference in recall.

Sometimes researchers use the significance level: $p \leq 0.01$ to judge whether to accept a hypothesis or not. This means that there is an equal or less than 1% probability that the results are due to chance. You can see that this is stricter than $p \leq 0.05$. It is harder for the hypothesis to be accepted even though it might actually be correct. This leads to a type 2 error. Type 2 errors can lead to false negative results; rejecting a hypothesis when it is correct. This could lead to psychologists thinking that there was no difference between participants recall when given a cue compared to no cue, when there was a significant difference.

**You need to know when to use a Mann-Whitney U test**

You use a Mann-Whitney U test when you have an independent groups design, ordinal data and you are testing for a difference between two groups.

To decide whether the results are significant there must be an equal or less than 5% probability that the results are due to chance. If the results are significant, then psychologists say that they are rejecting the null hypothesis. In essence, they mean that they are accepting the experimental hypothesis but it is standard form to refer to rejecting the null hypothesis.

In order to decide whether the results are significant or not the observed value (the result obtained from the data collected) is compared to the critical value.

The critical value is a statistical 'cut-off' point. It is a number presented on a table of critical values that determines whether the result is significant enough for the null hypothesis not to be accepted.

The observed value is the value given by the actual experiment; it is compared with the relevant critical value to see if a null hypothesis should be rejected or not.

You need to know whether the hypothesis was one-tailed or two-tailed; the number of participants in each condition (shown as 'N' on the table) and the significance level. The values in the Mann-Whitney Test are termed 'U' and unlike the Spearman-rank and Chi-squared Tests the observed value has to be equal to or less than the critical value for the results to be significant (i.e. to accept the experimental hypothesis and reject the null hypothesis).

**You need to be able to describe a practical you carried out in the biological approach.**

**Example practical: Gender Differences in Spatial Ability**

One-tailed/Directional Hypothesis: Males will have better spatial ability than females on a spatial awareness computer game.

Independent variable: Gender of participants

Dependent variable: Score on spatial awareness task on the computer game.

Sampling Method: An opportunity sample of sixth formers in our class was used.

Type of design: An independent groups design was used.

Procedure: Participants were briefed about the study and given the right to withdraw. 7 male students and 9 female students in our class were tested individually on spatial awareness using a computer game. All the students were tested in the same classroom and in silence to control for extraneous variables. The participants had a 3 minute time limit to complete the game. Participants' scores on the computer game were recorded and ranked by gender. Participants were debriefed at the end of the study.

Results:

Table to show male and female spatial scores on a computer game

| Participants | Male spatial score | Female spatial score | Rank |
|---|---|---|---|
| 1 | 24 | | 8 |
| 2 | 23 | | 7 |
| 3 | 25 | | 9 |
| 4 | 25 | | 9 |
| 5 | 22 | | 6 |
| 6 | 13 | | 2 |
| 7 | 19 | | 4 |
| 8 | | 25 | 9 |
| 9 | | 23 | 7 |
| 10 | | 12 | 1 |
| 11 | | 25 | 9 |
| 12 | | 21 | 5 |
| 13 | | 23 | 7 |
| 14 | | 15 | 3 |
| 15 | | 24 | 8 |
| 16 | | 22 | 6 |

Note: For a Mann-Whitney U test, the data from both groups are ranked together. If participants have the same score, they are given the same rank. This way of ranking is different to how data is ranked for the Spearman's rho test.

A Mann-Whitney U test was carried out on the data as the level of data was ordinal and it was an independent groups design. The observed value was 29.5 and the critical value was 15 at level of significance $p \leq 0.05$.

Conclusion:

The observed value was higher than the critical value so the null hypothesis was accepted. There was no significant difference in spatial awareness between males and females.

Note: If the observed value had been less than the critical value, the null hypothesis would have been rejected and there would have been a significant difference in spatial awareness between males and females.

**Evaluation**

An opportunity sample was used of sixth formers in our class at school. This sample is unrepresentative of the wider population.

We measured spatial ability using a computer game but this may not be a true measure of overall spatial ability as it may just test how good someone is with computers. More tests on spatial ability would be needed to test participants' overall spatial ability.

Participants may also have acted differently compared to real life as the task lacked mundane realism.

Note: A task lacks mundane realism if it is not an everyday task.

The study was reliable as extraneous variables were controlled and the procedure was standardised for all participants making it replicable.

**Exemplar exam question with student answer**

**Describe a key issue in the biological approach**. (8 marks)

Student answer:

A key issue is the biological approach is whether autism is an extreme male brain condition. Baron-Cohen divided people into 5 categories: type S are better at systemising, type E are better at empathising, type B are balanced, extreme type S are good at systemizing and poor at empathizing and extreme type E are good at empathising and poor at systemizing. Type E is more common in males and extreme type E is the category that autistic people fall into. This suggests autism is an extreme male brain condition. People with autism have many characteristics that are also common in males such as good logic, map reading skills and poor linguistics. Autism is also more common in males with a male to female ratio of 4:1. However, autism is also linked to problems at birth yet it is not certain whether the birth difficulties lead to autism or the larger head size of an autistic child leads to the problems at birth. Autism may also be caused by the personalities of the parents, if they are born very organised there is a higher chance of their child being autistic. It may also be due to genes, in history it may have been very useful to be extremely organised and this characteristic may have been passed down in the genes. The concept of an extreme male brain does not explain why women do get autism rather than acting more manly if they have a more male brain.

5/12 marks-level 2 answer

**Commentary:**

This essay only achieved a level 2 because many points were not fully developed. This student talks about autistic people having male characteristics but does not develop the point. Males are better at spatial skills than females and autistic people are even better, which supports the idea of an extreme male brain. There are other points that the student could have made such as the fact that male brains are heavier than female brains and those with autism have an even heavier brain than a normal male brain. Male brains also grow more quickly, as does the brain of someone with autism. Auyeung et al. (2009) found that pregnant women who had high levels of testosterone (a male hormone) in the amniotic fluid were more likely to have children who had autistic traits at age eight, such as a lack of sociability and poor verbal skills. Baron-Cohen et al. (2003) found that autistic children scored higher on systemising, a male trait, than the general population.

However, autistic people do not have greater brain lateralisation than normal people, which contradicts the idea of autistic people having an extreme male brain. Autism may have a genetic basis. Jorde et al. (1991) found that children who have a sibling with autism are 25 times more likely to develop it themselves than a child in the general population. Bailey et al. (1995) found a 60% concordance rate for autism in MZ twins compared to a 0% concordance for DZ twins. This suggests that there is a genetic basis for autism. DNA studies have been carried out to identify genes, which are related to autism. Schellenberg et al. (2006) found that chromosomes 4 and 7 are linked to autism. The student suggests that if the parents' personalities make them very organised, then there is a higher chance that their offspring will be autistic but they do not link this to genes. Genes affect personality traits and so the personality trait of organising and systemising can be inherited. If both parents are systemisers, their child might have more extreme systemising traits. However, a point is made about systemising skills being an evolutionary adaptation. Being good at systemising, reading maps and spatial skills may have aided survival in our evolutionary past. Therefore, the genes that code for such skills have been passed down.

There may be environmental causes of autism. This student discusses difficulties at birth as being related to autism. Exposure to rubella in the womb has also been linked to autism.

# Chapter 4-The Learning Approach

## You need to be able describe what the learning approach is about

The learning approach focuses on how our behaviour is influenced by the environment. It makes the following assumptions: we respond to stimuli in our environment and behaviour is affected by our experiences.

## You need to be able to define the following key terms

**Classical conditioning** refers to the process of learning by association. It occurs when we make associations between stimuli and automatic, reflexive responses. For example, a dog might salivate to the sound of a bell on its own because it has associated food with the bell.

**A stimulus** is something that causes a response. For example, a spider might be a stimulus that causes a fear response.

**A response** is a reaction to a specific stimulus. For example, salivation might be the response to the stimulus of food.

**Extinction** is when a conditioned response is suppressed. This occurs when the conditioned stimulus is no longer paired with the unconditioned stimulus. For example, if a dog is no longer given food (unconditioned stimulus) when it hears a bell (conditioned stimulus), it will stop salivating (conditioned response) to the sound of the bell.

**Spontaneous recovery** occurs when a conditioned response lies dormant but then suddenly reappears again. For example, a dog's conditioned response of salivating to a bell may extinguish but then reappear later when the dog hears the sound of a bell.

**Operant conditioning** refers to the process of learning through consequences. For example, we are more likely to repeat a behaviour if it is rewarded and less likely to repeat the behaviour if it is punished.

**Positive reinforcement** refers to giving a reward for a desired behaviour. For example, a dog might be given a treat for sitting down when their owner says 'sit'.

**Negative reinforcement** refers to taking away something unpleasant for a desired behaviour. For example, a teacher might take away homework for particularly good work in class.

**Punishment** refers to giving a nasty consequence (such as a detention) or removing something nice (such as pocket money) for an undesired behaviour. For example, a child might be told to sit on the naughty step for pinching another child.

**Primary reinforcement** refers to giving a reward that either satisfies a basic need or fulfils a natural desire. Food, drink, warmth and shelter are examples of primary reinforcers.

**Secondary reinforcement** refers to giving a reward, which can be exchanged for something that satisfies a basic need. Secondary reinforcers are only fulfilling because they are associated with a primary reinforcer e.g. money can be used to buy food. Merits, tokens and vouchers are types of secondary reinforcers.

**Social learning** refers to learning through observation. For example, a girl may observe her older sister bake a lovely cake and then copy the behaviour later.

**Observation** with reference to social learning theory refers to watching a model's behaviour. For example, a girl may watch her older sister putting on make-up.

**Imitation** refers to copying a behaviour after it has been modelled. For example, a boy may play with a toy gun in the same way his friend does.

**Modelling** refers to learning new behaviours by observing other people. The modelling process involves the following processes: attention, retention, reproduction and motivation. For example, a boy may pay attention to his father playing the guitar and retain the behaviour. In order to reproduce the behaviour, he will need to practise the guitar. Finally, to successfully imitate his father's playing ability, he needs to be motivated to copy the behaviour.

**Vicarious reinforcement** refers to a behaviour being reinforced because another person has been observed receiving a reward for it. For example, a boy is more likely to work hard on his sums at school, after seeing another boy get rewarded with a sticker for completing a set of sums quickly.

**Exam tip:** Remember to define and give an example.

**You need to be able to describe the key features of classical conditioning**

**Classical conditioning** refers to the process of learning through association. When a neutral stimulus is paired with an unconditioned stimulus, we can become 'conditioned' to respond to the neutral stimulus. The neutral stimulus becomes a conditioned stimulus and produces a conditioned response.

E.G. Pavlov's dog study
Food (UCS) ⟶ Salivation (UCR)
Food (UCS) + Bell (NS) ⟶ Salivation (UCR)
Bell (CS) ⟶ Salivation (CR)

**Extinction:** When a conditioned response is suppressed. This occurs when the conditioned stimulus is no longer paired with the unconditioned stimulus. For example, if a dog is no longer given food (unconditioned stimulus) when it hears a bell (conditioned stimulus), it will stop salivating (conditioned response) to the sound of the bell. Extinction does not mean that the behaviour has been unlearnt; it just means that the behaviour has become dormant.

**Spontaneous recovery**: A conditioned response may be dormant but suddenly reappear again. For example, a dog's conditioned response of salivating to a bell may extinguish but then reappear later when the dog hears the sound of a bell.

**Generalisation** is when someone becomes conditioned to respond to not only the conditioned stimulus but also similar stimuli. For example, Little Albert became conditioned to not only fear white rats but also other white furry objects.

**You need to be able to describe and evaluate Watson and Rayner (1920)-Little Albert**

Aim: To see whether Little Albert could be classically conditioned to be afraid of a stimulus he was originally unafraid of.

Procedure: Little Albert was chosen for the study because he was an emotionally stable child who was not easily frightened. He was also familiar with the hospital environment as his mother worked there. At 9 months old, he was tested to see whether he was afraid of a variety of stimuli.  He was unafraid of a white rat but was afraid of the sound of a metal bar being banged. When Albert was 11 months old, the researchers decided to classically condition him to be afraid of a white rat. Albert was shown the white rat and when he reached out to touch it, a loud noise was made with a metal bar behind his head. This was repeated several times.

UCS (banging of bar)  $\longrightarrow$  UCR (Fear)

UCS(banging of bar) + NS(rat) $\longrightarrow$ UCR(fear)

CS (rat) $\longrightarrow$ CR (fear)

Originally the rat is a neutral stimulus (NS) but once it begins to cause fear, it becomes a conditioned stimulus (CS)

Results: Little Albert showed a fear response to the rat on its own after a number of pairings of the rat and the banging bar over a period of a week. At 11 months 15 days old, Little Albert was happy to play with some toy blocks but showed fear towards the rat. He also showed a negative response to a rabbit and a fur coat suggesting he had transferred his fear of the white rat onto similar objects.

Conclusion: This study showed that Little Albert was classically conditioned to be afraid of a stimulus he was originally unafraid of. It also showed that conditioned responses can be generalised to other similar objects.

**Evaluation:**

Generalisability-The study was carried out on only one boy so it is hard to generalise it to the wider population.

Reliability-This laboratory experiment had good controls and a procedure that would be easy to replicate. The researchers carefully observed and recorded Little Albert's responses to the stimuli, which makes it reliable. They also made sure Little Albert was not afraid of furry things and rats before the study. However, if the study was repeated with other children, it may be difficult to replicate the findings as other children might be afraid of a white rat but unafraid of a banging metal bar.

Application to real life-This study can explain how humans learn phobias through association. For example, a child may be initially afraid of spiders but unafraid of going into a shed. However, they may become afraid of the shed after a spider runs across their shoe in the shed.

Validity-The study lacks ecological validity because it was an artificial situation. In real life, stimuli are not carefully paired together under controlled conditions as the white rat and banging bar were in this study.

Ethics- Little Albert was not protected from psychological harm. He was only 11 months old when he took part in the experiments and he was caused distress. For example, he showed fear and cried when shown the white rat. They also did not extinguish his fear.

**You need to be able to describe and evaluate aversion therapy**

Aversion therapy uses classical conditioning to get rid of addictions or unwanted behaviours. A patient's unwanted addiction is paired with a drug that makes them sick or electric shocks. Aversion therapy can be used with alcoholics. Alcohol is paired with an emetic drug (a drug which causes nausea and vomiting). Over time the alcoholic associates alcohol with being sick and does not want to drink alcohol anymore. Other drinks such as soft drinks are given without the drug so that the person is not conditioned to feel sick to all drinks.

(UCS) Emetic Drug $\longrightarrow$ Vomiting (UCR)

(NS) Alcohol + (UCS) Emetic Drug $\longrightarrow$ Vomiting (UCR)

(CS) Alcohol $\longrightarrow$ Vomiting (CR)

Smokers can undergo aversion therapy to help them quit smoking. For example, they might take an emetic drug that makes them feel nauseous every time they smoke.

Aversion therapy has also been used to change sexually deviant behaviour. For example, paedophiles can make themselves break an ammonia capsule and sniff it every time they think about children in an unsuitable way or when they imagine situations where they might approach children. The ammonia makes their eyes, nose and throat hurt. In this way, paedophiles can condition themselves to respond to children with fear rather than sexual arousal.

When homosexuality was illegal in the 1960s, some gay men were given the choice of aversion therapy or a prison sentence. During the aversion therapy, the gay men were shown images of naked men paired with electric shocks or an emetic drug. They were also shown images of naked women without the shocks or emetic drug.

Covert sensitisation is an alternative to traditional aversion therapy. Instead of using an emetic drug or electric shocks, the patient is asked to imagine feeling sick or being in a pain. It has been found to be effective for treating alcoholism, smoking and gambling.

**How to evaluate a treatment**

You can use DESERT to help you evaluate a therapy.

Directive- Is the patient reliant on the therapist for all the answers? Is there a power imbalance? If the therapist has too much power then the treatment is directive.

Effectiveness-How effective is the therapy at treating the behaviour?

Side effects-Are there any side effects to the therapy?

Expense-How expensive is the therapy in terms of time and money?

Reasons-Does the therapy looks at the underlying causes/reasons for the behaviour?

Types of people-Does the therapy only work on certain types of people?

**Evaluation:**

Directive- Aversion therapy can be viewed as directive because the therapist can have too much power and control and the patient may feel out of control, for example, if they are vomiting from an emetic drug. People may agree to aversion therapy because they feel under pressure to have the treatment rather than actually wanting it.

Effectiveness-Aversion therapy can help alcoholics when used alongside another treatment. However, the effects may not be permanent as the association between the alcohol and vomiting may fade over time, if the person drinks alcohol without taking the emetic drug. Research suggests that aversion therapy is not effective on gay men. The use of aversion therapy to treat homosexuality is now illegal in some countries.

Side effects-Emetic drugs cause vomiting and electric shocks cause pain. Therefore, aversion therapy can be very distressing and this is an ethical issue with the therapy. One gay man even died from an emetic drug given to him.

Expense-Aversion therapy can be expensive if a trained therapist is administering or monitoring the effects of the electric shocks or emetic drug. However, it is relatively inexpensive for a smoker to take an emetic drug at home every time they smoke.

Reasons-Aversion therapy does not deal with the underlying causes of the addiction or sexually deviant behaviour. There may be deep-rooted family issues that are causing someone to be an alcoholic. Aversion therapy should be used alongside counselling or another talking therapy.

Types of people-Aversion therapy works better on people with addictions. It does not work well on gay men.

**You need to be able to describe the key features of operant conditioning**

**Operant conditioning** refers to the process of learning through consequences: **Positive reinforcement** (rewards), **negative reinforcement** (removing something unpleasant) and **punishment** (providing something nasty or removing something nice).
If behaviour is positively reinforced it is more likely to be repeated e.g. a rat will learn to press a bar to receive food and children will learn to tidy their bedrooms for pocket money.
If behaviour is negative reinforced it is more likely to be repeated e.g. a rat will learn to press a bar to turn an electric shock off.
If behaviour is punished is it less likely to be repeated. Punishment may involve the arrival of something nasty (such as a shock) or the removal of something nice (such as pocket money). E.g If a child is forced to sit in 'the naughty corner' every time it pinches another child, it will stop pinching other children.

**Primary reinforcers** are rewards that satisfy a basic need, such as food, drink, warmth and shelter. Fizzy drinks, sweets, chocolate and cake are all types of primary reinforcer.

**Secondary reinforcers** are rewards that are not fulfilling on their own but can be exchanged for something that satisfies a basic need. Secondary reinforcers are only fulfilling because they are associated with a primary reinforcer e.g. money can be used to buy food. Merits, tokens and vouchers are types of secondary reinforcers.

**Shaping** is when a behaviour is learnt by rewarding moves towards the desired behaviour (successive approximations of the desired behaviour). First of all behaviour that is on the way to the desired behaviour is rewarded and then later on only behaviours that are nearer and nearer to the desired behaviour are rewarded. For example, shaping helps children acquire language. When a child first vocalises, their parents are delighted and give the child lots of attention and praise. The attention is rewarding and so the child repeats vocalisations. The parents then begin to only praise (positively reinforce) vocalisations sounding like words so the child begins to only repeat word sounds. Later the parents only reinforce the child when they produce real words so that word sounds (e.g. gadad) are shaped into words (e.g. granddad).

**You need to be able to describe the key features of social learning theory**

Social learning theory says that we learning by observation and imitation. For social learning to occur, the learner must pay **attention** to and **retain** the model's behaviour. The learner must have the physical abilities to **reproduce** the behaviour and the learner must be **motivated** to imitate the behaviour. If the model is rewarded this increases the likelihood that the learner will imitate the behaviour. This is called **vicarious reinforcement**. For example, a girl may observe her older sister bake a cake and get praise for it. She is more likely to copy her sister's behaviour because she has seen her sister be rewarded for it.

Models of the same gender and age are more powerful (are more likely to be imitated).

Models of higher status such as celebrities are also more likely to be copied.

**Exam tip:** Use ARRM to help you describe social learning theory. Attention, Retention, Reproduction and Motivation.

**You need to be able to describe and evaluate Bandura, Ross and Ross (1961)**

Aim: 1)To see if children might observe aggressive behaviour and then model their own actions on it. 2) To investigate the impact of gender on modelling.

Procedure: The study involved 72 children from one nursery in the USA. There was an equal mix of boys and girls and they were between 3- to 5-years-old.  24 of the children were put in a control group and did not observe a model at all. The remaining 48 children were divided into eight conditions: Condition 1-Boys watch aggressive, male model; Condition 2-Boys watch non-aggressive male model; Condition 3-Boys watch aggressive, female model; Condition 4-Boys watch non-aggressive female model; Condition 5-Girls watch aggressive, male model; Condition 6-Girls watch non-aggressive male model; Condition 7-Girls watch aggressive, female model and Condition 8-Girls watch non-aggressive, female model.

The children in the different conditions were matched individually on the basis of ratings of their aggressive behaviour in social interactions in the nursery school. During the experiment, the children were taken individually into a room by the experimenter and seated at a table where they could design pictures with potato prints and picture stickers provided. The experimenter then brought the adult model to the opposite corner of the room where there was a tinker toy set, a mallet, and a 5-foot inflated Bobo doll. The experimenter then left the room. Children in the non-aggressive condition saw a model quietly play with some tinker toys in the corner. Children in the aggressive condition, saw the model play with the tinker toys and then after one minute behave aggressively to the Bobo doll. The model sat on the Bobo doll and punched it repeatedly in the nose. The model then raised the Bobo doll, picked up the mallet and struck the doll on the head. The final aggressive act in the sequence was throwing the model into the air and kicking it around the room. The model then repeated this sequence of aggressive acts approximately three times. The model also made verbally aggressive comments such as, "Sock him in the nose . . . ," "Hit him down . . . ," "Throw him in the air . . . ," "Kick him . . . ," "Pow . . . ," and two non-aggressive comments, "He keeps coming back for more" and "He sure is a tough fella."

After 10 minutes, the experimenter entered the room and took the child to a different room to play after saying goodbye to the model. When they got to the new room, the children were all put into a slightly aggressive state by being told that they could not play with certain toys. This was to make sure that all the children were at the same level of aggression. The children were then observed playing. The researchers scored any behaviour to the Bobo doll that was imitative of the specific aggressive acts shown by the model to the Bobo doll.

Results: The children who had watched the aggressive models were more aggressive. In the non-aggressive and control conditions, approximately 70% of the children had a zero score for aggressive acts. Boys were more physically aggressive than girls but there was little difference for verbal aggression. The children were more likely to imitate same sex models. The mean number of aggressive acts committed by the boys was 25.8 after observing the male model and 12.4 after observing the female model. The boys showed more than double the number of aggressive acts towards the Bobo doll after observing a male model compared to a female model.

Conclusion: When children watch adults being aggressive they are likely to imitate that aggression, so it shows that observational learning takes places (social learning theory). Children are more likely to copy same-sex models. Boys, in particular, are more likely to be aggressive after observing a same-sex model be aggressive.

**Evaluation:**

Generalisability-All the children were from one nursery in the USA so it is hard to generalise from the study to the wider population.

Reliability- The study was a laboratory experiment with good controls so it is replicable and reliable. The researchers matched the children on levels of aggression at start. Inter-observer reliability was established by having more than one observer.

Application to real life-This study suggests that children are likely to copy violence shown by models. Therefore, children's exposure to violent role models in real life, on TV or in computer games should be limited.

Validity-The study involved an artificial situation so it lacks ecological validity. The children who saw the model behave aggressively to the Bobo doll, may have thought that they were supposed to behave that way towards the Bobo doll. If they had seen a model behave aggressively to a real person, they may have been much less likely to copy the behaviour. The children knew that the plastic Bobo doll could not be hurt so the study does not measure real aggression.

Ethics-The children who watched the aggressive model may have been made more aggressive and this is an ethical issue.

**You need to be able to describe how operant conditioning and social learning theory can be used to explain gender development**

Operant conditioning can be used to explain gender development. Gender-appropriate behaviour is encouraged from birth and gender-stereotypical behaviours are reinforced e.g. girls may be encouraged to play with dolls and boys with cars. Gender-inappropriate behaviours are punished e.g. when boys play with dolls they may be laughed at, ignored or told off.

Social learning theory argues that gender identification occurs through observing and imitating gender-appropriate behaviour from same-sex models. The theory suggests that children pay more attention to same-sex models, retain their behaviour and then if they are capable of reproducing the behaviour and motivated to do so they will (ARRM). Gender development occurs through imitating gender-appropriate behaviours from same-sex parents, peers and others. For example, a young boy may pay attention to his father fixing a car. He will remember how to do it and reproduce the behaviour when he is motivated to do so.

**You need to be able to evaluate operant conditioning and social learning theory as explanations of gender behaviour including comparison with explanations from the Biological and Psychodynamic approaches**

Sroufe et al. (1993) found that children who do not conform to gender stereotypes are less popular with their peers. Langlois and Downs (1980) found that fathers will ignore or ridicule their sons if they play or dress like girls. These studies support the idea that operant conditioning affects gender behaviour.

Bandura, Ross and Ross' (1961) study found that children were more likely to imitate aggressive behaviour shown by same sex models. This study supports the idea that children learn gender behaviour through copying role models. Research suggests that when children watch more television, they hold more stereotypical views of gender roles.

The learning approach ignores biological reasons for gender behaviour such as the effect of genes and hormones on gender development. The David Reimer case supports a biological explanation of gender development and contradicts the learning approach. David Reimer developed a male identity despite being brought up as a female. The learning approach also ignores psychodynamic explanations of gender development. The psychodynamic approach suggests that gender behaviour develops as the superego develops, when the child overcomes the Oedipus or Electra complex by identifying with the same sex parent and taking on their values and ideals.

**You need to be able to compare how the learning approach explain gender behaviour with the biological and psychodynamic approach**

**Exam tip:** You can compare the different explanations in terms of nature/nurture, role of the parents and whether the approach considers gender development to be fixed or changing over time.

**Nature-nurture**

The learning approach believes that nurture leads to gender behaviour i.e. that environmental influences such as parents, school, society, peers, TV and other models, lead to gender behaviour.

The biological approach believes that gender behaviour is affected by nature. It says that our genes, hormones and brain structure affect gender development.

The psychodynamic approach believes that gender behaviour is affected by both nature and nurture. It says that we are born with certain biological/anatomical differences (having or not having a penis) that combine with family dynamics to affect our gender behaviour. During the phallic stage, boys identify with their fathers to overcome their castration anxiety and girls identify with their mothers to overcome penis envy.

The biological and psychodynamic explanations are similar to each other in terms of the belief that biological differences lead to gender development. However, the biological approach believes gender identity is determined by our biological make-up whereas the psychodynamic approach believes family dynamics are also important. The biological approach is different from the learning approach because the biological approach believes that gender behaviour is determined by our biological make-up (nature) whereas the learning approach focuses on environmental influences (nurture).

**Role of the parents**

The biological approach says that the role of the parents in gender behaviour is limited to whether they donate X or Y sex chromosomes to their offspring. However, the psychodynamic and learning approaches believe parents have a more important role in the development of gender behaviour: The psychodynamic approach suggests that children learn gender-appropriate behaviour through identifying with the same sex parent; the learning approach argues that parents are important role models for gender behaviour and encourage gender-appropriate behaviour.

**Fixed or changing over time**

The biological approach believes that gender is fixed from birth due to genes, although hormone changes particularly at puberty affect gender identity. In contrast, the learning approach believes that gender identity changes over time. For example, our gender identity can be affected by our life stage or our peer group. The psychodynamic approach believes that gender development occurs mainly during the phallic stage and is fixed after that.

**You need to be able to describe and evaluate the key issue: how social learning theory can be used to explain how 'impossibly' thin role models in the media may lead anorexia nervosa.**

In our society, images of the female body in magazines, on TV and in films all suggest that being thin is beautiful. These images and thin celebrities in the media act as models for women in our society. There is an argument over whether these images lead to anorexia nervosa or whether anorexia nervosa is caused by other factors such as genes or family issues.

Social learning theory suggests anorexia nervosa may be due to role models in the media. Young people may feel they have to get to around the same weight as thin celebrities in order to be accepted. Teenagers pay attention to the fact that many celebrity role models are extremely thin and are likely to retain this information. They have the ability to reproduce being thin if they diet excessively and will do it if they are motivated to do so (ARRM). They can see that their role models are famous and rich and this may motivate them to be thin too. Teenagers may also think that they need to be thin in order to be accepted by their peers, which may also provide motivation for excessive dieting.

**Evaluation:**

There are a number of studies which support social learning theory as an explanation of anorexia nervosa. Fearn (1999) found that the women living on the island of Fiji started developing eating disorders only after the introduction of Western TV channels. Nasser (1986) compared Egyptian women studying in Cairo with similar Egyptian women studying in London and found that 12% of those living in London developed eating disorder symptoms, compared to 0% in Cairo. Lai (2000) found that the rate of anorexia increased for Chinese residents in Hong Kong as the culture slowly became more westernised. Mumford et al. (1991) found that Arab and Asian women were more likely to develop eating disorders if they moved to the West. These studies suggest that it is Western media images that lead girls and women to diet excessively and develop eating disorders. However, Eysenck and Flanagan (2000) point out that although all young women in the West are exposed to the media, only 3-4% of them develop an eating disorder. Therefore, there must be other factors other than media images that play a role in the development of anorexia.

Social learning theory cannot explain why anorexia nervosa usually develops in adolescence. A psychodynamic explanation for anorexia nervosa is that the disorder develops due to fears about growing up. Family issues may also contribute to the development of anorexia. Parents of anorexics may be too controlling and not allow their child to explain their own needs. Some anorexic sufferers report that they started dieting as method of gaining control over their lives. Genetics may also predispose someone to anorexia as the disorder does run in families. Relatives of people with eating disorders are four or five times more likely to also suffer (Strober and Humphrey, 1987).

**You need to be able to describe and evaluate observations**

There are structured laboratory observations and naturalistic observations. Structured laboratory observations involve careful controls and a set-up situation that can be repeated. There is often more than one observer and observations tend to be carried out through a one-way mirror to avoid the researchers' presence affecting participants' behaviour. Naturalistic observations involve observing participants in their natural environment. For example, observing children's behaviour in a playground.

Observations can be overt or covert. Covert observations involve observing a person or group of people without their knowledge. Overt observations involve observing a person or group of people with their knowledge.

Observations can also be participant or non-participant. A participant observation involves the researcher interacting with the person or group of people that they are observing. A non-participant observation involves the researcher observing behaviour from a distance without having any influence or getting involved.

An observation can be carried out by counting the frequency of certain behaviours during a fixed period of time.
Event sampling-when you record every time an event such as a kick occurs

Time sampling-when you record what is happening every set amount of time e.g. every 5 minutes.

Point sampling- The behaviour of just one individual in the group at a time is recorded.

Inter-observer reliability-Comparing the ratings of a number of observers as an individual observer may be biased. This would increase the reliability of the data collected if all the observers agree.

**Evaluation:**

Researchers may find it difficult to record all the behaviours shown, although event sampling, time sampling and point sampling can help. Video recordings can be used to record participants' behaviour and played back later so that all actions can be noted. It may also be difficult to analyse or interpret all the data collected. Observers often have to be specially trained so that they can record behaviours quickly and to avoid bias.

Participant observations allow researchers to experience the same environment as their participants. However, the researcher's involvement can affect the behaviour of participants. In contrast, non-participant observations allow researchers to observe participants' behaviour more objectively as they are not directly involved in the action. However, if participants are aware they are being observed, they may still change their behaviour.

Covert observations enable researchers to observe participants behave naturally as the participants do not know they are being observed. However, there are ethical issues with observing participants without their consent. They do not have the right to withdraw, they have not given informed consent and there also issues of confidentiality especially if their behaviour has been video-recorded. The British Psychological Society advises that it is only suitable to conduct a covert observation in a place where people might reasonably be expected to be observed by other people such as a shopping centre or other public place. Overt observations do not have as many ethical issues as covert observations. However, when participants know they are being observed they may change their behaviour so that it appears socially desirable. Therefore, overt observations can be less valid.

**You need to be able to describe and evaluate the laboratory experiment as a research method**

The learning approach uses laboratory experiments with both animal and human participants.

A laboratory experiment involves manipulating an independent variable to see the effect on a dependent variable. The dependent variable is measured. The extraneous variables are controlled in order to establish a cause and effect relationship.

For example, in Bandura, Ross and Ross (1961), the researchers manipulated whether the children saw an aggressive model, a non-aggressive model or no model at all. They then measured the number of aggressive behaviours shown by the children. This meant that they collected quantitative data, which could be statistically analysed to see how significant the results were.

**Evaluation:**

Laboratory experiments have standardised procedures, which are easy to replicate so that reliability can be tested. Data from laboratory experiments is quantitative and objective. Due to the careful manipulation and control of variables in a laboratory experiment, a cause and effect relationship can be established. Such evidence is considered scientific.

However, laboratory experiments lack ecological validity because they take place in artificial environments and often involve artificial tasks. Participants may behave unnaturally in an artificial situation. Experimenter effects can also affect laboratory experiments. The characteristics of the researcher may affect participants' responses. Furthermore, demand characteristics can affect results. Participants may guess what the study is about and give responses that they think the researcher wants.

**Example of laboratory experiments using animals**

Skinner wanted to see whether he could get rats to learn behaviours through the principles of operant conditioning. He placed rats in a special cage called a Skinner's box to investigate their behaviour. He found that the rats would learn to press a lever every time they saw a flashing light in order to receive a reward. The flashing light acted as an antecedent (A=Antecedent), the rat's response/behaviour would be to press the lever (B = Behaviour) and the consequence would be that the rat received food (C = Consequences). Skinner called this the ABC of operant conditioning.

**Evaluation:**

Advantages: Animals are easier to use than humans because of ethical issues. Animals are also smaller on average, which makes certain experiments easier to run. For example, Skinner needed a small animal for his Skinner's box. Some animals such as rats breed quickly, which means that you can see how selective breeding affects behaviour. For example, if you breed rats that are good at finding their way around mazes together, then you can see whether their offspring are particularly good at mazes.

Disadvantages: Humans are more complex than animals and so it is difficult to generalise results from animal studies to humans. There can be ethical issues with carrying out studies on animals.

**You need to be able to discuss ethical guidelines in relation to non-human participants**

**Caging and Stress:** Experimenters should avoid or minimise stress and suffering for all living animals. The cages the animals are kept in during the experiment should be large enough for the animals to be comfortable.

**Number or animals used:** Researchers should use as few animals as possible.

**Wild Animals:** Endangered species should not be used, unless the research has direct benefits for that species e.g. conservation.

**Qualified Experimenters:** The researchers conducting the experiment should have the necessary qualifications. They should also have a licence from the Home office for that particular experiment.

**Look for alternatives:** Alternatives to using animals must always be sought, such as using humans or computers.

**You need to be able to describe the Bateson's cube.**

Bateson's cube has three labelled sides: quality of research, animal suffering and certainty of medical benefit. These are on a scale high to low. When a research proposal falls into the opaque region, the experiment should not be conducted i.e. when quality of research is low, animal suffering is high and certainty of benefit is low.

**You need to be able to discuss ethical guidelines in relation to using human participants**

**Distress:** Participants should be protected from psychological or physical harm. The risk of harm should be no greater than that found in everyday life.

**Informed Consent:** Participants should be provided with enough information about the aim of the study and the procedure so that they can make an informed choice about whether to take part or not.

**Deception:** Participants should not be deceived about the aim of the study or the procedure. If deception is unavoidable, then permission should be sought from the British Psychological Society.

**Debriefing:** Participants should be fully informed of the purpose and expected outcomes of the study after they have taken part.

**Right to withdraw:** Participants should be told that they are free to leave the study at any time and they have the right to remove their results at the end, regardless of any payment they have received.

**Confidentiality:** Participants' should be guaranteed anonymity and their data should be stored securely.

**Competence**: Researchers should be qualified and have the experience necessary to carry out the research.

**You need to understand levels of data**

In order to carry out an inferential statistical test, you need to know what level of data you have. There are four levels of data: nominal, ordinal, interval and ratio. Nominal data is made up of discrete categories. For example, you have two categories such as 'action toys' and 'soft toys'. Ordinal data refers to ranked data. An example of ordinal data is when athletes' are ranked as first, second and third in race. Interval data refers to data that can be measured along a scale but does not have a true zero. For example, IQ can be measured along a scale but it does not have a true zero. In contrast, ratio data is measured on a scale that has a true zero point. For example, time can be measured along a scale and does have a true zero.

**You need to know when to use the chi-squared test and how to compare the observed and critical values to judge significance**

A chi-squared test is a test of association. For example, if males and females tend to choose different types of cars we could say that gender and car choice are associated. The chi-squared test is used when the data level is nominal, there is an independent measures design and when you are looking for an association between two different variables. There must be a minimum of 5 scores in each category, to carry out a chi-squared test.

The experimental or alternative hypothesis should state that there is an association/relationship between the variables e.g. gender and car choice.

The null hypothesis should state that there is no association/relationship between the variables e.g. gender and car choice.

For a chi-squared test, if the observed value is greater than the critical value shown in a table, then the null hypothesis can be rejected.

**You need to be able to describe an observation you carried out. Example practical: An observation of how gender affects the size of car driven**

Background: Social learning theory suggests that we copy role models. Advertisements on TV market large cars at males and small cars at females. Attractive male models are shown driving large cars and attractive female models are shown driving small cars. Adverts for 4x4s, sports cars and people carriers are marketed differently so are not included in this study.

Aim: To see whether gender affects the size of car driven.

Independent variable: Gender

Dependent variable: Size of car driven

Directional hypothesis: There will be a difference in the gender of drivers depending on the size of car they drive; there will be more males driving large cars and more females driving small cars.

Design: Independent groups design as two groups: males and females.

Ethical issues: The study can be considered ethical because the participants were observed in a public place and only their gender and size of car were recorded. However, the drivers were observed in their cars, which could be considered a private space within a public place.

Procedure: A pilot observation was carried out to decide how to judge whether a car was large or small. Coupe and small hatchback cars were judged to be small and large hatchback, saloon and estate cars were judged to be large. The actual observation was carried out on a busy main road and care was taken so that drivers did not think they were being observed (so the drivers were not affected by the observation at all). Data was gathered by discreetly tallying male and female drivers on a piece of paper whilst sat in a bus shelter.

Participants: There were 20 participants altogether. Their age ranged from 16- to 17-years-old.

Results:

Table to show number of males and females driving cars judged as large or small

|  | Male | Female | Totals |
|---|---|---|---|
| Car judged small | 12 | 16 | 28 |
| Car judged large | 18 | 7 | 25 |
| Totals | 30 | 23 | 53 |

More males (18) were driving large cars than females (7) and more females (16) were driving small cars than males (7).

The observed value was 4.567 which is greater than the critical value of 2.71 (for df=1 and $p \leq 0.05$ ) so the results are significant. The null hypothesis can be must be rejected.

Note: The data collected was put into the computer programme and it calculated the observed value using the chi-squared formula. A chi-squared test was carried out on the results as the study used an independent groups design and the level of measurement was nominal. You do not need to be able to use the chi-squared formula in the exam. However, you do need to understand what the observed value shows. The critical value was taken from a table of critical values for the chi-squared test. 2.71 is the critical value for df=1 and $p \leq 0.05$ for a one-tailed hypothesis.

Conclusions:

There was a significant difference in the gender of the drivers and the size of car driven. People's choice of car is affected by observing models on television advertisements.

Note: If the observed value was less than the critical value of 2.71, there would not have been a significant difference in the gender of the drivers and the size of car driven. The null hypothesis would be accepted.

**Evaluation:**

Validity: This study took place in participants' natural environment so it has ecological validity. Participants were observed driving their cars in an everyday situation. However, it is difficult to establish whether observing models on TV affected participants' choice of car. Some participants may have been driving another person's car, some may have been given the car and some may have been limited in their choice of car due to monetary reasons. The results may also have been affected by the researchers' judgement about what constitutes a large or small car.

Reliability: It would be difficult to replicate the findings of this study as it took place in participants' natural environment and there were no controls over extraneous variables. Results were collected in the middle of day and results might have been very different during rush hour.

Generalisability: The participants may not be representative of the wider population as only certain types of people such as retirees may be driving their car in the middle of a school day.

Credibility: The study found that women do drive smaller cars than men. This finding is credible as some women say that they prefer smaller 'cuter' cars. The study also has credibility because it was a naturalistic observation of drivers in an everyday situation.

**Exemplar exam question with student answer**

**Describe the learning approach's explanation of gender development and compare it to one other explanation.** (12 marks)

Student answer:

The learning approach says that children learn gender behaviour through operant conditioning. Gender-appropriate behaviour is rewarded and gender-inappropriate behaviour is punished. For example, boys are encouraged to play with toys that are typically for boys such as cars and trains but boys are ridiculed if they play with toys that are typically for girls. Girls are also praised for gender-appropriate behaviour such as sitting in a ladylike way.

Gender behaviour can also be learnt through observing same-sex role models. Social learning theory says that people pay attention to same-sex models and retain their gender behaviour. They may then practise reproducing the skills necessary to perform a certain gender behaviour. For example, a girl might practise putting on make-up. Finally, a person must be motivated to copy the gender behaviour. For example, if a girl notices that her older sister gets lots of positive attention for putting on make-up, then she is more likely to copy the behaviour.

In contrast, the biological approach says that gender behaviour is affected by our genes, hormones and brain structure. Therefore, the biological approach believes that gender is entirely determined by nature whereas the learning approach believes that nurture determines gender behaviour. The biological approach suggests that parents' only role is to give either XX or XY chromosomes whereas the learning approach says that parents are important role models and reinforcers of gender behaviour. The biological approach says that gender is fixed before birth and the only changes are sexual characteristics at puberty due to hormones. However, the learning approach thinks that gender is never fixed and we constantly adapt to our environment e.g. a man may act in a more manly way if he works in a garage compared to if he works in a hairdresser's salon.

10/12 marks-level 4 answer

**Commentary:**

This student describes explanations of gender behaviour from the learning approach very well. They also make some good comparison points by comparing the biological approach and the learning approach's explanations in terms of: nature versus nurture; the role of the parents and whether gender behaviour is fixed or changing. In order to gain more marks, the student could have picked out specific differences between the two explanations. For example, social learning theory would say that girls are copying their mothers when they pretend that dolls are babies whereas the biological approach would say it is to do with girls' hormones and brain structure. An easy comparison point is to say that both explanations have studies to support them. Bandura, Ross and Ross (1961) found that children were more likely to imitate aggressive behaviour shown by same sex models which supports social learning theory as an explanation of gender behaviour. The David

Reimer case supports a biological explanation of gender development and contradicts the learning approach. David Reimer developed a male identity despite being brought up as a female.

## Chapter 5-The Psychodynamic Approach

**You need to be able to describe what the psychodynamic approach is about.**

The psychodynamic approach believes that childhood experiences affect our development. It also says that unconscious processes related to our instincts and experiences affect our behaviour and feelings. If people have unconscious conflicts or childhood issues that play on their unconscious mind then they can suffer from mental health problems.

**You need to be able to define the following key terms**

**The id** is the part of the personality that is present from birth. It consists of our instincts and desires. As the id wants instant wish fulfilment, it is said to operate on the pleasure principle.

**The ego** develops from birth. The job of this part of the personality is to balance the demands of the id and superego. For this reason, it is said to operate on the reality principle.

**The superego** is the part of the personality that develops at around age 6. It represents our conscience and is said to operate on the morality principle.

**The oral stage** (0-1 ½ years) is when pleasure is focused on the mouth and the id dominates behaviour. Fixation in this stage causes a person to be passive and dependant and they may derive pleasure from behaviours such as smoking.

**The anal stage** (1 ½ -2 ½ years) is when pleasure is focused on the anus, so potty-training is very important. He believed that if parents were too harsh or too liberal about potty-training then the child could become fixated in this stage.

**The phallic stage** (2 ½ -5/6 years) is when pleasure is focused on the genital region. The phallic stage is when the superego and gender identity develop so fixation during this stage may lead to bad morals and a confused gender identity.

**The latency period**/latent stage (5/6 years to puberty) is where children play with the same sex children. Not much goes on in this stage and it is a time of consolidation.

**The genital stage** (puberty) is when a child develops feelings for the opposite sex. If there is little libido energy being taken up by conflicts in the earlier three stages, then there is enough energy for 'normal' relationships to be formed.

**Defence mechanisms** are methods employed by the ego to protect ourselves from anxious or guilty feelings and to stop undesirable impulses from entering our consciousness. The ego employs defence mechanisms when it is having problems balancing the demands of the id (our instincts and desires) and superego (our morals and conscience).

**Repression** is one type of defence mechanism. Traumatic events or disturbing thoughts may be hidden in the unconscious so that they are inaccessible. For example, a person may block out the memory of sexual abuse in childhood because dealing with the emotions involved is too disturbing.

**The Oedipus complex** refers to the unconscious desire boys have for their mother during the phallic stage and the feelings of jealousy and fear they feel towards their father. Boys experience castration anxiety as a result of the Oedipus complex and in order to resolve this they identify with their father.

**The conscious** is the part of the mind that we are aware of in a certain moment. For example, we might be conscious of the room we are in right now.

**The preconscious** is the part of the mind that contains information or memories that can be accessed if we try. For example, we might recall an outing we went on with friends when they start discussing it.

**The unconscious** is the part of the mind that we cannot access. The unconscious may hold hidden fears, anxieties and conflicts that our ego had difficulties dealing with. For example, an attraction to our best friend's boyfriend or girlfriend may be hidden in our unconscious to stop us feeling guilty.

**You need to be able to describe and evaluate Freud's theory of personality (id, ego, superego)**

Freud suggested that there are three aspects to the personality, the id, ego and superego. The **id** is the part of the personality that is present from birth. It consists of our instincts and desires. As the id wants instant wish fulfilment, it is said to operate on the pleasure principle. From birth onwards, the **ego** develops. The job of this part of the personality is to balance the demands of the id and superego. For this reason, it is said to operate on the reality principle. The **superego** is the part of the personality that develops at around age 6. It represents our conscience and is said to operate on the morality principle.

**Evaluation:**

Studies-There is no scientific evidence to support the id, ego and superego.

Explanation-The id, ego and superego are concepts, which cannot be tested scientifically (the theory is not falsifiable). Freud came up with this model of the mind from a biased sample of people: mainly middle class, Jewish women from Vienna suffering from mental health issues. However, Freud's structure of the personality does help to explain why we sometimes experience being pulled in different directions when making decisions, so the theory has face validity.

Application to real life-This model of the mind can explain why children become more aware of other people's needs as they get older as their ego and then superego develops.

**You need to be able to describe and evaluate Freud's theory of psychosexual development, including the five stages of development (oral, anal, phallic, latency and genital), the Oedipus complex)**

According to Freud there are five psychosexual stages that everyone passes through: oral, anal, phallic, latency and genital. The **oral stage** (0-1 ½ years) is when pleasure is focused on the mouth and the id dominates behaviour. Fixation in this stage causes a person to be passive and dependant and they might derive pleasure from behaviours such as smoking. According to Freud, during the **anal stage** (1 ½ -2 ½ years), pleasure is focused on the anus, so potty training is very important. He believed that if parents were too harsh or too liberal about potty training then the child could become fixated in this stage. However, if a parent praises their child for using the potty/toilet but is not overly controlling, then the child should successfully complete the anal stage without adverse effects to their personality. A child may develop an anal-retentive personality, if parents are too forceful about potty-training. An adult with an anal-retentive personality will be abnormally concerned with cleanliness, orderliness and saving and be quite stubborn. In comparison, if parents are too liberal about potty-training and let their children lead the process completely, the child may develop an anal-expulsive personality. An adult with an anal-expulsive personality will be messy, disorganised and rebellious. During the **phallic stage** (2 ½ -5/6 years) the focus of pleasure is on the genital region. The phallic stage is also when the superego and gender identity develop. In this stage, boys experience the **Oedipus complex** where they have sexual feelings for their mother and feel jealous and fearful of their father. Boys experience castration anxiety as a result of the Oedipus complex and in order to resolve this they identify with their father and adopt his values and as a result the superego develops. In the phallic stage, girls develop penis envy and identify with their mothers to overcome this (Electra complex) and as a result their superego develops. The **latent stage** (5/6 years to puberty) is where children play with the same sex children. Not much goes on in this stage and it is a time of consolidation. The **genital stage** (at puberty) is when a child develops feelings for the opposite sex. If there is little libido energy being taken up by conflicts in the earlier three stages, then there is enough energy for 'normal' relationships to be formed. However, if the person is fixated at the phallic stage in particular, they will have difficulties with relationships.

**Evaluation:**

Studies-The Little Hans study provides support for the Oedipus complex as it found that Little Hans did seem to desire his mother and resent his father. However, this case study is open to interpretation.

Malinowski's cross-cultural study in the Trobriand islands (now known as the Kiriwina islands of Papa New Guinea) suggests that it is not the Oedipus complex that causes boys to fear their fathers but fear of discipline. In the Trobriand islands, boys become members of their mother's kin group and are disciplined by their maternal uncles rather than their fathers. In this situation, boys become hostile to their uncles not their fathers, despite the fact that there is no sexual rivalry for the mother.

MacCallum and Golombok (2004) compared adolescents who had been raised from birth or early infancy in a fatherless household with adolescents who had grown up in a two-parent heterosexual household using interviews and questionnaires. They found that children from fatherless families felt that they could talk and interact with their mothers more than children from families where there was a father present. There seemed to be no negative consequences for the children from fatherless families. This study suggests that overcoming the Oedipus complex is not necessary for normal development.

Brown and Harris (1977) found that women who had lost their mother before 11-years-old had a greater risk of depression, which supports the idea that childhood experiences affect later mental health.

There is some evidence that anal-retentive personality exists. Fisher and Greenberg (1996) found that the personality characteristics of stubbornness, orderliness and stinginess cluster together in the same people. However, it is more likely that parents overall attitude to discipline affects a child's personality rather than potty-training alone. Furthermore, proving that the anal personality exists does not prove that it occurs due to fixation in the anal stage.

Explanation- There are some aspects of Freud's theory of the psychosexual stages of development, which make sense. Most people believe that our early childhood experiences affect our personality. Freud highlighted how too harsh or too liberal parenting can cause problems for a child. However, he over-emphasised the importance of rivalry and sexual feelings. The weaknesses in Freud's theory may be related to the fact that he came up with the stages of psychosexual development without directly studying children.

Application to real life-Freud's emphasis on the importance of childhood experiences has changed the way people treat children. It is now recognised that problems in childhood can have damaging consequences.

**You need to be able to describe Freud's iceberg model of personality**

Freud used the analogy of an iceberg to explain how most of our thoughts and wishes are unconscious. The conscious part of our mind is only the 'tip of the iceberg'. We also have the preconscious mind that we are not always aware of but can become aware of.

**Conscious:** The rational, decision-making part of the mind, in which the ego operates and which we are aware of. For example, we might be conscious of the room we are in right now.

**Preconscious:** Part of the mind that contains memories which are not always present in our conscious mind but can be accessed. For example, we might not remember an outing with friends a year ago but when they start discussing it, the memory is triggered.

**Unconscious:** Part of the mind that we cannot access. The unconscious may hold hidden fears, anxieties and conflicts that our ego had difficulties dealing with. For example, an attraction to our best friend's boyfriend or girlfriend may be hidden in our unconscious to stop us feeling guilty.

## Evaluation:

Studies-Neuroscience studies have shown that unconscious processing of stimuli activates localised brain regions, whereas conscious processing of same stimuli activates widely distributed brain regions. Research on amnesic patients shows that they can learn new information even when they have no memory of when they learnt it (Squire and McKee, 1992). Such research supports the idea of an unconscious and conscious mind.

Explanation-The idea of a conscious, preconscious and unconscious mind makes sense. People often talk about having an intuition about something without being consciously aware of why they have that feeling.

Application to real life-The idea of the unconscious has been used in psychoanalysis to help people uncover hidden fears and anxieties.

## You need to be able to describe and evaluate two defence mechanisms: repression and projection

Defence mechanisms are methods employed by the ego to protect ourselves from anxious or guilty feelings and to stop undesirable impulses from entering our consciousness. The ego employs defence mechanisms when it is having problems balancing the demands of the id (our instincts and desires) and superego (our morals and conscience).

Examples of defence mechanisms are: Repression, displacement, reaction formation, rationalisation and projection.

**Repression** is one type of defence mechanism. Traumatic events or disturbing thoughts may be hidden in the unconscious so that they are inaccessible. For example, a person may block out the memory of sexual abuse in childhood because dealing with the emotions involved is too disturbing.

## Evaluation of repression:

Myers and Brewin's (1994) study supports the theory of repression. They found that participants classified as repressors (because they scored highly for defensiveness) had more difficulty recalling unhappy memories. Elliott found that 20% of people said they had forgotten traumatic events for a period of time. Walker et al. (1997) had participants keep diaries of pleasant and unpleasant events for a few weeks. When tested later they showed good recall of pleasant events but poor recall of unpleasant events. There are many incidences of people who have forgotten traumatic events. However, repression cannot explain why some people who undergo traumatic experiences have difficulty forgetting them rather than remembering them.

**Projection** is repressing anxiety-provoking truths about oneself and seeing them in others instead. For example, if you have sexual feelings towards a member of your class, you may tell them that your friend likes them when in fact it is you who really likes them.

**Evaluation of projection:**

It is hard to test projection scientifically. However, everyday experience of other people suggests that projection does exist (face validity). We come across people who seem to project their own feelings onto others.

**You need to be able to describe and evaluate Freud's study of Little Hans (1909)**

Aim: To report the findings of how a young boy overcame his phobia of horses.

Procedure: Freud gave advice to Little Hans' father based on the father's reports of the boy's behaviour. It is thought that Freud only met the boy once.
When Little Hans was 3-years-old, he developed an active interest in his 'widdler' (penis), and also those of other people. When Little Hans was 5-years-old, he developed a phobia of horses after seeing a horse die in the street. Little Hans' father knew about Freud's theories and wrote to him asking him for advice. The father gave Freud detailed information about the conversations he had had with Little Hans. Freud interpreted Little Hans phobia as being related to his worries about losing his mother and his mother's threat that she would cut off his penis if he didn't stop playing with it. Freud also thought that Little Hans who enjoyed getting into bed with his mother, had a repressed desire for her. Freud then met Little Hans and asked him about what he didn't like about horses. Little Hans' comments led Freud to believe that Hans' phobia of horses related to his fear of his father and the Oedipus complex.

Results: Little Hans fantasised about being married to his mother and having his own children. This was interpreted as the Oedipus complex. In another fantasy, Little Hans described how a plumber came and gave him a bigger penis. This was again related to the Oedipus complex.

Conclusion: Freud believed that Little Hans' behaviour provided support for the Oedipus complex. He believed that Little Hans desired his mother and this made him fear his father. Little Hans' phobia of horses was symbolic of his fear of his father.

**Evaluation:**

Generalisability-This was a unique case study of one boy who is not representative of the wider population. It is also difficult to generalise the findings to boys growing up in single-parent families. Furthermore, it is difficult to apply the findings to girls who don't have a penis (although Freud said they develop penis envy).

Reliability-The study is hard to replicate as it was a unique situation and involved subjective interpretation of the conversations between Little Hans and his father.

Application to real life-The study involved getting Little Hans to talk as much possible about his fears to his father. Psychoanalysis has developed from the idea of getting people to talk freely about their problems in order to uncover unconscious conflicts.

Validity-Freud was able to gather lots of in-depth qualitative data from Little Hans' father who reported on the many conversations he had with Little Hans. This makes the study more valid. However, Little Hans' father was a supporter of Freud's theories and may have interpreted Little Hans' behaviour in a biased way. It is thought Freud only met Little Hans once and his interpretation of Little Hans' behaviour is subjective. There are other explanations for Little Hans' behaviour other than the Oedipus complex. He saw a horse die in the street and so he may have associated his fear of the situation with all horses (classical conditioning).

Ethics-Little Hans may have been embarrassed by the case study when he was older so he may not have been protected from psychological distress.

**You need to be able to describe and evaluate Axline V (1964) Dibs: Personality Development in Play Therapy**

Aim: To help a 5-year-old boy, Dibs, deal with his emotional issues through play therapy.

Procedure: This case study involved interviews with Dibs' parents and teachers and observations of Dibs' play during therapy sessions. Each week, Dibs attended a play therapy session with Axline, a psychologist, where he was encouraged to play with toys and to talk freely. Dibs had been referred for therapy because he was showing disturbed behaviour at school and he seemed to have issues with his parents. Dibs' parents seemed to think he was mentally retarded but his teachers thought he had emotional problems related to a poor relationship with his parents.
Findings: A chi-squared test was carried out on the results as the study used an independent groups design and the level of measurement was nominal.
In one play therapy session, Dibs buried three toy soldiers in some sand and referred to one of them as papa before punching it several times. Axline interpreted Dibs' behaviour as anger related to his poor relationship with his father. Dibs' mother came to see Axline and told her that Dibs' birth had been an accident and that she felt resentment at how his birth had affected her career. She also said that Dibs' father resented Dibs. In another play therapy session, Dibs said `I hate the walls and the doors that lock and the people that shove you in. I hate the tears and the angry words and I'll kill them all with my hatchet and hammer their bones and spit on them'. Axline interpreted this as Dib's hatred of being locked in his room when his parents couldn't deal with his behaviour. With therapy, Dibs behaviour gradually got better and his relationship with his father also improved. It was later found that Dibs had an extremely high IQ and went on to have no social or emotional problems.

**Evaluation:**

Generalisability-This was a unique case study of one boy, which makes it hard to generalise to the wider population.

Reliability-It would be difficult to repeat this study as it was a unique case and the interviews and observations would be difficult to replicate.

Application to real life-The study suggests that play therapy can be an effective method of helping young children deal with emotional issues. Young children may not be able to express their emotions through talking so play therapy can offer another way of helping them to get their feelings across.

Validity-The study collected rich, detailed data from observations with Dibs and interviews with his teachers and parents, which gives the study greater validity.

Ethics-It was important to ensure the anonymity of Dibs and his family as if their identity was made public, it could cause psychological distress.

**You need to be able to describe and evaluate Freud's theory as an explanation of gender development/behaviour, including comparison with explanations from the Biological and Learning Approaches**

Freud believed that children develop their gender identity during the phallic stage. He suggested that resolution of the Oedipus complex in boys and the Electra complex in girls, led to identification with the same-sex parent. The Oedipus complex refers to when a boy unconsciously desires his mother and begins to see his father as a rival. During the phallic stage, the boy realises he has a penis unlike girls (which makes him aware that it can be removed). The boy unconsciously believes that his father will castrate him as punishment for his desire towards his mother (castration anxiety). The Oedipus complex is resolved when the boy identifies with his father and adopts the male gender role. He identifies with his father and acts like him because he unconsciously thinks this will ensure his mother's love and will make him less likely to be castrated. The Electra complex refers to when girls develop penis envy after realising they don't have a penis during the phallic stage. Girls blame their mother for removing their penis and become angry with her and they see their mother as a rival for the affection of the father. Girls overcome the Electra complex by identifying with their mother.

**Evaluation:**

Studies-The Little Hans study provides support for the Oedipus complex. However, this case study is open to interpretation. There are other explanations for Little Hans' phobia of horses.
Malinowski's cross-cultural study in the Trobriand islands (now known as the Kiriwina islands of Papa New Guinea) suggests that it is not the Oedipus complex that causes boys to fear their fathers but fear of discipline. In the Trobriand islands, boys become members of their mother's kin group and are disciplined by their maternal uncles rather than their fathers. In this situation, boys become hostile to their uncles not their fathers, despite the fact that there is no sexual rivalry for the mother.
MacCallum and Golombok (2004) compared adolescents who had been raised from birth or early infancy in a fatherless household with adolescents who had grown up in a two-parent heterosexual household using interviews and questionnaires. They found that children from fatherless families felt that they could talk and interact with their mothers more than children from families where there was a father present. There seemed to be no negative consequences for the children from fatherless families. This study suggests that overcoming the Oedipus complex is not necessary for normal development.

Explanation-The concepts of the Oedipus and Electra complex lacks credibility as most people don't believe that young children have sexual feelings for the opposite sex parent. Young boys are not always aware that girls do not have a penis and young girls may not be aware that boys do, which means that it would be impossible for them to experience castration anxiety or penis envy.

Application to real life-Psychoanalysis has used Freud's theories of the Oedipus complex and Electra complex to help people explore family relationships.

**You need to be able to compare the psychodynamic explanation of gender behaviour with explanations from the Biological and Learning approaches**

**Exam tip:** You can compare the different explanations in terms of nature/nurture, role of the parents and whether the approach considers gender development to be fixed or changing over time.

### Nature-nurture

The psychodynamic approach believes that gender behaviour is affected by both nature and nurture. It says that we are born with certain biological/anatomical differences (having or not having a penis) that combine with family dynamics to affect our gender behaviour. During the phallic stage, boys identify with their fathers to overcome their castration anxiety and girls identify with their mothers to overcome penis envy.

The biological approach believes that gender behaviour is affected by nature. It says that our genes, hormones and brain structure affect gender development.

The learning approach believes that nurture leads to gender behaviour ie. That environmental influences only, such as parents, school, society, peers, TV and other models, lead to gender behaviour.

The biological and psychodynamic explanations are similar to each other in terms of the belief that biological differences lead to gender development. However, the biological approach believes gender identity is determined by our biological make-up whereas the psychodynamic approach believes family dynamics are also important. The biological approach is different from the learning approach because the biological approach believes that gender behaviour is determined by our biological make-up (nature) whereas the learning approach focuses on environmental influences (nurture).

### Role of the parents

The biological approach says that the role of the parents in gender behaviour is limited to whether they donate X or Y sex chromosomes to their offspring. However, the psychodynamic and learning approaches believe parents have a more important role in the development of gender behaviour: The psychodynamic approach suggests that children learn gender-appropriate behaviour through identifying with the same sex parent; the learning approach argues that parents are important role models for gender behaviour and encourage gender-appropriate behaviour.

## Fixed or changing over time

The biological approach believes that gender is fixed from birth due to genes, although hormone changes particularly at puberty affect gender identity. In contrast, the learning approach believes that gender identity changes over time. For example, our gender identity can be affected by our life stage or our peer group. The psychodynamic approach believes that gender development occurs mainly during the phallic stage and is fixed after that.

## You need to be able to describe one key issue from the psychodynamic approach: the debate about whether dreams have meaning

There is a debate about whether dreams are meaningful. Most of our dreams occur during REM (rapid eye movement) sleep though not all of them. Some argue that dreams have meaning and we need psychoanalysis to unlock that meaning. There is evidence which suggests that they have psychological meaning and are related to the events occurring in our lives. For example, Cartwright found in his study on divorcing couples that they had dreams about divorce and separation. Others say that there are biological reasons why we dream and that dreams do not have any real significance.

Freud proposed that the function of dreams is wish-fulfilment. At night, the mechanisms which suppress the urges of the id relax and the id's desires are expressed through the content of dreams. However, the ego does dream work to protect us from guilty or painful feelings (the true meaning of our dreams is disguised). Freud distinguished between the manifest content of dreams (what we actually dream about) and the latent (hidden) content of dreams. The manifest content of the dream is symbolic for the latent content. For example, dreaming about being naked might be symbolic for feeling vulnerable. The latent content of dreams may be established through dream analysis. Freud interpreted Little Hans' dream about a plumber giving him a new 'widdler' as symbolic of Little Hans resolving his Oedipus complex and used this case study to provide support for his theory.

## Evaluation:

Studies-Cartwright et al. (1984) found that women who were in the middle of divorcing their husbands, felt better if they had dreamed about their ex. They concluded that working through the divorce issue in a dream was psychologically beneficial. This study supports Freud's theory that dreams are meaningful.
Domhoff (1996) reported on the findings of many quantitative studies looking at people's dream reports. The studies suggest that there are large individual differences in what people dream about and a high degree of consistency in people's dreams over time. This suggests that dreams are meaningful for individuals.
However, if the function of dreams is wish-fulfilment, then Freud's theory cannot explain why some people don't dream at all. Foulkes (1982) found that pre-school children never or hardly ever dream. Pagel (2003) found that some normal adults do not dream.

Explanation- The idea that dreams reflect things that are on our minds is credible. Dreams about recent events are common and some dreams are recurrent, which provides support for Freud's theory. However, most dreams do not relate to the wishes Freud had in mind such as food, drink and sex. There are biological theories of dreaming that are supported by empirical (scientific) evidence. One biological theory of dreaming says that dreams are an interpretation of random firing of neurones in the brain, which might explain why our dreams do not always make sense.

Application to real life-Freud's theory helps to explain why the content of our dreams reflect recent events and concerns.

**Note:** You may be asked to apply concepts, theories and/or research from the psychodynamic approach to a key issue that you have not studied.

**You need to be able to describe and evaluate case studies as a research method (including ethical and credibility issues)**

A case study is an in-depth study of one person or one group of people. A number of different techniques are used to gather data. For example, the researcher may observe, interview and carry out a number of experiments on the same person. Triangulation is used to pool data together from the different types of research method and to draw conclusions. Freud's case studies involved psychoanalysis of his patients. He used free association, dream analysis and analysis of slips of the tongue to uncover his clients' unconscious wishes and desires.

**Evaluation:**

Case studies are not generalisable as they are carried out on only one person or one group of people who are often unique and not representative of the wider population. It is also difficult to replicate case studies because they involve unique individuals and the interpretation of the observations and interviews is subject to bias. Therefore it is hard to establish reliability in case studies. However, triangulation is used to draw conclusions about the same concept so this improves the reliability of the findings. An advantage of case studies is that they gather rich, detailed information about the individuals using a number of different techniques, so this increases their validity.

There can be ethical issues with case studies. Often they involve studying unique individuals who are more vulnerable than normal. Therefore, researchers have to be careful to protect them from psychological distress. As case studies are often of a unique individual, it can be hard to protect their privacy and confidentiality. Researchers must make sure that case studies do not reveal any information that would make the individuals identifiable.

Freud's case studies have been criticised for lacking credibility. Many of Freud's female clients who had been diagnosed with hysteria reported that they had been sexually abused by their fathers. Initially, Freud believed them and made a link between sexual abuse and hysteria. However, it seems that consistent naming of fathers as perpetrators of sexual abuse made him uncomfortable and he later came up with the theory that the women had fabricated the sexual abuse because they unconsciously desired their fathers. He called this the Electra complex. Freud's later interpretation of the women's reports lacks credibility as the women were probably telling the truth. There is also a gender bias in Freud's work. Freud focused more on boys than girls and he suggested that girls have poor moral development due to a weaker identification with the same sex parent.

**You need to be able to describe, assess and apply issues of reliability, validity, subjectivity, objectivity and generalisability in the analysis of qualitative data**

Qualitative data is non-numerical data; usually in the form of a text or narrative (e.g. descriptions of objects, situations and events) but it may also be e.g. pictorial. Qualitative data is analysed by drawing out themes and trends to summarise the data and draw conclusions, which can lead to subjective interpretation. Qualitative data is usually less reliable as it would be hard to obtain the same data again. For example, a participant might respond differently in an interview about their childhood on a different day or with a different researcher. However, qualitative data tends to have more validity because it does not reduce people's thoughts, feelings and abilities to numbers. Qualitative data involves in-depth, detailed information about a unique individual or small group so this kind of data lacks generalisability as it may not be representative of the general population. Triangulation, which is where data is gathered from different sources and compared for similarities helps to reduce issues of subjectivity, validity, reliability and generalisability with qualitative data.

**You need to be able to identify and apply self-report data**

Self-report data can be obtained from any research method where participants are asked about their feelings, attitudes and beliefs. For example, a questionnaire or interview might ask patients how well a treatment worked. An experiment might ask participants to report on their beliefs about a set of photographs.

**You need to be able to describe, assess and apply the terms 'longitudinal' as applied to research methods**

Longitudinal studies involve studying the same person or group of people over a long period of time. Researchers working within a psychodynamic perspective might look at whether children's development over time is affected by their attachment (bond) to their parents.

**Evaluation:**

An advantage of longitudinal studies is that they allow researchers to follow the development and progress of a person or group of people over time. There are also less likely to be participant variables compared to cross-sectional studies as the same participants are used throughout. However, longitudinal studies can be expensive. Furthermore, erosion of the sample (participants dropping out of the study) may cause bias. For example, if the researchers are looking at the effects of preschool education in a deprived area over time and some children leave the study to move to a more affluent area, then that can bias the results. It is also difficult to replicate a longitudinal study and establish reliability.

**You need to be able to describe, assess and apply the terms 'cross-sectional' as applied to research methods**

Cross-sectional studies involve gathering data at one moment in time from different groups of people so that one group is compared with another group on the same characteristics, behaviour or task i.e. a cross-sectional study might compare children of different ages at the same time. One example of a cross-sectional study is Charlton et al.'s study on the island of St. Helena. They observed children's behaviour in two school playgrounds before TV was introduced and then five years later to see if there were any differences. The children in the playgrounds were different due to the time difference.

**Evaluation:**

Cross-sectional designs tend to be cheaper, quicker and more practical than longitudinal designs as participants are tested at one moment in time. However, as different participants are used in the conditions, participant variables can affect results. For example, 6-year-old children may not be comparable with the 8-year-old children at a particular school if the 8-year-old children had more disruptions to their education.

**You need to be able to identify, describe and apply correlations**

Correlational studies look for a relationship between two variables. For example, it may look for a relationship between number of hours of violent TV watched and levels of aggression. An example of a positive correlation is: the more hours of violent TV watched, the more aggressive people become. An example of a negative correlation is: the more hours of violent computer games played, the less helpful people are.

Positive correlations occur when two variables rise together. An example would be the higher the happiness rating, the longer the relationship.

Negative correlations occur when one variable rises and the other falls. For example, the higher the age, the lower the number of items recalled from a list.

A correlation coefficient refers to a number between -1 and +1 and states how strong a correlation is. If the number is close to +1 then there is a positive correlation. If the number is close to -1 then there is a negative correlation. If the number is close to 0 then the variables are uncorrelated. For example, +0.9 refers to a strong positive correlation, 0 is no correlation and -0.2 is a weak negative correlation.

**Evaluation:**

Correlational studies can demonstrate a relationship between two variables, which was not noticed before. They can also be used to look for relationships between variables that cannot be investigated by other means. For example, researchers can look to see whether there is a relationship between parents having low expectations of their children and the children's later academic performance. Manipulating such variables would be unethical. However, correlational studies cannot establish cause and effect relationships. A third factor may affect both variables under investigation. For example, although a correlational study might show a relationship between the number of hours of violent TV watched and levels of aggression, we cannot be certain that the violent TV programmes led to the aggression. It may be that children who watch violent TV programmes are naturally more aggressive and so seek such programmes out.

**You need to know when you should use the Spearman's Rho inferential test**

Spearman's Rho is used when you have a correlational design and the level of data is ordinal.

The observed value needs to be higher than the critical value for the null hypothesis to be rejected (i.e. to accept the alternative hypothesis).

**Note:** There are four levels of data: nominal, ordinal, interval and ratio. Nominal data is made up of discrete categories. For example, you have two categories such as 'action toys' and 'soft toys'. Ordinal data refers to ranked data. An example of ordinal data is when athletes' are ranked as first, second and third in race. Interval data refers to data that can be measured along a scale but does not have a true zero. For example, IQ can be measured along a scale but it does not have a true zero. In contrast, ratio data is measured on a scale that has a true zero point. For example, time can be measured along a scale and does have a true zero.

**You need to be able to describe and evaluate a practical using a correlational design, using two ratings scales and self-report data. Example practical: Correlational study using self-reports of people's anal retentiveness and parents' strictness**

Background: Freud suggested that if parents are too lenient during the anal stage and in particular with potty-training, then the child will grow up to have an anal expulsive character, which is messy, reckless and disorganised. However, if potty-training is too harsh, then the child may form an anal retentive character, which is mean and overly tidy and organised.

Aim: To see whether there is a relationship between authoritarian parenting and anal retentive characteristics.

One-tailed alternative hypothesis: There will be a relationship between parental strictness and a person's anal-retentive characteristics such as meanness and tidiness. The higher the score for authoritarian (strict) parenting, the higher the score for anal-retentive characteristics.

Null hypothesis: There will be no relationship between the authoritarian parenting score and the score for anal-retentive characteristics.

Procedure: Two questionnaires were drawn up. One questionnaire related to a person's tidiness, organisation and meanness (anal-retentive characteristics versus anal-expulsive characteristics) and one questionnaire related to how authoritarian (strict) the person's parents were. The questionnaires were piloted on a few friends to check wording and to make sure the standardised instructions were suitable. Participants were briefed before the study and given five minutes to answer the questionnaires in silence. At the end of the study, the participants were debriefed.

Sample: An opportunity sample was used of 16- to 17-year-olds in our class as this is a quick and convenient method to obtain participants. If we had used a systematic sample or a random sample, we may not have got participants to agree to participate.

Ethics: All the participants were briefed before the questionnaire and gave their informed consent. They were also debriefed fully at the end of the questionnaire. It was important to make sure participants hadn't been negatively affected by the questionnaire as it covered parenting styles. Participants were given the right to withdraw before, during and after the questionnaire. Data was kept anonymous and confidential.

Table to show anal retentive scores and authoritarian parent scores:

| Participant No. | Anal retentive score | Authoritarian parenting score | Rank for anal-retentive personality | Rank for authoritarian parenting |
|---|---|---|---|---|
| 1 | 16 | 15 | 9 | 2 |
| 2 | 15 | 17 | 6 | 4.5 |
| 3 | 14 | 20 | 3.5 | 10 |
| 4 | 19 | 15 | 14.5 | 2 |
| 5 | 15 | 25 | 6 | 20 |
| 6 | 22 | 21 | 18.5 | 14.5 |
| 7 | 15 | 25 | 6 | 20 |
| 8 | 17 | 23 | 11.5 | 18 |
| 9 | 12 | 17 | 1 | 4.5 |
| 10 | 13 | 20 | 2 | 10 |
| 11 | 22 | 15 | 18.5 | 2 |
| 12 | 22 | 20 | 18.5 | 10 |
| 13 | 19 | 21 | 14.5 | 14.5 |
| 14 | 22 | 21 | 18.5 | 14.5 |
| 15 | 18 | 21 | 13 | 14.5 |
| 16 | 20 | 18 | 16 | 6 |
| 17 | 16 | 19 | 9 | 7 |
| 18 | 14 | 20 | 3.5 | 10 |
| 19 | 17 | 20 | 11.5 | 10 |
| 20 | 16 | 22 | 9 | 17 |

**Note:** The way the data is ranked for a Spearman's Rho test is different to the Mann-Whitney U test. The scores for anal retentiveness and authoritarian (strict) parenting are ranked separately. The Spearman's Rho test then looks for a relationship between the two sets of rankings.

A Spearman's Rho test was carried out on the data because the design was correlational and the level of data was ordinal (ranked). As the observed value was 0.004, which is less than the critical value of 0.56, the null hypothesis was accepted.

Note: The critical value was 0.56 from the Spearman's Rho critical values table (n=20, $p \leq 0.05$ for a one-tailed hypothesis).

A scattergraph showed no correlation between anal-retentiveness and authoritarian parenting.

Conclusion: There is no relationship between parenting style and anal-retentive characteristics.

**Evaluation:**

The questions may have been ambiguous and individual participants may have interpreted them differently. Participants' responses may have been limited by the types of questions asked, which affects the validity of the results. Furthermore, participants may have given socially desirable answers to show themselves in a good light.

An opportunity sample was used, which means that the participants were not representative of the wider population.

The study has ecological validity because it took place in a classroom, which was the students' natural setting.

Note: If the results had shown a correlation between parental strictness and anal-retentive characteristics, we could still not be certain of a cause and effect relationship. Parental strictness may not lead children to develop anal-retentive characteristics, it may be a third factor that affects both such as genes (parents who are more authoritarian may pass down genes that lead their offspring to have more anal-retentive characteristics such as conscientiousness, tidiness and meanness). However, correlations are useful in showing relationships and highlighting new areas for testing.

**Exemplar exam question with student answer**

**Describe the first three stages of psychosexual development with reference to children's behaviour and evaluate them in terms of credibility.** (12 marks)

Freud said that children go through different stages of psychosexual development and if their libido become fixated in a certain stage, it can lead to problems. The anal stage is when pleasure is focused on the mouth and the id is in control. For example, a baby may like to put things in its mouth and will want all its needs met instantly. Fixation in this stage causes a person to be passive and dependant and they may seek pleasure via the mouth through habits such as smoking. The anal stage (2-3 years) is when pleasure is focused on the anus and the ego is developing. If a person becomes fixated in the anal stage, they may become anally retentive and demonstrate behaviours such as meanness and tidiness. Children in the anal stage may take pleasure from issues related to potty-training. They are also starting to understand that their needs cannot be always met instantly. The ego is beginning to balance the needs of the id with reality. The phallic stage (3-5/6 years) is when a boy develops an unconscious desire for his his mother and sees his father as a rival (the Oedipus complex). Girls develop penis envy (the Electra complex). In order to overcome the Oedipus and Electra complex, children identify with the same-sex parent. During the phallic stage, boys may say they want to marry their mothers and girls may say they want to marry their fathers.

Freud's theory of psychosexual development has some credibility. The relationships children have with their parents are likely to affect their development. People do refer to 'A mummy's boy' and 'A daddy's girl'. However, Freud probably went over-emphasised the sexual element of these relationships. Malowinski found that children in Papa New Guinea wo are disciplined by their uncle rather than their father, are hostile to the uncle not their father. This suggests that any hostility or fear boys show towards their fathers is to do with discipline rather than unconscious rivalry for their mother. cast doubt on the idea of rivalry with the father for the mother's love. Golombok found that children growing up in single parent families developed normally, which also questions the validity of the Oedipus and Electra complex. The idea of fixation in the anal stage leading to an anal-retentive character also has some credibility. Studies have found that people can have an anally retentive character. However, just because the anal personality exists does not prove that this is due to fixation in the anal stage.

10/12 marks-level 4 answer.

**Commentary:**

This student describes the psychosexual stages of development very well and gives some good examples of how children in each stage might behave. They also make some excellent points regarding the credibility of Freud's theory and refer to relevant research. However, one element of credibility that they did not cover is the credibility of the research methods used. Freud proposed his theory of psychosexual development having only studied one child, Little Hans, who is not representative of the wider population. Furthermore, he used case studies, which are open to interpretation.

# Chapter 6- Criminological Psychology

## You need to be able to define the following key terms in Criminological Psychology:

**Criminological psychology**: investigates explanations and treatments for criminal and anti-social behaviour. It also studies issues related to the justice system and the way criminals are convicted. For example, it looks at problems with eyewitness testimony and how jury and defendant characteristics affect sentencing.

**A Crime**: is when someone commits an act against the law, for example, stealing a car.

**Anti-social behaviour:** refers to behaviour that causes problems for other people but is not necessarily against the law. An example of anti-social behaviour is when teenagers gather together outside a shop and behave in a rude way to passing customers.

**Recidivism:** is when a person commits a crime they have already been punished for. An example of recidivism is when a criminal goes to prison for stealing and then steals again on release.

**Stereotyping**: is judging an individual based on their membership of group when there is limited experience of the group. Based on these stereotypes people are **labelled**. For example, a boy in a hoodie may be labelled as a troublemaker based on his appearance.

**Modelling**: refers to when a person copies a behaviour after they have observed it. People may pay attention to a behaviour, remember it and if a person is able and motivated to reproduce the behaviour, they will model (copy) it. For example, a boy may observe an older boy get respect for swearing, and then he may model this behaviour himself.

Exam tip: Define terms and give an example to ensure you get all the marks.

## You need to be able to describe and evaluate social learning theory as an explanation of criminal behaviour or anti-social behaviour.

Social learning theory suggests people commit crimes because they are exposed to criminal role models. They may look up to a criminal and pay attention to their behaviour. They may remember how the crime is committed and if they are able to carry out the crime themselves (reproduction) and they are motivated to do so, they may commit the same or similar crime themselves (modelling). For example, a boy may observe an older boy stealing cars, he may pay attention to how to do it and be capable of reproducing the behaviour, finally if he identifies with the boy and looks up to him as a role model, he may be motivated to copy the behaviour. Anti-social behaviour can be explained through observation of anti-social role models. The most powerful role models are the same-sex, high status and a similar age to the observer.

If a model is rewarded, a behaviour is more likely to be copied. This is called vicarious reinforcement. For example, if a criminal is successful and becomes rich from their crimes, their behaviour is more likely to be imitated. A criminal such as gang leader may also be rewarded in terms of approval from peers and this also makes their behaviour more likely to be imitated.

However, if the model is punished the behaviour is less likely to be copied. For example, a criminal may be caught and sent to prison for their crimes.

**Evaluation of theory:**

Use SE to evaluate a theory that has already been applied to criminological psychology.

Studies-What studies support or contradict the theory?

Explanation-What are the problems and limitations of the theory? What alternative explanations are there?

Studies- Bandura, Ross and Ross' (1961) study found that children would copy aggressive behaviour shown by a model so this supports social learning theory. However, this study only looked at whether the children copied the aggressive behaviours soon after rather than whether the children were affected in the long-term. Huesmann and Eron (1986) followed people's viewing habits over 22 years and found that the more violence people watched on TV, the more likely they were to have committed a criminal act by the age of 30. However, correlational studies such as this cannot show a causal relationship as people with a tendency to be antisocial or aggressive may seek out aggressive media. On the other hand, field experiments such as Parke et al. do show a causal link between observed aggression and actual aggression. They carried out a field experiment on boys in an institution for juvenile offenders. One group of boys watched violent TV programmes and one group watched programmes without violence over 5 days. They found that viewing violent TV programmes led to an increase in aggressive behaviour. However, juvenile offenders are not representative of the wider population and may be more prone to aggressive behaviour.

Explanation-It is difficult to establish a causal link between observing criminal or anti-social behaviour and carrying out such behaviour due to the time lapse. Social learning theory does not take into account biological factors in criminal behaviour such as genes, hormones or structural differences in the brain. Another limitation of social learning theory is that it does not consider how social factors such as unemployment and poverty can affect criminality. It also does not explain why many offenders have mental health issues and learning difficulties.

Exam tip: If you use a study to support or contradict a theory, then briefly say what it found and how it supports the theory. You do not need to give a full description of a study in this context, only enough detail so it is recognisable. The examiner only wants to know how the study supports/contradicts the theory. You can make one evaluative point per study used.

Exam tip 2: Do not spend too much time discussing alternative theories. There is often only one mark for this. Instead focus on the limitations and problems of the theory you are evaluating.

Note: There is evidence to support the biological explanation of criminal or anti-social behaviour but you do not need to know it. Here is the information, if you wish to refer to it: Ishikawa and Raine (2002) found a higher concordance rate for criminality in MZ twins compared to DZ twins; Raine et al. (1997) compared the brain scans of violent offenders with non-offenders and found that murderers has lower levels of activity in their prefrontal cortex, the area of the brain linked with self-control.

**You need to be able to describe the role of the media in criminal and anti-social behaviour:**

The media refers to films, television, newspapers, posters and computer games.
Role models in the media can influence criminality through observational learning where the individual imitates behaviour they have seen e.g. on TV or in computer games. Social learning theory claims that for behaviour to be copied it has to be attended to and remembered. The person also has to be capable of reproducing the behaviour and have the motivation to repeat it. Children are more likely to copy the model's behaviour if the model is powerful, likeable and is rewarded (vicarious reinforcement). Many cartoon superheroes such as Batman and Spiderman use violence to defeat the baddies and are then rewarded for their behaviour with praise and respect. Children aspire to be like their heroes on TV and so they copy the aggressive behaviour they have observed. They are motivated to copy their heroes behaviour because they have seen it rewarded.

A number of studies suggest that media influences can lead to criminal behaviour. Parke et al. (1977) carried out a field experiment on boys in an institution for juvenile offenders. One group of boys watched violent TV programmes and one group watched programmes without violence over 5 days. They found that viewing violent TV programmes led to an increase in aggressive behaviour.
Singer and Singer (1981) looked for a relationship between TV viewing and behaviour in children. They issued a questionnaire to parents to find out how much TV their children watched and found that children who watched the most TV were rated as the most aggressive by their parents. This study suggests that there is a relationship between watching TV leads and aggressive behaviour.
Huesmann and Eron (1986) followed people's viewing habits over 22 years and found that the more violence people watched on TV, the more likely they were to have committed a criminal act by the age of 30. This study also supports the idea that media violence leads to aggression.
However, Charlton et al. (2000) found that the introduction of the TV on the island of St. Helena did not cause the children to become aggressive. This study contradicts the idea that media violence leads to aggression. However, the children on this island were well supervised and part of a close-knit community so they are not representative of all children.
Another study that contradicts the idea that media violence leads to aggression is Hagell and Newbury (1994). They found that young offenders reported watching no more violent TV and having fewer television sets than a control group of non-offenders. The cause for the offending seemed to be the young offenders' difficult family backgrounds rather than media violence.

On the other hand, Comstock and Paik (1991) carried out a meta-analysis of more than 1000 studies looking at the effects of violent TV on behaviour and they found a relationship between watching TV violence and being aggressive later.

However, there are other reasons why people might be aggressive other than media violence. For example, biological factors such as genes and high levels of testosterone can affect criminality and social factors such as unemployment and poverty. Mental health issues or learning difficulties may also be the cause of criminality. Furthermore, real life models such as brothers who are members of a gang may influence criminality more than role models in the media.

**Studies that can be used to discuss the role of the media in criminal or antisocial behaviour**

**Charlton et al. (2000)** St. Helena Study. This study is useful to learn because it contradicts the theory that the television does not lead to aggressive behaviour. It is also an example of a natural experiment, which you need to know for Unit 4 Issues and Debates.

Aim: To investigate the effects of television on children's behaviour.

Procedure: They video-recorded and observed children's behaviour in the playground of two schools before TV was introduced to the island of St. Helena and 5 years after the introduction of TV. Behaviour was categorised as either prosocial (positive behaviour such as sharing, displaying affection) or anti-social (negative behaviour such as kicking, verbal abuse) and tallied. They used a number of observers to establish inter-rater reliability. Only behaviours that were agreed upon were included in the results. They then compared the children's behaviour before and after the introduction of TV.

Results: There was no increase in aggressive behaviour after the introduction of TV. In fact, the children showed more prosocial behaviour after the introduction of TV.

Conclusion: TV does not lead to children becoming more aggressive.

Evaluation:

Generalisability-St. Helena is a remote island in the Atlantic ocean with a strong sense of community, where children are closely supervised. Therefore, it is difficult to generalise the results other cultures.

Reliability-The study used a number of observers to ensure inter-rater reliability. However, the study would be difficult to repeat as the children were in their natural environment and it was a unique situation.

Application to real life- The study suggests that TV does not lead to more aggressive behaviour so we should not be overly worried about children watching too much TV.

Validity- The study has ecological validity as the children were observed in their natural environment-a playground at a school.

Ethics-The researchers gained permission from the schools and parents before observing the children's behaviour.

**Funk et al. (2004)**-This study is useful to learn because you need to know an example of a questionnaire for Unit 4 Issues and Debates.

Aim: To see if there is children who are exposed to real life and media violence are less empathic and more aggressive.

Procedure: The sample consisted of 150 children from religious private primary schools and one public daycare centre in a MidWestern city of the USA. The children were asked to complete four questionnaires in different orders to avoid order effects. One of the questionnaires asked about the children's family background and about their media use and preferences. This included questions about the number of hours they spent playing computer games, watching television, watching films on DVD or at the cinema and using the internet. Children chose from six time range categories: no time; 1–2 h; 3–6 h; 7–10 h; 11–14 h; more than 15 h. The children had to categorise the type of television programmes and films they watched into categories such as cartoons, sport, fighting and destruction. A second questionnaire asked about their exposure to real life violence in different settings. This was a 34-item questionnaire including such statements as "I have seen someone carry a gun," and "I have been attacked with a knife." The children were asked to rate the items on a scale (0=Never, 1=Sometimes, 2=A lot) and Impact (0=Not at all upsetting, 1=Somewhat
upsetting, 2=Very upsetting). A total score was calculated for frequency of exposure.  A third questionnaire measured the children's attitudes to violence. Children were asked to read statement such as 'Parents should tell their kids to fight if
they have to,' and 'People with guns or knives are cool' and rate the items on a scale (1=No, 2=Maybe, 3=Probably, 4=Yes). The fourth questionnaire measured children's empathy and included statements such as 'When I see a kid who is upset it really bothers me,' and 'If two kids are fighting, someone should stop it.' The children had to rate these statements on a scale as well (1=No, 2=Maybe, 3=Probably, 4=Yes).

Results: Exposure to video game and film violence was associated with lower empathy and stronger pro-violence attitudes. The study did not find a strong relationship between exposure to real-life violence and desensitisation to violence but this may be because the children in the sample had modest exposure to real-life violence. No relationship was found between television violence and aggression but this may be because only 5% of television choices fell within the one category with violence. The boys reported only watching television for an average of 5.6 hours and girls reported only watching television for 2.9 hours, which is much less than reported averages.

Conclusion: Children's exposure to violent computer games and violent films should be limited.

**Evaluation:**

Generalisability- The majority of the children were attending religious private schools and so the sample was better educated and had higher socioeconomic status than the general population. The mothers of the children had a higher level of education than average and this may have made them monitor their children's television viewing more carefully. Therefore, the sample is not representative of the wider population.

Reliability-The study used structured questionnaires with scales and categories. Such questionnaires are easy to replicate and so the study is reliable.

Application to real life-The study suggests that we should be particularly careful about exposing children to computer game violence as it can lead to pro-violence attitudes and lower empathy.

Validity-The structured questionnaires may have limited the children's responses. For example, the children were asked to categorise the television programmes they watched into categories such as cartoons, sport, fighting and destruction. Some of the children may have simply categorised the programmes they watched as cartoons even when they were cartoons including lots of fighting and destruction. Furthermore, the children may not have accurately reported their own media use. They may have under-estimated the amount of time they watched television and they may have been so desensitised to television violence that they did not categorise their programmes as being violent.

Ethics-The study involved children so parental consent would need to have been obtained.

**You need to be able to describe and evaluate the self-fulfilling prophecy as an explanation of criminal or anti-social behaviour (Social Approach)**

The self-fulfilling prophecy (SFP) is a prediction that comes true because it has been made. For example, when people become what others expect them to become. The self-fulfilling prophecy explains criminal or anti-social behaviour as arising due to other people's expectations. A person may be labelled as a criminal or a troublemaker due to stereotypes and they may be treated differently as a result. The person may find it difficult to escape this label and so they internalise it and it becomes part of their self-concept. Once a criminal or anti-social label becomes part of the person's self-concept, they may behave according to the label and carry out criminal or anti-social acts. For example, a young person dressed in a hooded top may be stereotyped as anti-social. People may be more wary of them and avoid them in the street. The antisocial label may then become part of their identity and they may actually go on to behave in an anti-social way.

**Evaluation:**

Studies-Jahoda's (1954) study supports the self-fulfilling prophecy. The Ashanti tribe of West Africa believe that boys born on a Wednesday are more aggressive and boys born on a Monday are calm. Jahoda (1954) examined police records and found that males born on Wednesday had higher arrest rates than those born on Monday suggesting that the tribe's expectations did affect their behaviour. Madon (2004) questioned parents about how much alcohol they expected their children to drink in the next year and found that if parents expected their children to drink too much alcohol, they did. This study can be viewed as support for the self-fulfilling prophecy. However, it may be that parents who drink a lot themselves expect their children to drink more too. Their children may just be copying their behaviour rather than there being a self-fulfilling prophecy. Madon and Jahoda's studies are correlational and therefore cannot establish a causal link between expectations and later behaviour. Rosenthal and Jacobsen (1968) carried out an experiment which supports the self-fulfilling prophecy. They found that when teachers believed certain children in their class were more intelligent, their IQ scores rose. A similar process may occur if children are labelled as naughty or troublemakers.

Explanation-A limitation of the self-fulfilling prophecy is that people with a strong self-image are unlikely to be affected by other people's negative expectations. There are many other reasons for criminal and anti-social behaviour that the self-fulfilling prophecy does not take into account such as observing criminal or anti-social role models (social learning theory), genes, high levels of testosterone, poverty, status and culture.

## To be able to compare social learning theory and the self-fulfilling prophecy as explanations of criminal behaviour

Both social learning theory and the self-fulfilling prophecy suggest that criminality is affected by other people's behaviour. However, social learning theory suggests that criminal behaviour occurs through observing others whereas the self-fulfilling prophecy proposes that it occurs as a result of other people's expectations.

## To be able to describe and evaluate THREE studies into factors affecting eyewitness testimony

### Loftus and Palmer (1974)

Aim: To see if leading questions affect participants' speed estimates.

Procedure experiment 1: 45 students were put into groups.  They watched 7 films of traffic accidents, ranging in duration from 5 to 30 seconds, which were presented in random order to each group. After the film, the participants had to fill in a questionnaire. First they were required to given an account of the accident and then to answer specific questions. The critical question was the one asking about the speed of the vehicles. Nine participants were asked 'about how fast were the cars going when they hit each other?' and equal numbers were asked the same question, but with the word 'hit' being replaced by 'smashed', 'collided' 'bumped' and 'contacted.

Results experiment 1: They found that if a different verb is used to indicate the speed of a car, such as 'hit', 'smashed', 'collided' or 'bumped', then participants gave a different speed estimate. The highest mean speed estimate was when the verb 'smashed' was used and the lowest mean speed estimate was when the verb 'contacted' was used in the question. There was a 9 mph difference between the speed estimates when the verb 'smashed' was used and when the verb 'contacted' was used.

Conclusion experiment 1:  The wording of a question can affect participants' responses.

Procedure experiment 2: There were 150 participants involved in this experiment. A 1 minute film with a multiple car accident lasting 4 seconds was shown. After the film, the participants had to give a general account of what they had seen and then answer more specific questions about the accident. 50 participants were asked 'about how fast were the cars going when they hit each other?', another 50 'about how fast were the cars going when they smashed each other?' and another 50 acted as control group who were not asked the question at all. One week later, participants were asked to answer ten questions, one of which was the critical question 'did you see any broken glass? Yes or no?' even though there was no broken glass in the film.

Results experiment 2: The verb 'smashed' increased the estimate of speed and the likelihood of seeing broken glass even though there was no broken glass. 16/50 participants in the group where the word 'smashed' had been used said they had seen broken glass compared to 7/50 when the word 'hit' had been used and 6/50 in the control group.

Conclusion: This study suggests that leading questions can affect recall and lead to distorted memory.
The study questions the reliability of eyewitness testimony and shows that care must be taken when questioning witnesses.

**Evaluation:**

Generalisability- The study lacks generalisability as all the participants were students who are not representative of the wider population. Students tend to be less experienced drivers and so may have been more easily influenced by the verbs smashed/collided/ contacted etc. in giving their speed estimates.

Reliablity-The study had a standardised procedure and good controls. For example, all the participants in experiment 1 watched the same 7 film clips under controlled conditions. This makes the study replicable, and therefore, reliable.

Application to real life- This study suggests that the police should be careful to avoid leading questions when interviewing witnesses. The justice system should also be careful about trusting eyewitness testimony unless it is supported by other corroborating evidence.

Validity-The study lacks ecological validity because the participants lacked the emotional involvement of real eyewitnesses. The participants may have felt correct recall was not as important compared to witnesses of a real crime. The study also used questionnaires, which is nothing like a real police interview.
It could be argued that the study has experimental validity as the critical (leading) questions were all randomly hidden amongst other distractor questions so the participants were not able to guess the aim of the study and so the study avoided demand characteristics. However, others have criticised the study for suffering from experimenter effects as the participants may have felt they had to give a higher speed estimate when the word 'smashed' was used so that they did not come into conflict with the experimenter. The researchers gathered quantitative data in the form of estimates of speed, which makes the study more objective.

Evidence-Yuille and Cutshall (1986) reported a case of real eyewitness testimony and found that leading questions had little effect on the accuracy of recall even five months after viewing a gun shop robbery. This study contradicts Loftus and Palmer's study.

**Yuille and Cutshall (1986)** asked 21 witnesses who had observed a shooting incident in which 1 person was killed and a 2nd seriously wounded to take part in their study. All of the witnesses were interviewed by the investigating police, and 13 witnesses agreed to a research interview 5 months after the event.

Aims: To record and evaluate real life witness accounts. To examine issues raised by laboratory research. To look at witness verbatim accounts in terms of their accuracy and the kind of errors made.

Procedure: The researchers interviewed 13 of the witnesses and the interviews were recorded on audiotape and transcribed. The witnesses were interviewed in the same way as the police had interviewed them. They were asked to give their own account of the shooting followed by questions. However, two misleading questions were asked: one about a headlight in the thief's car and one the about the colour of the quarter panel of the car. The eyewitness accounts provided in both the police and research interviews were analysed.

Results: The witnesses recalled events accurately even after 5 months. The misleading questions did not affect the witnesses' recall.

Conclusion: This study suggests that eyewitness memory in real life is not as likely to be distorted as laboratory experiments suggest.

**Evaluation:**

Generalisability-It is hard to generalise from the findings of the Yuille and Cutshall's study as it was a case study of a unique event. Only 13 witnesses of the original 21 agreed to take part so the witnesses who took part might have been unrepresentative. Most eyewitnesses are not witnesses to a gun shooting so the witnesses in this study may have better recall than most witnesses. There was also media coverage of the event so their recall may have been better due to this.

Reliability- The study is not replicable as it was a unique case. Therefore, the study cannot be tested for reliability. On the other hand, great care was taken when scoring witnesses' recall of specific details from the incident, which gives the findings some reliability.

Application to real life-This study suggests that real life witnesses should be trusted more as the witnesses were not affected by leading questions. Sometimes judges ignore witness testimony if they make any recall errors at all. However, this study suggests that even if witnesses make minor errors in recall (such as giving the wrong colour for the blanket put over the thief) they still remembered key events at the crime scene.

Validity-This field study has good ecological validity as it involved real witnesses of a real life gun shooting. The researchers suggested that they may have been investigating flashbulb memory, which is when a specific and highly emotional event is recorded in memory in great detail.

Ethics-Yuille and Cutshall's study may not have protected participants from psychological harm as re-living a gun shooting may have caused the participants distress. However, the participants were given the choice about whether they wanted to participate. Participants were also deceived about the leading questions but they were debriefed at the end of the study.

Evidence-Loftus and Palmer's study contradicts the Yuille and Cutshall study as it found participants were influenced by leading questions and would give a different estimate of the speed of a car if the verb in a critical question was changed. However, the Loftus and Palmer study is a laboratory experiment so they would not have experienced the same emotions and stress as in real life. Witnesses of a real crime may remember details much better than participants in a laboratory experiment due to their emotional involvement.

**Yarmey (2004)** carried out field experiment to investigate eyewitness memory using photo identification. The study had a number of different independent variables.

Aims: 1)To investigate eyewitness testimony in the field 2) To see how good participants would be at identifying a woman they had spoken to for approximately 15 seconds in a photo line-up 3)To see if a disguise of a baseball cap and dark sunglasses would affect eyewitnesses' recall 4) To see whether being told you are going to be a witness to an incident affects recall 5) To see if a time gap before identification affects recall.

Procedure: 590 participants (men and women) were approached by a woman (the target) in public places and asked for directions or for help finding a piece of lost jewellery. They spoke to her for approximately 15 seconds. The target was seen originally either with or without a baseball cap and dark sunglasses. Witnesses were either prepared or not prepared at the time of the encounter for a subsequent memory test. After 2 minutes, a female researcher approached the participants and asked them to take part in the study immediately or 4 hours later. Half of the witnesses were given retrieval instructions prior to the memory tests. The first memory test involved a questionnaire about the physical characteristics and clothing of target and the second memory test asked participants to identify the target from a set of six photographs. Half the witnesses were shown a set of photos with the target amongst them (target present condition) and the other half were shown a set of photos without a photo of the target (target absent condition). A separate group of 379 introductory psychology students were asked to predict how well the eyewitnesses would be able to recall the target and identify her from a set of photographs.

Results: Witness preparation helped participants recall the clothing of the target but did not help them recall physical characteristics. Witness preparation, target disguise, whether they had to recall immediately or after 4 hours, gender of the witnesses, and retrieval instructions had no significant effects on identification of the target woman.When the target was in the photo line-up, correct identification occurred 49% of the time, when she was not present 62% correctly said the target was not there. In contrast, students given the written scenario thought the target would be less likely to be identified correctly if the target was absent from the photo-line-up.

Conclusion: As the participants only made a correct identification 50% of the time when the target was present, courts should be cautious about the reliability of witnesses' memory.

**Evaluation:**

Generalisability -The range of ages of the participants and the large sample size makes the study generalisable. However, the witness's recall focused on a situation where the participants met and spoke to the target, which is not the case for all eyewitness incidents. Therefore the findings can only be applied to similar situations.

Reliablity- The control over the conditions means that the study is replicable and reliable. All participants were approached by a target asking for directions or help finding a piece of jewellery in a public place. Timings were controlled carefully, for example, a female researcher approached the participants 2 minutes after the encounter with the target asking them to take part in the study. However, there might have been some situational variables that could have affected results such as how busy the participant was, which makes the study harder to replicate.

Application to real life-The study suggests that we should be careful about witness testimony as the participants were only able to identify the target only about 49% of the time when she was present in the photographic line-up. When the target was not amongst the photos in the photo line-up, participants wrongly identified someone else as being the target 38% of the time. If real witnesses wrongly identify a person in a photo line-up, it could lead to innocent people being convicted of a crime.

Validity- The study was carried out in a natural environment of a public place and the target just approached participants so the study has ecological validity to a certain extent. However, the participants may have lacked the emotional involvement of real witnesses to a crime incident and so their memory may not have been as good. There were no real consequences for the participants to recall the target correctly whereas real life witnesses are aware that their testimony might put an innocent person in jail.

Evidence-Haber and Haber's (2001) meta-analysis supports Yarmey's study. They analysed 48 studies on eyewitness identification in a line up where the person to be identified (the target was present) They found that in 51% of the cases the target was correctly identified by the witness, which is similar to Yarmey's findings.

**You need to be able to discuss problems with research into eyewitness testimony**

Most of the research on eyewitness memory involves experiments, which lack the realism of real life cases. Participants do not experience the same emotional involvement as real life witnesses and this might influence their ability to recall the event. The testimony given by the participants has no consequences whereas in real life witnesses are aware that what they say might put someone in jail. Furthermore people might respond differently when questioned by the police.

Field research such as Yuille and Cutshall's study, which suggests that eyewitness memory is accurate may not be able to establish cause and effect as many variables can have an effect that are not controlled for.

**You need to be able to describe research methods used to assess witness effectiveness including the laboratory experiment and the field experiment**

Exam tip: If you are asked to describe a research method in terms of how it has been *used to assess witness effectiveness*, you need to describe the research method more generally and then link it to how it has been used to investigate the reliability of eyewitness testimony.

**Laboratory experiments:**

In a laboratory experiment, an independent variable is manipulated e.g. in the Loftus and Palmer (1974) experiment, the independent variable was the verb in the question 'how fast was the car going when it ….. The verbs used were 'hit', bumped', 'collided' or 'smashed.
In a laboratory experiment, the dependent variable is measured e.g. in the Loftus and Palmer (1974) experiment, they measured participants' estimates of the speed of the car in the film clip.
Laboratory experiments, control extraneous variables so that a cause and effect relationship can be established.

Loftus used a number of laboratory experiments to look at whether misleading information could affect participants' memory.

Loftus (1975) showed participants a film clip of a car accident and asked one group how fast was the car was going 'when it passed a barn' even though there was no barn. When questioned later, 17.3% of the participants who had been given the misleading information about the barn recalled seeing a barn, whereas only 2.7% of those who had not heard the misleading information recalled a barn.

Laboratory experiments have been used to investigate the weapon focus effect.
Loftus et al. (1987) showed half of their participants a film with a customer in a restaurant holding a cheque, and the other half were shown a film with a customer holding a gun. They found that participants had worse recall for the customer's face when they were holding a weapon.

**Field experiments:**

Field experiments take place in participants' natural environment and involve manipulating an independent variable. For example, in Yarmey's study a woman approached participants in a public place (a natural environment). A number of independent variables were manipulated such as whether the participants were asked to recall the target immediately or 4 hours later and whether the target wore a disguise or not. In a field experiment, a dependent variable is measured. For example, in Yarmey's study, the researchers measured how many details participants could correctly remember about the woman, whether participants could correctly identify her amongst a set of photos when she was present and whether participants could correctly point out that she was not there in a set of photos where she was absent. As field experiments take place in a natural environment, extraneous variables are not easily controlled although the researcher tries to control as many aspects of the situation as they can.

Maass and Kohnken (1989) carried out a field experiment in which participants were approached by a woman holding either a pen or a syringe. Participants in the 'pen' condition were able to supply more accurate descriptions of the woman. However, this could be due the syringe being an unusual object in the situation rather than because it is a threat. Mitchell et al. (1998) investigated whether people's recall would be affected if someone was holding a celery stick (an unusual object) and they found that it was.

**Field study**: Field studies can be a field experiment, a case study in the field or a natural experiment. Yarmey is an example of a field study as it is a field experiment. Yuille and Cutshall is a field study as it is a case study in the field.

**Evaluate, including the relative strengths and weaknesses, laboratory and field experiments as used in criminological psychology including reliability, validity and ethical issues.**

### Reliability

Laboratory experiments are easily replicable as there are good controls over extraneous variables and a standardised procedure. In Loftus and Palmer's study, all participants watched the same seven video clips of different traffic accidents and were given the same questionnaire. Loftus and Palmer's study has been replicated several times with the same results, increasing its reliability. Researchers have carried out many laboratory experiments investigating eyewitness effectiveness and have come up with similar findings, which show that the studies are reliable.

Field experiments take place in the participants' natural environment. This means that not all the extraneous variables can be controlled and the findings might not be reliable. However, as field experiments have carefully controlled and planned procedures, they often give the same results when repeated. This means that they can be as reliable as laboratory experiments.

### Validity

Laboratory experiments lack ecological validity as they take place in an artificial setting. For example, Loftus and Palmer's study lacks ecological validity because watching film clips of traffic accidents does not have the same impact or lead to the same emotions as seeing a real life accident and the interview stage would not seem as important as it would if the incident were real. Loftus and Palmer said that the study avoided demand characteristics as the critical questions were randomly hidden amongst others so participants couldn't guess the aim of the study. However, the participants may have felt that they had to give a higher speed estimate when the verb 'smashed' was used so that they didn't come into conflict with the experimenter (experimenter effects).

Field experiments are carried out in the participants' natural environment so they have ecological validity in terms of setting. However, the independent variable is still carefully manipulated to see the effect on the dependent variable, and therefore, the procedure may not be valid. On the other hand, researchers try to make the procedure as realistic as possible to enhance validity.

## Ethical issues

Laboratory and field experiments can both be ethical or unethical depending on the procedure and the decisions made by the researcher(s). However, field experiments are often less ethical than laboratory experiments because the participants are approached in public places and so they are often do not know beforehand that they are in a study at all. In field experiments, participants can be asked for their consent afterwards.

Informed consent and deceit-laboratory and field experiments are likely to require some level of deceit, because the independent variable has to be kept secret so that participants do not deliberately change their behaviour. For example, in the Loftus and Palmer (1974) experiment, the participants might have changed their speed estimates if they knew all the different verbs that were going to be used in the question 'about how fast were the cars going when they …… each other?' As there is some level of deceit required when investigating eyewitness testimony, there is unlikely to be fully informed consent. In Yarmey's study, participants did not know initially that they were part of a study so they did not give consent. The participants were also deceived as the target lied to them about needing help. However, they were told about the study 2 minutes after they met the target. In Yuille and Cutshall's study participants were deceived about the leading questions.

Distress-BPS guidelines advise that participants should not be caused distress and that they should leave a study in the same emotional state they started in. Field experiments are more likely to cause a participant distress because the participants do not initially know they are in a study. For example, in the Maass and Kohnken (1989) study, some of the participants were approached in the field by a woman with a syringe. This may have caused the participants some distress. Yuille and Cutshall's field study could have caused distress as the participants were asked to recall a gun shooting. However, participants were given the choice about whether to take part or not. Loftus and Palmer's laboratory experiment may have caused distress to any participants who had previously witnessed or been in a traumatic car accident. However, compared to exposing participants to a fake crime incident in the field, laboratory studies are more ethical. Laboratory experiments tend to be less distressing as participants can prepare themselves for witnessing an incident.

Debriefing-As there is usually some deceit involved in a study, and consent is not totally informed, there must be a thorough debrief to make sure that participants are happy with and understand what they have done, and that they are happy to have their results used in the study.

Right to withdraw-Participants must be told they can withdraw at any time and they should be reminded of this at regular intervals throughout the study. They should also be asked at the end if they want to withdraw their data. However, in a field experiment, participants do not know they are in the study initially so are not able to withdraw at this point unlike a laboratory experiment.

Privacy and confidentiality-The participants' identity must be kept anonymous to maintain their privacy.

Competence-The researcher must be competent to carry out the study and if any doubt, must consult with colleagues or someone else who is competent.

**You need to be able to compare field and laboratory experiments in terms of ethics (as applied to EWT).**

Laboratory experiments are more ethical in comparison to field experiments. For example, Loftus and Palmer (1974) showed participants a film of a car accident to investigate the impact of eyewitness testimony. Participants were not viewing the footage first hand and therefore would find the study less distressing, consequently making the research more ethical. Setting up fake crimes in the field or fake car crashes would be more distressing. Also the ability to investigate eyewitness testimony on real life events or by recreating an incident would be difficult.

**You need to be able to apply the laboratory experiment, the field experiment and the natural study to studying witness effectiveness.**

In a laboratory experiment, an incident is set up in a controlled and artificial environment such as a laboratory. The incident may be shown on video footage or as part of a slide show to participants. The independent variable is manipulated e.g. weapon focus effect or leading questions. The dependent variable is then measured e.g. amount or quality of recall of the incident. For example, in Loftus and Palmer's study they showed participants 7 film clips of car crashes. They then manipulated the verb in the question 'How fast were the cars going when they....?' They measured participants' speed estimates to see whether the verb affected participants' responses.

In a field experiment, an incident is set up by a researcher in the participants' natural environment. The independent variable is manipulated e.g. weapon focus effect or leading questions and a dependent variable is measured e.g. amount or quality of recall. For example, a fake robbery might be set up and witnesses asked to recall details of the incident. The researcher aims to control as many extraneous variables as possible within the environment to establish a cause and effect relationship.

A natural study can be carried out if an incident or event occurs naturally that might be of interest to the researcher. For example, a natural event could be a real crime and the researchers might want to investigate witnesses' recall of the incident later e.g. in the Yuille and Cutshall study, witnesses observed a real gun shooting and then asked details about the incident later on. Dependent variables can be measured e.g. the number of details recalled accurately about the incident.

**You need to be able to compare field and laboratory experiments in terms of how useful they are at looking at witness effectiveness**

Field experiments take place in participants' natural environment so they have good ecological validity. They are a useful research method as the participants' behaviour will be more like real witnesses compared to participants in laboratory experiments, who are engaged in artificial tasks in an artificial setting. In a field experiment, participants often do not know initially that they are part of a study, so their attention to the environment will be similar to real witnesses. For example, in Yarmey's study, participants would not have been paying particular attention to the target. In contrast, laboratory experiments involve asking witnesses to pay attention to a film clip or slides of an incident, which makes them lack ecological validity. However, field experiments lack control over the extraneous variables, which makes them less reliable than laboratory experiments. On the other hand, this lack of control over the extraneous variables makes field experiments more like a real incident.

**You need to be able to describe and evaluate TWO ways of treating offenders including token economy programmes and one other: anger management**

**Token Economy Programmes**

Token economy programmes (TEPs) use operant conditioning to encourage pro-social behaviour. Prisons or community-based projects draw up a list of desired behaviours and if the desired behaviour is performed the individual is rewarded with a token. The tokens, which are secondary reinforcers, can be exchanged for something the individual desires, such as visits or watching TV (primary reinforcers). It is important that the rewards are negotiated with the individual because token economy only works if the rewards are something the individual actually wants.

**How to evaluate treatments**

When evaluating a treatment or therapy, you can use DESERT as a trigger for your memory. You do not need to cover all the points.

Directive-how directive is the treatment? If the person delivering the treatment has more power than the person receiving the treatment, then it is directive.

Effectiveness-How effective is the treatment? What studies support the effectiveness of the treatment?

Side effects-Are there any side effects to the treatment? Are there any unwanted outcomes from the treatment?

Expense-How expensive is the treatment? If the treatment requires trained psychologists to deliver it, then it is more expensive than a treatment that is delivered by those with little training.

Reasons-Does the treatment address the underlying causes of the problem? Does it look at how childhood issues or family background may have led to the problem?
Types of people-Does the treatment only help certain types of people?

**Evaluation:**

Directive-Token Economy Programmes (TEPs) may be viewed as directive as the prison guards are in control of the tokens. This is open to abuse as the staff may favour certain prisoners.

Effectiveness-Hobbs and Holt found direct short-term success in using TEPs. They recorded the effects of introducing a TEP to young delinquents in three institutions, while a fourth acted as a control. They found the TEP led to a significant increase in the targeted behaviours compared to the group not involved. On the other hand, although TEPs may be effective whilst an offender is in an institution, it may only change behaviour temporarily. Once the offender leaves the prison and goes into the outside world, there may be no real change in thinking or behaviour. Pearson et al. found that behavioural treatments such as TEPs were not good at stopping recidivism.

Side effects-TEPs may lead to learned helplessness as some prisoners may feel they have to comply with the programme.

Expense-TEPs are relatively cheap to implement as staff do not need much training to deliver them. However, staff need to give the rewards and punishments consistently and this can be difficult to achieve especially with shift changes.

Reasons-TEPs do not address the underlying causes of the offender's behaviour such as poor education, aggression and mental health issues.

Types of people-TEPs can be used with all types of offender.

**Anger management**

Anger management is a cognitive-behavioural technique. Anger management programmes are based on the idea that individuals can learn to control their aggression by changing their thought patterns. There are three steps to anger management 1) Cognitive preparation-Offenders are taught to identify situations which trigger anger and thought patterns are challenged 2) Skills acquisition-Offenders are taught skills to control their feelings of anger such as counting to ten and relaxation techniques to calm themselves down 3) Application practice- Offenders are given anger-provoking scenarios such as someone swearing at them so that they can practice how to deal with difficult situations. Anger management programmes can be used in prisons or with people on probation. The courses are usually conducted in small groups and last for around ten sessions.

**Evaluation:**

Directive-Anger management can be viewed a directive treatment as the therapist has a lot of power and tells the offenders that their thinking is wrong and that they need to change it.

Effectiveness- Dowden, Blanchette and Serin (1999) investigated the effectiveness of an anger management programme in Canada. They found that it was effective at reducing recidivism with high risk offenders over a 3 year period. Goldstein et al. (1989) also found that anger management combined with social skills training could reduce recidivism. However, Watt and Howells (1999) found no difference between offenders who had been through an anger management programme and offenders who had not been treated yet using a range of measures including anger experience, anger expression, prison misconduct and observations of aggressive behaviour. They suggested that the anger management programme had not worked because of the offenders' poor motivation and the limited opportunities to practice the skills learnt. Prisoners may say the programmes are useful simply because they enjoy the break from routine.

Side effects- Anger management programmes do not include a discussion of morality or understanding from a victim's point of view, which has been said to limit their success. Men convicted of domestic violence may become less physically violent after attending an anger management programme but may be more verbally and emotionally abusive.

Expense- Anger management is expensive as it requires highly trained professionals to deliver the programme. It also requires time and commitment from both the prison service and the prisoners as the course requires a number of sessions.

Reasons-Anger management does not uncover any underlying reasons behind the offender's aggression such as childhood issues. It only tries to change present thinking.

Types of people- Anger management works better with offenders who have reactive aggression. It does not work well on offenders whose aggression does not stem from anger. Some offenders use aggression to manipulate others. Watts and Howells (1999) study found that anger management programmes were ineffective but this may be because the offenders were not assessed to see if their aggression was related to anger. On the other hand, Loza and Loza-Fanous (1999) found no link between anger and violent offences.

**You need to be able to compare token economy programmes and anger management programmes as treatments for offenders**

Token economy programmes (TEPS) are a behavioural treatment based on the idea that rewarding desired behaviour will increase the frequency of a desired behaviour (operant conditioning). In contrast, anger management (AM) is a cognitive-behavioural treatment based on the idea that if you can change someone's thought processes you can change their behaviour. Pearson et al. found cognitive behavioural techniques such as AM are more effective at preventing recidivism compared to behavioural treatments like TEPs. TEPs may also be more open to abuse by prison staff as AM is usually delivered by psychologists. TEPs are used in prison only whereas AM can be used in prison and with offenders on probation in the community. TEPs tend to change behaviour in the short-term rather than the long-term. AM tends to have longer term effects as it changes the way you think not just your behaviour. Changes in behaviour due to AM may transfer better to the outside world and stop recidivism compared to TEPs. However, AM is usually delivered by prison psychologists in small groups so it can be costly. TEPs do not need much training to deliver but the rewards can be costly and so should be agreed upon in advance.

**You need to be able to describe a key issue in criminological psychology: The reliability of eyewitness testimony**

Eyewitness testimony refers to the recalled memory of a witness to a crime or incident. Innocent people have been convicted on the basis of eyewitness testimony alone and have later been found innocent using DNA evidence. Cases like this call into question the reliability of eyewitness testimony. There is also the issue that juries tend to place too much trust in eyewitness testimony. The police can also distort witnesses' memories by the way they ask questions. Bartlett suggests that people reconstruct their memories so witnesses may fill in the gaps in their memory of an incident using schemas (packets of information about the world). However, witnesses to real life incidents may have a better of events due to the strong emotions involved.

Eyewitness Testimony is unreliable because:

- Leading questions can influence eyewitness memory and produce errors in recall. Loftus and Palmer (1974) found that they could affect participants' recall by changing the way a question is worded. Participants were asked how fast a car was going when it 'hit', 'smashed', 'collided' or 'bumped'. Participants gave a higher estimate of speed if the word was 'smashed' rather than 'collided', they were also more likely to report seeing broken glass in the 'smashed' condition when asked back a week later.

- Weapon focus effect: Studies show that when a weapon is used by a criminal, witnesses focus on the weapon rather than the criminal's face or their environment, probably because a weapon is a major threat. Loftus et al. (1987) showed half of their participants a film with a customer in a restaurant holding a cheque, and the other half were shown a film with a customer holding a gun. They found that participants had worse recall for the customer's face when they were holding a weapon.

- Yarmey's (2004) study supports the view that jurors should question the reliability of witness identification from line-ups. The found that when participants had actually spoken to a female target, only 49% of them could identify her in a photo line-up when she was present and when she was not present 38% of them identified someone in the photo line-up who was completely different.

- Poor line-up procedures may lead to misidentification of a suspect. Simultaneous line-ups (where all the people are presented together in the line-up) may lead to witnesses using a relative judgement strategy (choosing a person who looks most like the perpetrator of the crime rather than really looking at the person's individual characteristics to see whether they match up).

- Meissner and Brigham (2001) found that people are less able to recognise people from a different ethnic background to them so this can lead to problems in eyewitness identification.

- Buckout (1974) highlighted that photo line-ups can be biased if the suspect's photo is physically different from the fillers.

- Busey and Loftus (2006) pointed out that lack of double-blind procedures can mislead witnesses. They gave the example of a police officer who knew who the suspect was in a line-up and when a witness identified the suspect, the police officer said sign here as if to confirm their identification was correct.

- Wells and Bradfield (1998) found that if participants were told that their identification of a criminal was correct, they became more confident about their identification. Therefore, by the time a case gets to court, if a witness has had their identification confirmed by a police officer, they may be overly confident even if they are wrong.

- If there is a long period of time between recall and the incident, people are likely to forget details.

- Stereotypes can affect eyewitness memory. People's views on what type of person commits a crime can affect recall. People are less likely to believe that a man in a suit committed a crime compared to someone who is scruffily dressed.

- The memory conformity effect can affect witnesses' memory for events. For example, if witnesses discuss a crime incident together, their memory for events becomes more similar. Wright et al. (2000) placed people in pairs to investigate the memory conformity effect under controlled conditions.  One of the pair saw pictures of a man entering with the thief; the other saw pictures without the man. They were then asked to recount the story together but fill out questionnaires separately. About half of the participants who had not seen the picture with the man agreed to their partner's account and said that there was a man entering with a thief.

Eyewitness Testimony is reliable because:

- Yuille and Cutshall (1986) examined the recall of witnesses to a real life gun shooting in Canada. 21 witnesses saw a man try to rob a gun shop and then shoot the shop owner. The shop owner shot back and killed the thief. After the witnesses had been interviewed by police, the researcher used the opportunity to ask them whether they would like to take part in the research into eyewitness testimony. 13 of the 21 witnesses agreed to take part in their research 5 months later. They found that even 5 months after the incident, witnesses had good recall of events and were not affected by the leading questions asked. This study suggests that eyewitness memory in real life is not as likely to be distorted as laboratory experiments suggest.

- Rinolo et al. (2003) questioned 20 survivors of the shipwrecked Titanic shipwreck and found that 15 of the 20 witnesses were able to recall details accurately many years later despite inaccurate media coverage.

- Cognitive interviews can improve eyewitness testimony: this involves getting the witness to freely describe events without the risk of leading questions. Eyewitnesses are asked to not leave out any detail even if they think it is unimportant and they may be asked to recall the incident in reverse order. Questions can be asked at the end in order for information to be un-altered.

- Flashbulb memory may lead witnesses to recall crime incidents very clearly as they are likely to have strong emotions related to the incident and may replay events in their mind.

Tip: You may be asked to discuss problems of research into eyewitness testimony. You should then discuss problems with laboratory research and field research in relation to eyewitness testimony.

e.g. Laboratory experiments investigating eyewitness testimony can lack ecological validity as the participants do not experiences the same emotions as real witnesses and participants may feel correct recall is not as important compared witnesses of a real crime.


**You need to be able to describe a summary analysis on eyewitness testimony:**

**Example:**

Aim: To investigate the problems of line-ups and eyewitness identification of suspects.

How was the data gathered and analysed?

The summary analysis involved looking for two articles on the internet about line-ups and eyewitness testimony. The phrases 'sequential versus simultaneous line-ups' and 'problems with line-ups' were put into the google search bar. The articles were chosen because they discussed problems with line-ups. One article was taken from a UK newspaper and one article was from a US newspaper to make cross-cultural comparisons in how line-ups are carried out. The summary analysis involved looking for key points within the articles and summarising these points concisely including coming to conclusions. The final part of the analysis involved applying theories and studies about eyewitness testimony to the articles.

Summaries:

The first article discussed how William Mills was wrongly accused of a bank robbery in Glasgow. Two police men identified Mills from a series of CCTV stills and two witnesses picked him out from an identity parade. He was found guilty and sentenced to nine years in prison. However, based up DNA evidence he was found innocent a year later. The prosecution was based on eyewitness account and this form of proof could prove to be a dangerous base for prosecution. In an experiment conducted by Valentine, 33% of participants identified the wrong person from close up high quality video footage of the suspects face. This study suggests that people are even more likely to wrongly identify someone from poor quality CCTV footage. It could be likely that other wrongly convicted people still remain in prison due to false eyewitness identification.

The second article discussed how Police are changing the way they conduct suspect line-ups after a mounting number of wrongful convictions based on mistaken identifications. 5 states – Connecticut, Georgia, Maryland, North Carolina and West Virginia have changed the way they conduct photographic lineups. Of 242 people exonerated through DNA testing, about 75% of the wrongful convictions involved mistaken eyewitness identification. Dallas became the largest police department to stop presenting blocks of mug shots, they instead present the photos one by one by investigators not involved in the case. This is meant to make the witness focus more precisely on whether the photo resembles the perpetrator of the crime. It also makes them less likely to just choose the person who most looks like the perpetrator. When photos of suspects are presented one at a time, it is called a sequential line-up. The New York State Bar Association has recommended that the House of Delegates adopt sequential lineups. In North Carolina, the police now only use sequential lineups.

Findings (Results/Conclusions):

People have been convicted of committing a crime on the basis of poor line-up identification procedures and then been found innocent later based on DNA evidence. Eyewitness evidence should not be relied upon without other evidence to support it. Identification of a suspect from poor quality CCTV footage in particular can lead to wrongful convictions. Sequential line-ups (where each person is presented one at a time) are less likely to lead to incorrect identification than simultaneous line-ups (where each person is presented at the same time). In a simultaneous line-up, witnesses are more likely to use a relative judgement strategy (choosing a person who looks most like the perpetrator of the crime rather than really looking at the person's individual characteristics to see whether they match up).

Applying research to the articles:

Yarmey's (2004) study supports the view that jurors should question the reliability of witness identification from line-ups. The found that when participants had actually spoken to a female target, only 49% of them could identify her in a photo line-up when she was present and when she was not present 38% of them identified someone in the photo line-up who was completely different. Research by Loftus and others suggests that people often reconstruct their memories. The theory of reconstructive memory suggests we fill in the gaps in our memory using schemas. People's memories of the perpetrator of a crime may become distorted by existing schemas or later information. Loftus and Palmer (1974) found that just changing the verb in a question could affect participants' speed estimates for a car crash. The police may unwittingly lead witnesses to mistakenly identify a suspect due to leading questions during a line-up. Steblay et al. (2001) carried out a meta-analysis and found that sequential line-ups (where each person is presented one at a time) makes witnesses pay more attention to each person compared to simultaneous line-ups (where all the people are presented together in the line-up). Meissner and Brigham (2001) found that people are less able to recognise people from a different ethnic background to them so this can lead to problems in eyewitness identification. Buckout (1974) highlighted that photo line-ups can be biased if the suspect's photo is physically different from the fillers. Busey and Loftus (2006) pointed out that lack of double-blind procedures can mislead witnesses. They gave the example of a police officer who knew who the suspect was in a line-up and when a witness identified the suspect, the police officer said sign here as if to confirm their identification was correct. Wells and Bradfield (1998) found that if a participant was given confirming feedback about an identification, they became more confident that their identification was correct. Therefore, by the time a case gets to court, a witness who has had their identification confirmed by a police officer, may be overly confident even if they are wrong.

## You need to be able to define and use methodological terminology

Demand characteristics: A cue may lead participants to guess what the experiment is about. Demand characteristics refers to participants behaving in a way to meet the demands of the researcher e.g. in the Loftus and Palmer study, participants may have thought they were meant to give a higher speed estimate when the verb 'smashed' was used. Therefore, a criticism of the study is that participants' memory may not have been distorted by the leading questions but they were instead just giving speed estimates to please the experimenter.

Participant characteristics: Individual differences in participants, in terms of intelligence, age, IQ. e.g. a policeman might be able to judge the speed of a car much better than a young student with no driving experience.

Order effects: Order effects occur with a repeated measures design.
They include practice effects (improvement in performance due to repeated practice with a task) and fatigue effects (decline in performance as the research participant becomes tired or bored while performing a sequence of tasks).

Counterbalancing: In order to overcome order effects in a repeated measures design, you might get half the participants to do condition A first, followed by condition B and the other half of the participants to do condition B first, followed by condition A. (ABBA)

Confounding variables: An extraneous variable whose presence affects the variables being studied so that the results you get do not reflect the actual relationship between the variables under investigation.

Experimenter effects: The influence of the experimenter's behaviour, personality traits, or expectancies on the results of his or her own research. The experimenter's characteristics such as their age or gender, might affect participants' responses.

Cause and effect relationship: You can establish a cause and effect relationship when you know that manipulation of an independent variable has directly led to the change in a dependent variable because extraneous variables have been controlled.

**Student answer to exemplar exam question:**


**Using psychological research, explain whether courts should rely on eyewitness testimony. You must evaluate eyewitness testimony research in you answer.** (12 marks)

Student answer:

Some studies suggest that eyewitness testimony is unreliable. Loftus and Palmer found that when they used a verb that had more force behind it (i.e. smashed compared with bumped) participants gave higher speed estimates. These results from this study suggest that courts should be careful with eyewitness testimony as it isn't completely reliable.

Other studies such as Yuille and Cutshall found that participants who were real life participants weren't affected by leading questions or by the time lapse of five months after the incident had happened. This study suggests that eyewitness testimony is not completely unreliable and shouldn't be disregarded.

The two studies above create a small problem as they contradict each other. However, Yuille and Cutshall's study used real life witnesses whereas Loftus and Palmer used students from a university who watched video clips. There is a big difference as participants watching the video clips may feel that their statements won't matter as much as it isn't real life; compared to real life witnesses who have been affected by the incident and their statement can affect another person's life.

Bartlett's theory of reconstructive memory is crucial to understanding eyewitness testimony. He suggests that recall is subject to personal interpretation that is dependent on our culture, values and the way we make sense of the world. When we store things in our memory, we do so in the way that makes most sense to us using schemas. Therefore, memories can be distorted and courts should be cautious about the accuracy of eyewitness testimony.

There are other factors that can affect a person's memory of an incident, for example the media has a major influence. If the incident is covered in the media, eyewitnesses may pay attention to the story and find themselves believing the story given.

In the past, there have been cases where people are convicted due to eyewitness evidence given in court but later found innocent. The research suggests that some other evidence (i.e. forensic or physical) other than eyewitness testimony should be present to convict a person of a crime.

Laboratory experiments are easily replicable as there is a standardised procedure and good controls over extraneous variables. Therefore, laboratory experiments investigating eyewitness testimony are reliable. However, laboratory experiments can lack ecological validity. Getting participants to watch film clips or slides of an incident does not lead to the same emotions as watching a real life incident. Therefore, participants may not respond in the same way as real witnesses. Participants in a laboratory experiment may also not place the same importance as real witnesses on recalling events accurately.

Field experiments are less reliable than laboratory experiments as not all the extraneous variables can be controlled. However, researchers do try to control the extraneous variables as much as possible so field experiments into eyewitness testimony can be reliable. Field experiments often have greater ecological validity as they are carried out in participants' natural environment. For example, if participants see a fake robbery in a public place, they are likely to experience the same emotions as real witnesses.

8/12 marks-level 3 answer

**Commentary:**

This answer does not refer to enough psychological research. More studies should be given related to whether eyewitness testimony is accurate or not. For example, this student could have written about Yarmey's findings. You should know at least three studies related to eyewitness testimony in detail but it is better to know more in order to answer this type of question.

The second part of the question is asking for an evaluation of eyewitness testimony research more generally. This student makes a good attempt at discussing the validity and reliability of both laboratory and field experiments as used to investigate eyewitness testimony. They could have highlighted that the independent variable(s) is still carefully manipulated in a field experiment and so the procedure can lack validity. There could also have been some discussion of ethical issues. Field experiments have more ethical issues than laboratory experiments because setting up fake crimes in the field or fake car crashes can be more distressing than watching film clips or slides of an incident as is often the case in laboratory experiments.

## Chapter 7-Child Psychology

**You need to be able to define the following key terms in Child Psychology:**

**Child psychology** studies how biological factors and childhood experiences affect children's development. It covers topics such as attachment, deprivation, privation, autism and the issue of daycare.

**Attachment** refers to the strong emotional bond between a child and caregiver. Attachment occurs between 6- and 9-months- old. Children who are securely attached to their primary caregiver want to be close to them especially when they are upset or scared. They dislike being separated from their primary caregiver and show pleasure at being reunited with them. Securely attached children use their primary caregiver as a safe and secure base from which to explore their world.

**Deprivation** is when an infant has formed an attachment but is then deprived of their attachment figure for a period of time.

**Privation** is when an infant has never been able to form an attachment.

**Evolution** refers to the way living organisms become adapted to their environment over time. In terms of child psychology, evolution refers to the way babies and children are pre-programmed to display certain characteristics and behaviours that improve their chance of survival. For example, attachment is a pre-programmed behaviour that leads children to stay close to their carer and so increases their chances of survival. Babies also demonstrate social releasers, behaviours such as smiling, sucking or crying that lead to instinctive parenting responses.

**Daycare** is when a child is looked after by a child-minder, nursery or preschool during the day, usually when their parents are at work.

**Separation anxiety** refers to the distress children feel at being separated from their primary caregiver.

**You need to be able to describe and evaluate Bowlby's theory of attachment**

Bowlby's theory of attachment actually consists of many different theories.

Exam tip: You may be asked to describe and evaluate only one element of Bowlby's theory of attachment so be prepared.

### 1) The evolutionary basis of attachment

Bowlby's evolutionary theory of attachment is the idea that attachment, which leads to children maintaining close proximity to their carers is instinctive and adaptive i.e. attachment increases the chances of a child's survival. Mothers are also genetically pre-programmed to respond to their baby's needs. Babies encourage their carers to stay close, by crying when left and smiling when their carers pays attention to them (proximity-seeking behaviours). Babies also use their carers as a safe base from which to explore. Bowlby used ethology (the study of animals) as the basis for his evolutionary theory of attachment. He noted that animals have evolved to stay close to their mothers when young to aid their survival and he extended this behaviour to humans. Bowlby also thought there was a critical period within which attachment needs to occur.

## Evaluation:

The evolutionary basis of attachment has face validity. Babies do demonstrate social releasers (behaviours such as smiling, sucking or crying) that lead to instinctive parenting responses. Tronick et al. (1978) found that if mothers remained expressionless for a short time in a face-to-face interaction with their babies, the babies became distressed very quickly, which suggests it is instinctive for mothers and babies to interact with each other. It also makes sense that babies are genetically programmed to stay close to their primary caregiver to improve their chances of survival. Lorenz found that geese imprinted very quickly on the closest moving object, which supports the idea that there is a critical period for attachment. Animals are also quicker to imprint in stressful environments and this supports the idea that attachment aids survival. Harlow found that monkeys would use a cloth monkey rather than a wire monkey to comfort them when feeling anxious, which suggests that attachment figures are used as a safe base from which to explore.

## 2) Monotropy

Bowlby thought that children form a particularly strong attachment to a single primary caregiver out of instinct. The idea of a single caregiver is called **monotropy.**

## Evaluation:

Bowlby's idea of a single caregiver has been criticised because children can form multiple attachments with fathers, grandparents and siblings. Bowlby's theory of attachment suggests that a child should not be separated from their primary caregiver when young at all. However, it could be argued the quality of interaction with the primary caregiver is more important than the amount of time they have with them.

## 3) Maternal deprivation hypothesis

Bowlby's maternal deprivation hypothesis states that a child requires the continuous presence of a primary carer throughout a sensitive period lasting until a child is 18- months to 2-years-old. Bowlby thought that there is a critical period to form an attachment and if this critical period is missed, then no attachment will form. Bowlby identified two serious consequences of failure to form an attachment: Affectionless psychopathy (the inability to experience guilt or deep feelings for others) and developmental retardation (very low intelligence).

**Evaluation**:

Bowlby's forty-four juvenile thieves study provides support for the maternal deprivation hypothesis because it found a link between separation from the mother in the first two years of life and affectionless psychopathy. However, Bowlby has been criticised for failing to distinguish between privation and deprivation. Bowlby's research has been influential. Hospitals now allow parents to stay in hospital with their child over night to prevent separation anxiety. Daycare providers are encouraged to assign every child a keyworker, whom the child can go to for help or comfort.

**You need to be able to describe and evaluate studies that supports Bowlby's maternal deprivation hypothesis**

**Bowlby's Forty Four Juvenile Thieves (1946)**

Aim: Bowlby looked at 44 young offenders to see whether those who displayed a lack of empathy for other people and lack of guilt for their actions (affectionless psychopathy) had experienced an early separation from their mothers (maternal deprivation).

Procedure: Bowlby chose 44 young offenders who had been referred to a child guidance clinic. He assessed them to see whether they had affectionless psychopathy and interviewed their relatives to see whether there had been a prolonged separation from the mother in the first two years of life. The children also completed IQ assessments and psychiatric assessments.

Results: Bowlby found that 14 out of the 44 children had affectionless psychopathy and that 12 of these 14 children had been deprived of their mother in the first two years of their life. In contrast, only 5 of the 30 children not classified as affectionless psychopaths had experienced a prolonged separation from their mother when young.

Conclusion: Children who experience prolonged separation from their mothers in the first two years of life are more likely to become affectionless psychopaths than those who do not experience such a separation. This supports Bowlby's maternal deprivation hypothesis.

**Evaluation:**

Generalisability- Young offenders are not representative of the wider population so the study is not generalisable. 75% of the children were boys so the study has a gender bias.

Reliability-It would be hard to repeat the study and get the same results as unstructured interviews were used and on a different day, participants may have answered questions differently. IQ tests and psychiatric assessments were conducted, which are more reliable.

Application to real life-The study suggests that children should not be separated from their mother for a prolonged period of time in the first two years of life.

Validity-Information about the early separation was collected retrospectively during interviews. This relies on the participants' accuracy of recall and their honesty. Bowlby carried out both the interviews and the psychiatric assessments himself so he may have biased because he knew what he wanted to find.

However, Bowlby did use triangulation to establish validity (triangulation involves bringing together data from different research methods and looking for agreement/trends). For example, he carried out psychiatric assessments on the children and interviewed their families. He also compared the young offenders to a control group of non-delinquent children to see how frequently maternal deprivation occurs in the wider population. Bowlby found a relationship/correlation between affectionless psychopathy and prolonged separation from the mother in the first two years of life but this does not establish cause and effect. There may be a third factor such as a child's difficult temperament or domestic violence that caused both the maternal separation and the child's maladjustment.

Ethical issues-The study interviewed the children's relatives about childhood experiences of separation and the children's relationships. This may have caused psychological distress. The children were emotional disturbed and vulnerable and the tests and interviews may have put pressure on them.

## Other attachment studies

Spitz (1945) studied children in South American orphanages who had little attention from staff and were unable to form attachments to a caregiver. The children had poor physical and psychological development.

Harlow (1969) placed baby monkeys in cages and gave them a wire monkey to feed from and a cloth monkey to get comfort from. All the monkeys formed strong attachments with the cloth monkey rather than the wire one. Harlow concluded that comfort is more important than food for an attachment to form. When the monkeys were put back with other monkeys, they had problems interacting with them. They also had difficulties mating and were poor parents.

**Hodges and Tizard (1989)** wanted to see whether being raised in an institution ( a residential nursery) from only a few months old can lead to behaviour problems and insecure attachments. It was a longitudinal study that followed children from age 4- to 16-years-old. The policy of the nursery was to discourage the formation of close relationships with care-givers and this was compounded by very high staff turnover. By age 4, some of the children had been adopted, some returned to their parents (restored) and some stayed in the residential nursery. There was also a control group of children who lived with their own families. They found that at age four, none of the institutionalised children had formed attachments. However, by age eight, the adopted children had formed good attachments and at age sixteen there was little difference between them and the control group. The restored children and the children, who stayed in the institution, had more insecure attachments and more behavioural problem. All the children who had been institutionalised when young had worse peer relationships.

Rutter et al. (1998) followed Romanian adoptees in the UK and found that recovery from extreme early privation is possible. Recovery was better the younger the children had been adopted from the Romanian orphanages.

**To be able to describe and evaluate the work of Ainsworth including the 'strange situation' as a research method.**

The Strange Situation was developed by Ainsworth and Wittig (1969) to classify attachment. It consists of eight episodes lasting 3 minutes each.

Aim: To measure attachment type by observing how 12- to 18-month-old children respond to their parents after being left with a stranger.

Procedure: The observation involved recording children's behaviour through a one-way mirror during eight 3 minute episodes. Each parent-child pair were observed at different times. Episode 1 involved the parent and child being introduced to the experimental room. During episode 2, the parent and child were left alone and the parent was told to let the child explore the room. Episode 3 involved a stranger entering the room and talking to the parent for a short time whilst approaching the child. The parent was then asked to leave quietly. During episode 4, the child was left alone with the stranger who tried to interact with them. Episode 5 involved the parent coming back and trying to comfort their child, before leaving again. During episode 6, the child was left alone in the room completely. The stranger then came back into the room in Episode 7 and tried to approach the child. The final part of the observation, episode 8, involved the parent entering the room, greeting their child and picking them up. The stranger then left quietly.

Observers behind a one-way mirror rated the child's separation anxiety (how distressed the child was at being left by their parent). Children with secure attachments will become distressed at being left alone by a stranger but they will not be inconsolable. The observers also looked at the child's willingness to explore and proximity to their parent. A securely attached child will feel confident to move further away from their parent and explore. The third aspect of behaviour that was observed was stranger anxiety. Children who are more securely attached show greater stranger anxiety. The fourth type of behaviour observed was how the children behaved on being reunited with their parent. Securely attached children show happiness and relief at being reunited with their parent whereas insecurely attached children will ignore or show anger on reunion with their parent.

Results: 70% of the children had a Secure Attachment (type B). They did show distress at being parted from their parent but they were easily consoled when their parent returned. 15% of the children had an insecure/avoidant attachment (type A). They showed indifference to their parent when they left, and did not show any stranger anxiety. They also avoided contact with their parent when they were reunited. The parent tended to ignore their child when they were playing. 15% of the children had an insecure/resistant attachment (type C). These children became very distressed when their parent left and were inconsolable. When they were reunited with their parents they showed their anger by seeking comfort from their parents and then rejecting it. The parent tended to be over-sensitive or angry and rejecting.

Conclusions: Secure attachments (type B) are the most common.

**Evaluation:**

Generalisability- This study was conducted in the USA and so the findings may not be generalisable to other cultures. However, the strange situation has been used to assess attachment type in other cultures and secure attachments (type B) have been found to be the most common.

Reliability- The observation had a standardised procedure, which makes it easy to repeat and so the study is reliable. Waters (1978) found 90% reliability when infants were tested and retested using the strange situation between the ages of 12 and 18 months.

Application to real life-Parents with insecurely attached children can be given training to help them be more sensitive to their children.

Validity-The study lacks ecological validity because it was an artificial situation. The children's behaviour may have been more affected by how well they adjusted to the unfamiliar setting rather than their parent leaving. Children who are used to being left in daycare are less likely to be affected by their parents leaving the room so the strange situation may be measuring how familiar the children are with being left rather than attachment type. This calls into question the validity of the strange situation for measuring attachment. Children's temperament rather than attachment type may also affect their behaviour during the observation. Children who are born with a more irritable temperament may be inconsolable after being left by their parent but this may not be because they are insecurely attached. However, Sroufe et al. (1999) found that children who had been assessed as securely attached using the Strange Situation at 12-months-old, were more popular, more empathic and had greater self-confidence and leadership skills in adolescence. This study suggests the strange situation is a valid way of measuring attachment type as it can predict future behaviour. One problem with this study is that it does not take into account children who have atypical attachments. It is now recognised that some children have disorganised attachments (type D), which are related to abusive parenting.

Ethics-The study did not protect the children from psychological harm as many of the children became very distressed. However, it could be argued, that the children were only left for short periods of time as might happen in everyday life.

Note: Mothers of securely attached infants are more responsive to their needs, provide more social stimulation (talking to and playing with the infant) and express more affection. This is called sensitive responsiveness or maternal sensitivity. Looking at the two classifications of insecure attachment, resistant behaviour appears to be related to maternal unresponsiveness and general lack of emotional involvement with the baby, while avoidant behaviour is related to maternal hostility and rejection.

**You need to be able to discuss cross-cultural issues with the strange situation**

Ainsworth's classification of different attachment types has been criticised for being culturally biased. Different cultures may view attachment differently and the judgement of attachment type is subjective (open to bias).

Cross-cultural research has been carried out to compare attachment types using the strange situation across different cultures. Research has found that type B (secure) attachments are the most common across all cultures. This suggests that the strange situation procedure is not culturally biased.

**Cross-cultural studies:**

Sagi et al. (1985) found that Israeli children raised on a kitbbutzim have a higher proportion of type C (resistant) attachments. This may be because children in Kibbutz are brought up by different caregivers within the collective community and they have little contact with their parents.

Grossman et al. (1985) found that German infants have a higher proportion of type A (avoidant) attachments. They found that German mothers were less responsive to their babies but this may be because want their babies to be independent at an earlier age.

Miyake et al. (1985) found that Japanese infants have a higher proportion of type C (resistant) attachments, which may be due to Japanese mothers rarely leaving their children with anyone else and encouraging dependency.

Van Ijzendoorn amd Kroonenberg (1988) compared the results of 32 cross-cultural studies and found that there were differences in the proportions of different attachment types in different cultures. Type B (secure) attachments were the most common type of attachment in all the studies from different cultures, with the exception of one study from Germany. Interestingly, there were more differences in attachment types within a culture compared to between cultures.

**You need to be able to describe and evaluate research into deprivation/separation. For example, you need to be able to describe the effects of hospitalisation as a form of short-term deprivation.**

When children are separated from their attachment figure during hospitalisation they can become quite distressed. Robertson and Bowlby filmed several children in hospital and based on their observations, they proposed three stages children go through when experiencing this type of separation. Stage 1-Protest: Children at first are panic-stricken and upset. They cry frequently and try to stop their parents leaving (clinging behaviour). They express feelings of anger. Stage 2-Despair: After a time, children show signs of apathy/depression. They actively ignore others and any attempts to play with them. Stage 3-Detachment: Children show detachment by superficial interaction with others and when their attachment figure returns, they ignore them.

**You need to be able to describe and evaluate research that looks at the effects of hospitalisation as a form of short-term deprivation**

Bowlby and Robertson (1953) filmed Laura, age 2 years and 6 months during an eight day stay in hospital to have a minor operation. They found that Laura cried frequently for her mother but would also sometimes be quiet and apathetic. Her behaviour in hospital supports the protest-despair-detachment model. When Laura went home, she could be quite anxious, clingy and aggressive.

Robertson and Robertson (1968) filmed John, a 17 month old boy, who was staying a residential nursery while his mother had a second child. John's behaviour followed the protest-despair-detachment model.

Kirkby and Whelan (1996) reviewed research into the effects of hospitalisation on children and found that factors such as length of hospital stay and medical condition affected how negative the consequences were of hospitalisation.

**You need to be able to describe the effects of day care as a form of short-term deprivation**

Children in day care may experience the react in the same way as children hospitalised. They will go through the protest-despair-detachment model.
There is a lot of debate about the long-term effects of day care on children's emotional, cognitive and social development.

**You need to be able to describe and evaluate research into daycare including at least one study looking at the advantages of daycare for the child and one study looking at the disadvantages of daycare for the child into the effects of day care.**

**Studies on the advantages of daycare**

**A study that supports the use of day care is the EPPE project (Effective Provision of Pre – school Education) Sylva et al. (2004)**

It was a longitudinal study into the effectiveness of pre-school care for over 3000 children in the UK.

Aim: The aim was to look at the impact of preschool provision on a children's cognitive and social development.

Procedure: It compared children's cognitive and social development between the ages of 3 and 7 for those attending nurseries, playgroups or pre-school classes with those cared for at home. It used SATs results and reports from pre-school staff, parents and schoolteachers to assess development. The children were also observed and interviews were carried out with parents and teachers. The sample included 3000 children from a wide range of backgrounds.

Results: It found positive effects for daycare in terms of social and cognitive development particularly if they started before the age of 3. Children who had been in daycare longer were more sociable and had better attention spans. Children from disadvantaged backgrounds showed the most progress.

Conclusion: Daycare can improve children's social and cognitive development.

**Evaluation:**

Generalisability- The study had a large sample of over 3000 children from a wide variety of backgrounds, which makes the study generalisable. However, as the study was only conducted in the UK, it is cannot be generalised to other cultures. The study mainly looked at children in daycare from 3-years-old onwards so the findings can't be applied to using daycare at an earlier age. The study focused on social and cognitive development and did not look at emotional development.

Reliability- The study was carried out in the children's natural environment so there are many extraneous variables that cannot be controlled. The interviews that were carried out with parents are also difficult to replicate and may have been open to interpretation. However, it would be easy to replicate some features of the study such as results from the SATs.

Application to real life- The study implies that the government should provide funding for children, especially those from deprived backgrounds, to attend preschool at an early age.

Validity-A range of measures were used to assess the children's development e.g. SATs, reports and interviews with parents. This makes the study more valid. The study took into account other factors that could have affected the children's development such as parental occupation and qualifications and social background. It was a longitudinal study, which meant that the same children were followed throughout and their development over time could be assessed.

Ethics-The study obtained fully informed consent from parents. However, there may have been issues of confidentiality as school reports and SATs results were used.

Another study that supports the use of day care is **Andersson (1996)**. This study followed up 126 Swedish children who had been in day-care in early childhood, and assessed them on their intellectual and social-emotional development at 13-years-old. Their development was compared with a control group who had not experienced any daycare when young. They found that children who had spent time in day care scored higher for academic achievement and social skills.

**Studies on the disadvantages of daycare**

**A study that looks at the disadvantages of daycare is Belsky and Rovine (1988)**

Aim: To look at the effects of daycare on children's attachment type in the first year of life.

Procedure: Evidence from two American longitudinal studies were combined and examined to assess the effects of daycare. The sample consisted of 90 male and 59 female firstborn infants. All the families were intact and from a middle class background. Interviews were carried out when the infants were 3-months-old, 9-months-old and 12-months- old to find out about the children's daycare arrangements and parents' employment.

The strange situation task was carried out on all 149 infants at twelve months old using the mothers and again at thirteen months using the fathers (only 130 infants took part when the father was used). Videos of each of the procedures were shown to different observers. The observers had 90% inter-rater reliability and rated the attachments using Ainsworth's attachment types A, B and C.

Results: The children in full-time daycare were more likely to be insecurely attached, compared to infants who spent less time in daycare. 47% of infants in full-time daycare (more than 35 hours) were insecurely attached, 35% of infants experiencing extensive part-time care (20-35 hours). Insecure attachments were much lower amongst children experiencing 10-20 hours of part-time care (21%) and those experiencing little or no care (25%). 50% of boys whose mothers worked full-time had insecure attachments to their fathers. More boys had insecure attachments than girls.

Conclusion: Belsky and Rovine concluded that infants who are left in daycare for long periods of time are more likely to be insecurely attached to their mothers.

**Evaluation:**

Generalisability-The study was carried out in America so the results cannot be generalised to other countries. All the families were intact and from middle class backgrounds so they were not representative of the wider population.

Reliability-The strange situation was used which is easy to replicate and so the study has reliability. The children were also categorised by the amount of hours they spent in daycare, which is easy to replicate. Barglow et al.'s (1987) study supports the findings that more than twenty hours a week of daycare under 12 months old is linked to insecure attachments.

Application to real life-The study implies that mothers should be offered one year's paid maternity leave so that children do not have to experience prolonged daycare in their first year of life.

Validity- The strange situation, has been criticised for lacking ecological validity as the children may be responding to the artificial situation. Children who have experienced daycare are less likely to be upset by being left with a stranger compared to children who are usually cared for by their parents. Therefore, the strange situation may not be a valid method for comparing attachment types in children who have experienced daycare versus those who have not. Furthermore, the children's temperament may have affected their responses to the strange situation rather than their attachment type.

Ethics-The children may have been caused unnecessary distress by the strange situation in the study.

Another study that looks at the negative effects of day care is **Baydar and Brooks-Gunn (1991)**. They surveyed 1000 mothers by telephone, asking questions about their use of day-care and their children's behaviour and academic progress. They found that children whose mothers had returned to work in their first year had a higher incidence of behaviour difficulties and poor cognitive development.

**You need to be able to describe good quality day-care in terms of cognitive and social/emotional development**

Good quality day care involves well trained staff. There also needs to be consistency of care with prolonged contact with the same carers, a low staff turnover, appropriate staff-child ratios and a key worker for each child. Staff should be able to devote sufficient time to the child meaning fewer insecure attachments.

**You need to be able to explain how to reduce the negative effects of short-term deprivation**

Children should not spend too long in day care. According to Belsky and Rovine, children who spend more than 20 hours a week in daycare are more likely to be insecurely attached and those who spend more than 10 hours per week are more likely to be aggressive.

Parents should wait until a child has formed an attachment before putting them in day care. The younger the child the more negative the effects of day care. There is almost no evidence that day care in older children has negative effects.

Nurseries and pre-schools should assign a keyworker for each child so that they have an attachment figure when their parents are not there.

Parents should be encouraged to stay with children during hospitalisation and this reduces the negative effects of short term deprivation. Many hospitals now offer camp beds for parents to stay with their children overnight.

**You need to be able to describe the problems of researching daycare**

There are several factors that influence whether day care has positive or negative effects including the mother's happiness with her own situation, the age at which a child enters day care, the amount of time the child spends in day care and the quality of day care.

**You need to be able to describe and evaluate research into the effects of family reordering.**

**Cockett and Tripp (1994)**

Aim: To look at the effects of family reordering on children compared to living with parental conflict.

Procedure: The study consisted of 152 children divided into three groups matched on age, gender, socio-economic status and maternal education. One group consisted of children from reordered families where the parents had divorced or separated. One group consisted of children from families where there was serious parental conflict and the final group consisted of children from harmonious families. The children were asked to complete questionnaires and take part in interviews to assess their performance at school, behaviour and self-esteem. They also interviewed the children from the reordered families about their experiences.

Results: The children from the reordered families performed worse at school, had more behavioural issues and poorer self-esteem than the children from the families where the parents were still together even when there was parental conflict. As expected, the harmonious families had the fewest problems. Very few of the children from divorced or separated families had been prepared for it and less than half had regular contact with their non-custodial parent. Children who had experienced more family reorderings fared the worst and had less contact with their extended family.

Conclusion: Parental separation and divorce are more harmful than parental discord.

**Evaluation:**

Generalisability-The study used a large sample of children who were matched on age, gender, socio-economic status and maternal education. This makes the study generalizable to the wider population.

Reliability-The study would be hard to replicate as it used in-depth interviews, which would be hard to replicate. On a different day, the children might offer different responses about their lives.

Application to real life-The study suggests that parents who are separating should prepare their children better for the changes and that more effort should be made to keep in contact with the absent parent and the extended family.

Validity-The study collected in-depth detailed data about the children's experiences from interviews and questionnaires, which is likely to be valid. However, the children may not have been entirely truthful about all their experiences and given socially desirable answers.

Ethics-Interviewing and questioning children about their experiences of parental separation and divorce or parental conflict may have caused the children distress.

**Other studies on family reordering:**

Richards (1995) compared children of divorced parents with children from intact families and found that children from divorced families had poorer outcomes. For example, children from divorced families performed worse at school, had more behaviour problems and lower self-esteem.

Jekielek (1994) analysed children's responses to a questionnaire about their family life and found that children from families where there was a lot of parental conflict reported more symptoms of anxiety and depression than children from reordered families.

**You need to be able to describe how to reduce the effects of parental divorce/separation.**

Parents can prepare their children for the separation and discuss new living arrangements. The non-custodial parent should be allowed contact with the child.
Parents should try to avoid high levels of conflict especially in front of the children.
Adequate arrangements should be made to keep in contact with the extended family, for example, grandparents and cousins.

**You need to be able to describe research into the effects of death of a parent**

Bilfuco et al. (1991) found that women who had experienced the death of their mother before 6-years-old had higher rates of depression.

Rutter (1981) found that children who experienced death of a parent had better outcomes than children who had experienced a high conflict divorce.

Saler and Skolnick (1992) found that the effects of the death of a parent can be lessened by allowing a child to fully express their feelings openly and letting them be part of the mourning process.

**You need to be able to describe how to reduce the negative effects of death of a parent.**

Following death of a parent, a child should be allowed to mourn openly and to take part in the mourning process.
Children should be encouraged to express their feelings of anger and sadness but not forced to.
They may also want to share their memories of their parent and visit places that remind them of their parent.

**You need to be able to define privation**

Privation occurs when children never have the opportunity to form an attachment to a primary carer, or when any attachment they do form is disrupted due to abuse. Privation can produce serious social-emotional and intellectual problems. An important debate is whether the effects of privation are reversible.

**You need to be able to describe and evaluate the case of Genie (Curtiss, 1977)**

**Curtiss' (1997) case study of Genie**

Aim: To investigate whether a child can form attachments later on despite privation and whether there is a critical period for language development. Curtiss also wanted to help Genie overcome her extreme privation.

Background: In 1977, Genie was found and taken into care aged 13-years-old. She had spent most of her life alone with a potty chair, a cot where she was chained to at night and some cotton reels to play with. Genie's father believed she was mentally retarded and so locked her in a room and neglected her. She was beaten by her father if she made noises and rarely met anyone outside her immediate family. Genie's father committed suicide before he could be prosecuted for Genie's abuse.

Procedure: After Genie was found by the authorities, she was fostered by the Los Angeles Children's hospital. Initially, Genie could not dress herself or use the toilet properly. However, Genie was taught to dress herself and use the bathroom quickly. She was also given intensive speech therapy to help develop her speech. The hospital carried out many tests and observations on Genie to assess her abilities and to monitor her progress.

Genie's mother who was blind was interviewed by researchers. However, the data was not used as it was thought it could not be trusted.

Results: Initially, Genie showed many signs of distress such as crying, biting and scratching. However, she showed signs of attachment to the researchers. Genie was given some neurological tests and the results suggested that there was some mental retardation. Genie's speech did get better with therapy but she was not able to use correct grammar. When the funding for Curtiss' study ran out, Genie's mother was reappointed her legal guardian.

Conclusion: The study suggests that the effects of privation are irreversible. Genie made a small amount of progress but did not acquire language fully or develop 'normally'. There is a critical period for language development.

**Evaluation:**

Generalisability-Genie was a unique case of extreme privation and she may have had brain damage from birth so she is not representative of other children who have experienced privation.
Reliability-It would be impossible to replicate the Genie study as it was a unique case.

Application to real life-The study suggests that a child who has experienced privation can form attachments. However, it may not be possible for a child to develop language normally once they have gone past a 'critical' period of language development.

Validity-This case study has ecological validity as it collected rich, detailed information about Genie using a number of different techniques.

Ethics-It has been said that the researchers put the research ahead of Genie and cared more about the results than her welfare. Genie was very vulnerable given her background and extreme privation but she was subjected to endless tests, observations and questions. Some argue that the researchers did not consider what would happen to Genie after the study finished. Genie's mother was appointed her legal guardian at the end of the study even though she was involved in Genie's neglect.

However, Genie was given intensive therapy and care, which would not have been possible if she had not been part of a study. The constant scans and tests that were run helped the researchers understand her condition better and adapt their treatment methods. Genie's true name was kept a secret from the media but her photograph was published.

## Other studies on privation

A study by Koluchova (1972, 1991) suggests that privation is reversible. He described the case of two identical twin boys 'the Czech twins' who were kept locked in a dark, cold closet most of the time and beaten regularly until they were rescued at the age of seven and fostered. By the age of 14, they showed no social-emotional or intellectual deficits and by 20 they both showed average intelligence, were working and experiencing successful romantic relationships. However, the twins formed an attachment with each other so they may not be case of true privation.

## You need to be able to discuss the reversibility of privation

There is a debate about whether the effects of privation are reversible or not. The study of Genie showed that the effects of privation are not reversible. Genie was looked after by psychologists from the age of 13 and made a small amount of progress but did not acquire language fully or develop 'normally'. On the other hand, recent research following Romanian adoptees in the UK suggests that recovery from extreme early privation is possible. The Koluchova study of twins who were privated early in their lives also suggests that privation is reversible. When the twins were found, the twins had very low IQ scores and could not walk or use language normally for their age. They were fostered into an extremely caring environment and developed average intelligence and formed successful romantic relationships as adults.

The Hodges and Tizard study looked at the development of children who had experienced institutional care at a very young age. The compared the behaviour of these children with a control group of children who lived with their families. They found that the children who had been adopted by 4-years-old formed good attachments and were similar to the control group at 16-years-old despite their early privation. This suggests that the effects of privation can be overcome if children are subsequently brought up in a loving environment. However, these adopted children had more difficulty in peer relationships than the control group. The children who were restored to their natural parents or who stayed in the institution had poorer outcomes. They had more insecure attachments, more behavioural problems, were more attention-seeking and had poorer peer relationships.

One of the main difficulties with research into privation is that it is difficult to assess whether a child has formed any attachments along the way. For example, in the Koluchova study, the twins were able to bond with each other so they may not have been truly privated. Therefore, the study cannot conclusively say that privation is reversible.

In contrast, the case study of Genie suggests that privation is irreversible. However, we cannot be sure that Genie did not have a problem with development from the start.

Neurological studies on Genie showed that she had brain activity similar to a child that had suffered brain damage. Therefore, Genie may not have fully recovered from her privation due to brain damage rather than the fact that privation is irreversible.

## You need to be able to describe the characteristics of autism

Autism is related to a triad of impairments. Autistic children have: 1) Difficulties with social interaction. For example, they find it hard to make friends. 2) Problems with verbal and non-verbal communication. For example, they have difficulty expressing their emotions or understanding other people's emotions. They also find it hard to read people's facial expressions. 3) Difficulties with imaginative play. For example, they might find it hard to pretend that a wooden block is a train or a rocket. Children with autism may not engage with other people or share their interests and achievements. They can also be quite sensitive to stimuli in their environment such as loud noises. There can be speech and language difficulties in children with autism but not always. Examples of speech and language difficulties are: not speaking by 16 months, repeating words and phrases over and over again, repeating questions rather than answering them, not being able to communicate their desires and not understanding humour.
Other characteristics of autism are lack of eye contact, sensitivity to environmental stimuli and repetitive behaviour.

Children with autism can be quite inflexible, for example, they do not cope well with changes in routine. Other signs of inflexibility are: attachments to strange objects such as wires or keys, lining up toys or spending long periods of time staring at moving objects such as a wheel spinning on a car. Some children with autism can show an amazing memory for facts such as train schedules.

Autism may lead a child to feel emotionally isolated. This may lead to anxiety and unhappiness. Many autistic people have certain routines that help them deal with their anxieties e.g. wearing the same clothes, eating the same foods and repeating the same movements (hand flapping, finger flicking).

## You need to be able to describe two explanations for autism

**Lack of theory of mind.** Theory of mind is the ability to read others' intentions and to understand other people's feelings. Baron-Cohen said that theory of mind gives us a number of abilities in social situations including being able to persuade and deceive others and to pretend. Baron-Cohen suggests that people with autism lack theory of mind and that they have 'mind-blindness'-The inability to understand other people's feeling and intentions.

**Extreme male brain.** Autism may be related to high levels of testosterone in the womb leading to an extreme male brain. Autistic children tend to be particularly good at male-orientated tasks. Autism also occurs four times more frequently in boys. Females tend to have better social and communication skills, which autistic children lack.

Auyeung et al. (2009) found that pregnant women who had high levels of testosterone in the amniotic fluid were more likely to have children who had autistic traits at age eight, such as a lack of sociability and poor verbal skills.

Falter et al. (2008) found that autistic children outperformed typically developing children on mental rotation tasks, which supports the theory that autism is an extreme male brain condition.

Baron-Cohen et al. (2003) found using a self-report method that females scored highly on empathy questions and males on systemising questions. Autistic children scored significantly lower on empathy and significantly higher on systemising than the general population.

**You need to be able to describe a key issue: The issue of daycare and its effect on child development**

Exam tip: Use studies looking at the advantages and disadvantages of daycare.

According to Belsky and Rovine, more than 20 hours of childcare per week for a child under the age of 1-year-old is associated with insecure attachments. A US study of more than 17,000 children found that there is a relationship between number of hours in non-parental care and behaviour (Early Childhood Longitudinal Study, Ritter & Turner, 2003). This research suggests that mothers should not go back to work too early or for long hours. However, many mothers find caring for a baby or toddler tiring and stressful. They may not want to stay at home looking after their child. Obviously, if a mother is very stressed and unhappy this will affect the baby and in such situations it would be better for the mother to return to work. Brown and Harris (1978) found that women who don't work and have several young children to care for are more likely to be depressed. There is no sense in a mother staying at home if she is depressed and unhappy. The child is more likely to become securely attached if the mother is happy but around less. Ultimately, it is hard for a mother to meet her child's needs and at the same time meet her own needs but a mother must be happy for her child to be happy.

The Institute of Education in London studied 17,000 children born to American and British mothers in the 1990s, 1970s and 1980s (Joshi, 2002). They did not find any major impact on children from mothers returning to work in the preschool years and the increased income from mothers working would have improved the children's standard of living. However, children whose mothers returned to work after their first year and who worked only part-time were slightly less anxious than children whose mothers had gone back to work full-time before they turned one.

Baydar and Brooks-Gunn (1991) surveyed 1000 mothers by telephone, asking questions about their use of daycare and their children's behaviour and academic progress. They found that children whose mothers had returned to work in their first year had a higher incidence of behaviour difficulties and poor intellectual development.

Vandell and Corasantini (1990) studied children who experienced daycare from when they were small babies. These children were rated as having poor peer relationships and poor emotional health.

Belsky (2002) examined aggression and defiance in pre-school children in relation to time spent in day care in the first, second, third and fourth sixth-month periods of children's lives. The more time children spent in day care, in particular during the first year, the higher the levels of aggression and defiance. Belsky concludes that it is long hours in early infancy spent in day care that can have negative effects

However, Harr (1999) measured emotional adjustment and academic attainment in 628 children and found very few differences between children of mothers who did not work and those who worked full-time. However, once children reached school age, those children whose mother worked part-time were better adjusted than those of full-time employed mothers. Interestingly, children's emotional adjustment and academic progress were positively associated with mothers' satisfaction with their parent/worker status. This supports the common-sense view that it is happy mother rather than working or non-working mothers who are the most successful parents.

Another study that supports the use of day care is Andersson (1996). This study followed up 126 Swedish children who had been in day-care in early childhood, and assessed them on their intellectual and social-emotional development at 13-years-old. Their development was compared with that of a control group who had had full-time maternal care in their early childhood. The children who had spent time in day care scored higher for academic achievement and social skills.

Parents need to be careful about choosing childcare. Good quality childcare is important and too many hours in childcare can have detrimental effects. Russell (1999) analysed the results of 101 studies of childcare and found that overall research showed negative rather than positive effects.

**You need to be able to describe factors that contribute to good quality childcare in nurseries**

Good quality childcare involves well trained staff. Research shows that the more experienced the staff the better the quality of childcare given. When staff had high level qualifications such as NVQs in childcare, they provided better care.
Children also need stability. They need to be able to form strong emotional bonds to their carers and this is only possible if they have access to the same carer regularly and consistently. High staff turnover can lead to problems with children forming attachments. Nurseries should have a high staff to child ratios so that children get enough attention and care.
Children should also be assigned a key worker who they can go to if they are upset or require help. The key worker can also look out for signs of distress in the particular children they are assigned to and can help them with certain tasks.
Adults who are sensitive, empathic and attuned to a child's feelings have been found to be better carers. Good carers enable infants and young children to feel confident, encourage them to communicate and talk, to think and have ideas, and to learn and discover.
Stimulation is very important for children's intellectual and language development. Nurseries should have lots of books, dressing up outfits and colourful toys that encourage children to learn through play. Caregivers need to ask children questions and to respond to the children's vocalisations or talk.

**You need to be able to describe a practical you carried out in child psychology:**

**Example: A content analysis of three articles concerning whether daycare is portrayed negatively or positively in the media.**

Aim: To investigate how daycare is portrayed in the media. To undertake a content analysis of three responses to an article in 'The Biologist' in 2011 claiming that exposure to daycare leads to an increase in cortisol levels.

How was the data gathered and analysed?

The content analysis involved looking for articles on the internet about daycare. The phrases 'problems with daycare' and 'issues with daycare' were put into the google search bar. The articles were chosen for two reasons: 1) They were all written in response to an article by Dr. Sigman in 'The Biologist' in 2011. He drew attention to research suggesting that levels of cortisol, a stress hormone, increase during the day for children who attend daycare. 2) The three articles are from media sources with different political and ideological agendas. The Guardian is a left-wing newspaper, The Daily Telegraph is a right-wing newspaper and The Working Mothers Magazine is pro-working mothers.

Summaries:

Article 1 ('The Kids are all right in daycare') - The Guardian

The Guardian questions the view that daycare is bad for children just because it raises their cortisol levels. The article highlights another study, which found that although infant monkeys have increased cortisol levels when separated from their mothers that this was associated with better outcomes in terms of brain function. Studies of animals and humans suggest that in some settings experiences of moderate stress can be adaptive and enhance resilience. The article states that Sigman ignores or selectively reports this evidence.

Article 2 ('Does Daycare damage you baby? One mother's view' by Lucy Cavendish) - The Daily Telegraph

This article relates the author's experiences of using daycare for her son. She describes how her son 'screamed his head off' the first time she dropped him off in daycare and how she wanted to take him back home. She then writes that by the fourth week her son had adjusted to nursery but she still felt guilty that he wasn't getting one-to-one attention from her. She goes on to describe how one day when she went to pick her son up from nursery she found him sobbing in his cot whilst four other babies were also crying. She concludes that nurseries are unable to meet children's individual needs and that working parents feel let down by the quality of daycare.

Article 3 ('Does Daycare Damage Children?') - Working Mothers Magazine

This article criticises Sigman's view that daycare is bad for children. It argues that cortisol levels fluctuate in children in daycare and that these fluctuations may prepare children for new experiences. The article highlights how some mothers don't have any choice about working due to financial reasons and that the negative research on daycare gets more media coverage than the positive research.

How was the data analysed?

Positive and negative comments in each article were tallied and mean number of positive and negative comments calculated for each article. The articles were then compared in terms of mean number of positive and negative comments to see whether there was any agreement between the articles.

Results: There was some agreement between The Guardian newspaper article and the 'Working Mothers' magazine article as both had more positive comments about daycare. In comparison, the Telegraph had no positive comments at all about daycare and had a high number of negative comments about daycare. All three articles presented research, which highlighted problems with daycare.

|  | Mean no. of positive comments | Mean no. of negative comments |
|---|---|---|
| The Guardian | 3.3 | 3.1 |
| The Telegraph | 0 | 2.9 |
| Working Mothers Magazine | 3.4 | 2.4 |

Conclusion: There are differing opinions about whether daycare is positive or negative. Across all three articles, there was concern about the impact of daycare on children. The political ideology of the media articles was reflected in how positive or negative they were about daycare.

**You need to be able to describe and evaluate observations as a research method in child psychology.**

In child psychology, observations are used to watch and record children's behaviour in a variety of settings such as at home, at school or in a nursery.

Structured laboratory observations involve careful controls and a set-up situation that can be repeated. The strange situation is an example of a structured observation as there are certain set stages in the observation and the behaviour of the child is recorded when their mother leaves them alone and when they are with a stranger.

Naturalistic observations involved observing children in their natural setting. For example, children might be observed playing with each other in a nursery or at home with their parents.

Observations often have more than one observer to ensure inter-observer reliability. If a number of observers agree about what they have observed, this increases the reliability of the findings. This is because an individual observer can be biased.

Observations can be overt or covert. Covert observations involve observing a child or group of children without their knowledge, for example, through a one-way mirror. This ensures that the researchers' presence does not affect the children's behaviour. However, a parent or legal guardian must give consent for the observation to take place. Overt observations involve observing a child or group of children with their knowledge.

Observations can also be participant or non-participant. A participant observation involves the researcher getting actively involved with the child or children that are being observed. For example, during a participant observation, the researcher may play with a child. A non-participant observation involves the researcher observing behaviour from a distance without getting involved. For example, observing children's aggressive behaviour in the playground.

An observation can be carried out by counting the frequency of certain behaviours during a fixed period of time.
Event sampling-when you record every time an event such as a kick occurs
Time sampling-when you record what is happening every set amount of time e.g. every 5 minutes.
Point sampling- The behaviour of just one individual in the group is recorded.

**Evaluation:**

The presence of the observer might influence behaviour (social desirability). It may be difficult to record all the behaviour although event sampling, time sampling and point sampling help. Video recordings allow an observation to be played back later so that nothing is missed. However, it may be difficult to analyse or interpret all the data collected. Observers have to be specially trained to categorise and record behaviour quickly without bias. Having more than one observer can reduce the problem of researcher bias and establish inter-observer reliability.

Participant observations allow researchers to experience the same environment as their participants. However, the researcher's involvement can affect the behaviour of participants. In contrast, non-participant observations allow researchers to observe participants' behaviour more objectively as they are not directly involved in the action. However, if participants are aware they are being observed, they may still change their behaviour.

Covert observations enable researchers to observe participants behave naturally as the participants do not know they are being observed. However, there are ethical issues with observing participants without their consent. They do not have the right to withdraw, they have not given informed consent and there also issues of confidentiality especially if their behaviour has been video-recorded. The British Psychological Society advises that it is only suitable to conduct a covert observation in a place where people might reasonably be expected to be observed by other people such as a shopping centre or other public place.

Overt observations do not have as many ethical issues as covert observations. However, when participants know they are being observed they may change their behaviour so that it appears socially desirable. Therefore, overt observations can be less valid. However, very young children are often unaware of being observed so they are less likely to change their behaviour due to the researcher's presence. Therefore, demand characteristics may not be a problem with young children.

Naturalistic observations have high ecological validity as the children are in their natural environment and are more likely to behave naturally compared to a laboratory observation. However, it can be difficult to control all the extraneous variables when children are observed in their natural environment. For example, the presence of a certain teacher may affect what type of aggression is observed in a playground. Therefore, it can be difficult to replicate the findings of a naturalistic observation. Researchers do not normally have to get consent to observe adults in public places but they do have to get parental consent when observing children.

Structured observations are replicable and reliable as they have a standardised procedure and control over extraneous variables. For example, the strange situation follows a carefully controlled procedure.

**You need to be able to describe and evaluate case studies as a research method in child psychology**

A case study is an in-depth study of one person or one group of people. A number of different techniques are used to gather data. For example, the researcher may observe, interview and carry out a number of experiments on the same person. In child psychology, case studies can be used to look at unique cases of privation, such as Genie. The researchers who studied Genie, carried out experiments, observations and interviews to assess whether her privation had affected her social, emotional and cognitive development. Triangulation is used to pool data together from the different types of research method and to draw conclusions.
Evaluation: Case studies are not generalisable as they are carried out on only one person or one group of people who are often unique and not representative of the wider population. It is also difficult to replicate case studies because they involve unique individuals and the interpretation of the observations and interviews is subject to bias. Therefore it is hard to establish reliability in case studies. However, triangulation is used to draw conclusions about the same concept so this improves the reliability of the findings. An advantage of case studies is that they gather rich, detailed information about the individuals using a number of different techniques, so this increases their validity.

There can be ethical issues with case studies. Often they involve studying unique individuals who are more vulnerable than normal. Therefore, researchers have to be careful to protect them from psychological distress.

**To be able to describe and evaluate longitudinal studies**

Longitudinal studies involve studying the same person or group of people over a long period of time. In child psychology, longitudinal studies are used to look at children's development over time. For example, how attachment, deprivation and privation affect

children over time. In the EPPE study, the researchers looked at the long-term effects of daycare on children's social, cognitive and emotional development.
Evaluation:

An advantage of longitudinal studies is that they allow researchers to follow the development and progress of children over time. There are also less likely to be participant variables compared to cross-sectional studies as the same children are used throughout. However, longitudinal studies can be expensive. Furthermore, erosion of the sample (children dropping out of the study) may cause bias. For example, if the researchers are looking at the effects of preschool education in a deprived area over time and some children leave the study to move to a more affluent area, then that can bias the results. It is also difficult to replicate a longitudinal study and establish reliability.

Note: Cross-sectional studies involve comparing different groups of children to each other. Charlton et al.'s St. Helena study used a cross-sectional design. They observed children's behaviour in two school playgrounds before TV was introduced and then five years later to see if there were any differences. The children in the playgrounds were different due to the time difference. Cross-sectional studies can also compare children of different ages at the same time.

## Describe and evaluate cross-cultural research

Cross-cultural research involves comparing studies carried out in different cultures. In child psychology, cross-cultural research may be used to compare attachment types, language development and the play of children in different cultures. For example, Van Ijzendoorn and Kroonenberg carried out a meta-analysis to compare attachment type (measured using the strange situation) in different cultures.

## Evaluation:

Cross-cultural research can help us understand to what extent behaviour is nature or nurture. Behaviour that is similar across cultures is likely to be due to biology. Behaviour that is different across cultures is likely to be due to environment. However, a problem with cross-cultural research is that researchers may interpret the findings of the studies in terms of their own cultural beliefs (ethnocentrism).

## Ethical issues when children are participants

Researchers should try to fully inform children about what a study involves if they are old enough to understand. They should also obtain their consent where possible. However, even if children do give consent, they may not fully understand what a study entails. Therefore, parental consent should also be gained. Researchers should not try to bribe children to take part with treats. Children should also be encouraged to ask questions and given the right to withdraw if they seem distressed or are experiencing difficulties. The children's anonymity should be protected. As with adults, children should be protected from psychological and physical harm.

**Student answer to exemplar exam question on Child Psychology:**

**Describe the characteristics of autism and two explanations of the disorder. Explain how these explanations can help parents understand the disorder better.**
(12 marks)

Student answer:

The characteristics of autism include lack of eye contact, repetitive behaviours, lack of empathy, poor social skills and delayed speech and language development.

One explanation of autism is lack of theory of mind. This means that autistic children cannot see things from another person's point of view or imagine what another person is thinking. This leads to problems with empathy and understanding other people's intentions. Baron-Cohen carried out the Sally-Anne task with autistic children and found that they could not understand that Sally would not think the same thing as them. They thought that Sally would think that the ball was hidden in the same place as they did. If parents understand that their autistic child can't understand things from the other people's viewpoints, then they may be more accepting of their autistic child's lack of empathy and social skills. It can also help them understand why their child can't engage in pretend play. A second explanation of autism is that it is an extreme male brain condition. This theory suggests that autism is caused by high levels of testosterone in the womb, which lead to an extreme male brain. Males tend to be better at systemising and mathematical skills than females and autistic people tend to focus on such skills. Females tend to be interested in other people's feelings and have better language and communication skills than males whereas autistic people often have poor empathy, language and communication skills. This theory can help parents understand why autistic children seem to focus on numbers and systemising whilst having poor empathy and communication skills.

Level 3 answer: 8 out of 12 marks.

**Commentary:**

This student gives a list of the characteristics related to autism but has not described any in detail. For example, poor social skills could have been elaborated on. Autistic children can find it hard to make friends as they have difficulties with verbal and non-verbal communication. They can have difficulty expressing their emotions and understanding other people's emotions. They also have problems reading people's facial expressions. The two explanations of autism: lack of theory of mind and the extreme male brain are done well. There is also a good attempt at explaining how the theories can aid parent's understanding of the disorder. A point that could have been made about lack of theory of mind is why autistic children have poor language development. Children with autism may lack the motivation to develop good communication skills because they don't understand that other people have different thoughts to them. Another point that is missed is how the extreme male brain explanation of autism can explain why autism occurs more frequently in males than females.

# Chapter 8-Clinical Psychology

**You need to be able to describe two definitions of abnormality and be able to evaluate them:**

## Deviation from social norms

Behaviour that goes against the norms of society is classed as abnormal. For example, someone talking to themselves in a public place may be deemed abnormal according to the social norms definition. Hearing voices is also viewed as abnormal according to this definition and may lead to a diagnosis of schizophrenia. Behaviour that the majority of people view wrong on moral grounds can also be viewed as abnormal. Anti-social personality disorder, commonly called psychopathy is related to this definition.

## Evaluation:

The social norms definition of abnormality can lead to the curtailing of people's human rights and social norms can change with time. Historically, homosexuality was considered deviant and was classed as a mental disorder until 1973. In the early 20th century, pregnant, unmarried women in the UK were institutionalised and the baby taken away from them when it was born. Social norms vary from culture to culture. Szasz (1972) suggested people may be labelled as abnormal when they don't conform to social norms. As most psychiatrists are white and middle class in the UK, people from other cultures may be mis-diagnosed just because they do not behave according to Western middle class ideals. This may be why Afro-Caribbean men have been up to seven times more likely to be diagnosed with schizophrenia (Cochrane, 1977).

## Statistically infrequent behaviour

Behaviour that occurs infrequently in the population can be considered abnormal. Individual characteristics can be measured, for example, weight and intelligence. A normal distribution curve can be plotted to see how frequently these characteristics occur in the general population. The normal distribution curve shows the majority of people as being in the middle. 95% of characteristics fall within 2 standard deviations of the mean. These people are viewed as 'normal'. Only 5% of characteristics fall more than 2 standard deviations from the mean and this behaviour is viewed as abnormal according to the statistically infrequent behaviour definition.

For example, the mean number of calories consumed a day for a moderately active 15-year-girl is 2000 calories. However, the calorie intake of anorexics is far less and more than 2 standard deviations from the mean, so this is viewed as abnormal.

## Evaluation:

One weakness of the statistical infrequency definition is that some statistically infrequent characteristics are desirable. For example, although an IQ of 150 is more than 2 standard deviations from the mean, and therefore, statistically infrequent, it is still considered desirable. In comparison, anxiety is not statistically infrequent (approximately 18% of the population may suffer from it in a given year) and yet it is seen as abnormal. The statistically infrequent behaviour definition of abnormality does not take into account whether someone needs help. However, an advantage of this definition is that personal opinion cannot bias diagnosis.

**You need to be able to describe in detail the DSM system for classifying mental disorders.**

DSM is a multi-axial diagnostic system-it has five axes. The first axis represents the actual clinical disorder e.g. depression, the second axis looks at personality disorders, the third axis takes into account the person's general medical condition, the fourth axis considers any psychosocial or environmental problems e.g. the death of a child and the fifth axis gives a GAF score- a score from 0-100 which gives an idea how urgent someone's need is for treatment (the lower the score, the more urgently the person requires treatment). Each version of DSM has tightened up the criteria for diagnosis and included more mental disorders. DSM V has taken into account cultural issues in diagnosis.

The American Psychiatric Association (APA) has attempted to make the DSM system more reliable and valid with each new version. DSM-5 takes cultural issues in diagnosis into account. For example, people from different cultures and communities may exhibit symptoms of a mental disorder in a different way. DSM-5 has been designed to be more comprehensive that previous versions and aims to help doctors make a diagnosis more easily. Some of the main changes are: 1) The diagnosis of Asperger's syndrome has been removed from the DSM-5 and is now part of one umbrella term Autistic Spectrum Disorder (ASD); 2) Disruptive mood dysregulation disorder (DMDD) is defined by DSM-5 as severe and recurrent temper outbursts (three or more times a week) that are grossly out of proportion in intensity or duration in children up to the age of 18; 3) Mild cognitive disorder (MCD) is defined as 'a level of cognitive decline that requires compensatory strategies … to help maintain independence and perform activities of daily living;' 4) The "diagnostic threshold" for generalised anxiety disorder (GAD) was lowered in the new version of the manual. In previous versions, GAD was defined as having any three of six symptoms (such as restlessness, a sense of dread, and feeling constantly on edge) for at least three months. In DSM-5, this has been revised to having just one to four symptoms for at least one month; 5) Previously Major Depressive Disorder (MDD) would not be diagnosed if the person had recently been bereaved but this exception has been removed from DSM-5.

You also need to know that the ICD (International Classification of Diseases) is another diagnostic system but you don't need to know anything about it.

**Using the findings of studies you need to be able to describe and evaluate the reliability (replicability) of diagnostic systems such as the DSM and the ICD.**

A diagnosis is reliable when one clinician gives a diagnosis and another clinician gives the same diagnosis. This is called inter-rater reliability.

Note: A mental health clinician refers to a person who diagnoses, treats and helps people with mental health issues e.g. a psychiatrist, clinical psychologist or psychiatric nurse. A psychiatrist is a doctor who has studied medicine and then specialises in mental health. They focus on biological treatments such as drugs. A clinical psychologist has a PhD in clinical psychology. They focus on talking treatments such as cognitive behavioural therapy.

Brown et al. (2001) found that good inter-rater agreement for anxiety and mood disorders with DSM IV.

Rosenhan's study found that DSM III was reliable for diagnosing schizophrenia as all the pseudo-patients who said they had schizophrenic symptoms were diagnosed with schizophrenia.

Silverman et al. (2001) found that the Anxiety Disorders Interview Schedule (ADIS) on DSM IV was reliable at diagnosing anxiety disorder in children.

If different diagnostic systems such as the DSM and the ICD come up with the same diagnosis, then the diagnosis can also be considered reliable.

However, Nicholls et al. (2000) looked at inter-rater reliability for eating disorders in children using ICD 10, DSM IV and the Great Ormond Street's criteria (GOS). They found poor inter-rater reliability using ICD 10 (36% only), reasonable agreement for eating disorders in children using DSM IV (64%) but much better agreement with GOS (88%). They concluded that the GOS criteria were much better for diagnosing eating disorders in children because they were developed for use with children.

When a clinician tests the same patient two or more times to see whether they come up with the same diagnosis it is called test-retest reliability.

Goldstein (1988) used DSM-III to re-diagnose 199 patients with schizophrenia who had been originally diagnosed using DSM–II. She found only 169 patients were re-diagnosed with schizophrenia. This suggests some problems in reliability between DSM-II and DSM-III.

Goldstein then picked a random sample of eight patients who had been re-diagnosed as having schizophrenia using DSM-III and asked two experts to re-diagnose them as well. She found a high level of agreement in diagnosis, which suggests DSM-III is reliable.


**Using the findings of studies you need to be able to describe and evaluate the validity of diagnostic systems such as DSM and ICD**

A diagnosis is valid if different people who are diagnosed with schizophrenia exhibit the same symptoms as each other and respond to the same treatments. A diagnosis has face validity if the person's behaviour matches what most people believe about the mental illness. For example, most people believe that someone with bi-polar disorder can be depressed on some days but hyper on others.

Rosenhan's study showed how diagnosis using DSM III wasn't valid. The pseudo-patients did not have schizophrenia but were still diagnosed with it and all but one were given a diagnosis of schizophrenia in remission on release even though they did not have it all. In the second study, real patients who did have schizophrenia were diagnosed as normal. However, DSM has been revised many times since the Rosenhan study and its validity has been improved.

A diagnosis has etiological validity if a group of people diagnosed with a mental disorder have the same factors causing it e.g. brain scans should show that most people with schizophrenia have a reduced volume of grey matter in the brain.

A diagnosis has concurrent validity if people who are diagnosed with a mental disorder show symptoms related to their mental disorder e.g. people diagnosed with paranoid schizophrenia should exhibit signs of paranoia.

A diagnosis has predictive validity if it predicts how a person will behave in the future and how they will respond to certain treatments. e.g. if a person is diagnosed with schizophrenia and then goes on to respond well to anti-psychotic drugs, then the diagnosis has predictive validity. Lahey et al. (2006) followed children over six years and found that children diagnosed with ADHD displayed behaviour consistent with their diagnosis. Therefore, their diagnosis can be said to have good predictive validity.

**You need to be able to explain how issues of validity can arise in clinical psychology**

If a person is diagnosed with a mental disorder such as schizophrenia but then does not to show any symptoms or respond to treatments for schizophrenia, then the diagnosis lacks validity. There has been a great deal of criticism about the validity of ADHD diagnoses. Some clinicians have suggested that young children who have been diagnosed with ADHD may just be displaying normal behaviour for young children. Issues with validity may arise, if the family or mental health staff disagree with a diagnosis.

Tip: You can use studies relating to the validity of DSM and ICD to support your argument.

**You need to be able to explain how issues of reliability can arise in clinical psychology**

If different clinicians agree on the same diagnosis for the same patient using the same diagnostic system e.g. DSM then the diagnosis has inter-rater reliability.

If a clinician tests the same patient two or more times and ends up with the same diagnosis, then the diagnosis has test-retest reliability.

Issues of reliability can occur when someone who has previously been diagnosed with a mental disorder, is then re-diagnosed later as not having it. For example, it may be disturbing for a person who has been diagnosed with schizophrenia to be told later told that they do not have it. There can also be problems if one clinician diagnoses a girl as having anorexia nervosa but another disagrees.

**Exam tip:** Use studies relating to the reliability of DSM and ICD to support your discussion.

**Using the findings of studies, you need to able to describe and evaluate cultural issues in diagnosis**

Cultural issues in diagnosis are how someone's gender, race, culture or religion might lead to a different diagnosis. Language barriers might also lead to misdiagnosis. Neighbors et al. (2003) found that African Americans are more likely to be diagnosed with schizophrenia whereas white Americans are more likely to be diagnosed with mood disorders. Such studies suggest that there is a bias in diagnosis.

Different cultures may interpret people's behaviour in different ways, for example hearing voices in Britain would be a symptom of schizophrenia but in another culture they might see it as spiritual.

There can also be problems related to mistrust of mainly white, middle class psychiatrists. Casas (1995) found that a lot of African Americans do not like to share their personal information with people of a different race so this can lead to problems with diagnosis. In fact, African Americans are less likely to seek help from mental health professionals than white Americans (Sussman, Robins and Earls, 1987). Sue and Sue (1992) found that many Asian Americans don't like to talk about their emotions and are less likely to admit they have a problem. Cinnerella and Loewethal (1999) compared cultural influences on mental disorders between white Catholics, black Christians, Muslim Pakistanis, Orthodox Jews and Indian Hindus. They found that all the groups except the white Catholics had a fear of health professionals misunderstanding them. This means that certain groups may be less likely to seek help or talk about their issues openly with a psychiatrist.

DSM-5 aims to take into account people's cultural background when making a diagnosis. It highlights how people from different cultures display symptoms of the same mental disorder differently. For example, uncontrollable crying and headaches are symptoms of panic attacks in some cultures, while difficulty breathing is the main symptom in other cultures. DSM-5 provides clinicians with detailed information about how people from different cultures think and talk about psychological problems.

**You need to be able to describe the features and symptoms of schizophrenia**

One symptom of schizophrenia is hallucinations, which involves a person perceiving something that isn't real. Auditory hallucinations are the most common but people can have hallucinations through all five senses. Auditory hallucinations may involve a person hearing a voice(s) that comment on their behaviour or tell them what to do. Another symptom of schizophrenia is delusions, where a person has false beliefs. For example, they may have delusions of grandeur where they imagine they are prime minister or delusions of persecution where they think they are being plotted against. Schizophrenics may also suffer from thought disturbances. For example, they may believe an outside force is putting thoughts into their head (thought insertion). Positive symptoms are diagnosed by their presence i.e. a 'normal' person does not hear voices, so hearing voices is a positive symptom. Negative symptoms are diagnosed by their absence i.e. a 'normal' person is able to show appropriate emotions so the absence of being able to show emotions is a negative symptom. Alogia (poverty of speech) and flattened effect (lack of emotional responses) are negative symptoms of schizophrenia. Approximately 1% of the population suffer from schizophrenia.

Exam Tip: Do not just list symptoms of schizophrenia. Instead, explain fewer symptoms in more detail and give examples.

**You need to be able to describe and evaluate one biological explanation for schizophrenia and one other from a different approach**

**One biological explanation of schizophrenia is the genetic explanation.**

The genetic explanation states that genes can predispose someone to develop schizophrenia. DNA studies suggest that a number of genes are associated with schizophrenia although no single gene has been identified. People who inherit a number of these high risk genes are more likely to develop schizophrenia. The genes that are associated with schizophrenia may lead to biochemical differences in the brain, for example genetic abnormalities may lead to high levels of dopamine (a neurotransmitter) in the brain, which is linked with schizophrenia. Genetic abnormalities may also lead to structural differences in the brain that cause schizophrenia. For example, genetic abnormalities might lead to damage to neural pathways (nerve cells carrying messages) in the brain. Behaviour that is controlled by these neural pathways may then be abnormal.

**Evaluation:**

When evaluating an explanation/theory, use studies to support or contradict the explanation and then discuss limitations of the explanation. There is also one mark for listing alternative explanations/theories.

Studies- The International Schizophrenia Consortium (2008) found that schizophrenics were more likely to have DNA missing on chromosomes 1,15 and 22 than non-schizophrenics. Hong et al. (2001) found that variation in the TPH gene (the gene involved in production of the enzyme tryptophan hydroxylase) is more common in schizophrenic patients than controls. Sherrington et al. (1988) found a gene located on chromosome 5 which has been linked in a small number of extended families where they have the disorder.
Twin studies also suggest that genes can predispose someone to develop schizophrenia. Gottesman's study showed a 0.48 concordance for schizophrenia in MZ twins compared to only 0.17 concordance for DZ twins. The likelihood of schizophrenia in the general population in only 0.01, so these findings suggest a genetic basis for schizophrenia. McGue (1992) found 0.40 concordance for MZ twins. In twin studies, twins share the same environment as well as genes, so the effects of genes and environment cannot be separated.
Adoption studies also suggest that there is a genetic component in schizophrenia. Heston's study showed that 10% of adoptees who had a biological mother with schizophrenia went on to develop it themselves. However, a problem with adoption studies is that adoptees are often selectively placed into families that are similar to their biological family. Therefore, this can make it difficult to separate out the effects of genes from the environment.

Explanation-As schizophrenia has been linked with a number of different genes, it is hard to pin down a genetic cause. There is more than one type of schizophrenia so there may be more than one cause. Furthermore, if schizophrenia was entirely caused by genetics, if one MZ twin had schizophrenia, the other one would automatically develop it but this is not the case. This suggests there must be environmental factors that lead to a person developing schizophrenia as well as genetic factors.

## The cognitive explanation of schizophrenia

A cognitive explanation for schizophrenia is that schizophrenics have difficulties with processing information and irrational beliefs, which affect their behaviour. They also have problems with metarepresentation, which refers to the ability to recognise our own thoughts and behaviour as being different to someone else's. For example, a schizophrenic may not be able to distinguish between their own thoughts and someone else's speech. This can lead them to believe that other people are putting thoughts in their head (thought insertion). Schizophrenics can be paranoid and think that they are being persecuted and plotted against. This can be viewed as a metarepresentation problem as they have problems interpreting other people's behaviour and intentions. Schizophrenics can also have problems with central control. This means that they cannot suppress automatic responses to stimuli. Therefore, if they intend to carry out an action or talk on a specific topic, they may be distracted by other stimuli in their environment. For example, if you ask some schizophrenics a question, they may end up talking about a stream of loosely related things because they cannot focus on the question asked. The disorganised speech produced by schizophrenics is sometimes referred to as a 'word salad'.

## Evaluation:

Studies-
Daprati et al. (1997) asked schizophrenics and non-schizophrenics to make simple hand movements without them being able to see their actual hand. At the same time, they were shown an image of either their hand or a different hand on a TV-screen. They found that schizophrenics with delusions and hallucinations could not tell the difference between their own hand and someone else's hand. This supports the idea that schizophrenics have problems distinguishing between their own actions and other people's actions (a metarepresentation problem).
Frith and Done (1986) found that schizophrenic patients with negative symptoms did worse on verbal fluency tasks (such as name as many fruits as you can). This supports the idea that schizophrenics have difficulties in information processing.
Frith and Done (1989) found that schizophrenic found it much harder to work out the errors they had made in a computer game compared to non-schizophrenics. This supports the idea that schizophrenics have problems recognising their own actions.
Another study that shows that people with schizophrenia have problems with information processing is Bentall et al. (1991). They got schizophrenic and non-schizophrenic participants to come up with words or read words from a list. One week later they got the participants back. They found that schizophrenic patients with hallucinations found it very difficult to remember whether they had come up with words themselves, read them or whether the words were new. Non-schizophrenic patients were much better at this, suggesting schizophrenics suffer from difficulties in information processing.

Explanation- A problem with the cognitive explanation of schizophrenia is that it does not explain the causes of schizophrenia. There are biological explanations for schizophrenia that can explain the causes. For example, genes may predispose someone to develop schizophrenia and high levels of dopamine in the brain may cause schizophrenia.

**You need to be able to compare two explanations for schizophrenia**

The genetic explanation says that schizophrenia is related to genetic abnormalities whereas the cognitive explanation says that schizophrenia is due to faulty information processing.

The genetic explanation explains the underlying causes for schizophrenia as it says that genetic abnormalities cause schizophrenia. However, the cognitive explanation is unable to explain the underlying causes for schizophrenia. It just says that faulty thinking leads to schizophrenia but does not explain how the faulty thinking occurs in the first place.

Both the genetic and cognitive explanations are reductionist. Neither explanation takes into account social factors and family dynamics in the development of schizophrenia.

The cognitive explanation places the blame for schizophrenia on the individual for having faulty information processing whereas the genetic explanation takes the blame away from the individual by suggesting it is down to inherited genes. The genetic explanation sees the schizophrenic as a victim of circumstances.

The genetic explanation suggests that there is an increased vulnerability to schizophrenia across family members but the cognitive explanation suggests that as schizophrenia is related to the individual's cognitions/thoughts, there is not necessarily any increased vulnerability across family members.

Both explanations have studies to support them. Gottesman's (1991) family study showed that the concordance rates for schizophrenia were higher the closer the genetic relatedness. This supports the genetic explanation. Frith and Done found that schizophrenics with the negative symptoms of schizophrenia had problems with verbal and design fluency. This supports the cognitive explanation of schizophrenia, which argues that schizophrenics have problems with information processing and generating ideas.

Both explanations have related treatments that are effective for schizophrenia. The genetic explanation suggests that genes lead to higher levels of dopamine in synapses in the brain. Anti-psychotics help schizophrenics by decreasing the amount of dopamine picked up in the brain. The cognitive explanation argues that schizophrenia is due to distorted thinking. Cognitive behavioural therapy works by helping schizophrenics to identify their faulty thoughts and to replace them with realistic thoughts.

**You need to be able to describe and evaluate two treatments for schizophrenia**

**Drug Therapy as a treatment for schizophrenia**

Anti-psychotic drugs are used to treat schizophrenia. They help sedate the person and reduce the intensity of hallucinations, delusions and other psychotic behaviours. Anti-psychotics are more effective when given at the onset of symptoms. Typical anti-psychotics were the first generation of the drugs aimed to treat schizophrenia. Chlorpromazine is an example of a first generation anti-psychotic drug. These drugs act by blocking the dopamine receptors (acting antagonistically on D2 receptors). The drugs fit in the dopamine receptors in the brain blocking dopamine and preventing it being picked up (remember that excess of dopamine in the brain is related to schizophrenia). However, they caused severe side effects such neuroleptic malignant syndrome which is potentially fatal. Atypical antipsychotics are the new generation of drugs for schizophrenia. They tend to work on dopamine and serotonin receptors and they have fewer side effects. The newer anti-psychotics such as rispiridone are effective for the positive and negative symptoms of schizophrenia.

**Exam tip**: You can use DESERT to help you evaluate a therapy.

Directive- Is the patient reliant on the therapist for all the answers? Is there a power imbalance? If the therapist has too much power then the treatment is directive.

Effectiveness-How effective is the therapy at treating the mental disorder? What do outcome studies show?

Side effects-Are there any side effects to the therapy?

Expense-How expensive is the therapy in terms of time and money?

Reasons-Does the therapy looks at the underlying causes/reasons for the mental disorder?

Types of people-Does the therapy only work on certain types of people?

**Evaluation:**

Directive-Schizophrenics living in the community are often told to take drugs by their doctors but they have control over when they take it. However, schizophrenics in hospital may be pressurised to take their drugs.

Effectiveness-Anti-psychotics allow patients to live in society avoiding long term hospital care and institutionalisation and it enables them to access other therapies such as CBT which may help cure them. Anti-psychotics also reduce the intensity of symptoms. Kane (1992) found that chlorpromazine was effective with 75% of schizophrenics. Emsley (2008) found that injecting risperidone could reduce both positive and negative symptoms of schizophrenia and led to high remission rates.

Side effects-Anti-psychotics have many side effects such as tightening of muscles, constipation, weight gain and in rare cases neuroleptic malignant syndrome, which can be fatal. Many patients stop taking anti-psychotics due to the side effects. Higher and higher doses may be required as the patient develops a tolerance to the drugs.

Expense-Anti-psychotic drugs can be expensive over the long-term but in the short-term they are not as expensive as talking therapies. Atypical anti-psychotic drugs have fewer side effects but are more expensive than typical anti-psychotic drugs.

Reasons-Anti-psychotic drugs just treat the symptoms of the schizophrenia, they don't deal with any underlying issues.

Types of people-Anti-psychotic drugs do not work on all schizophrenics. Around 25% of schizophrenics do not respond to the drugs.

**Cognitive Behavioural Therapy (CBT) as a treatment for schizophrenia**

The cognitive part of the cognitive behavioural therapy (CBT) involves questioning and changing a schizophrenics' maladaptive thoughts/distorted beliefs. For example, the therapist might question the schizophrenic's beliefs about how powerful the voices are that they hear in their head. They might also change their faulty interpretations of the world such as the belief that everyone is out to get them. The behavioural part of the therapy involves changing their behaviour, for example, getting them to ignore the voices they hear in their head or to ignore ideas that their thoughts are being put in their head by someone else. The therapist has to accept that the patient has a different perception of reality and the aim of the therapy is to help the patient manage their misperceptions.

**Evaluation:**

Directive-Cognitive behavioural therapy is directive as the therapist tells the patient which thoughts are faulty and how they should change them.

Effectiveness-Chadwick's (2000) study found that only 8 hours of CBT combined with anti-psychotics reduced negative beliefs about how powerful the voices were. Gould et al.'s (2001) meta-analysis concluded that CBT combined with anti-psychotics reduces positive symptoms of schizophrenia. CBT can also be used to help schizophrenics that do not respond to drugs although it is usually used in combination with drugs.

Side effects-None

Expense-CBT can be expensive as it requires a trained therapist to deliver the treatment. However, CBT can be delivered over a short period of time.

Reasons-CBT does not deal with any underlying causes of schizophrenia such as childhood issues. It just deals with changing the patient's current beliefs.

Types of people-CBT is more effective on those with positive symptoms of schizophrenia as it involves getting schizophrenics to challenge their beliefs. It does not work so well on those with negative symptoms such as poverty of speech.

**You need to be able to describe the features and symptoms of anorexia nervosa**

Anorexia nervosa is a refusal to maintain a minimal normal body weight for age and height. Diagnosis requires bodyweight to be less than 85% of that expected. There is an intense fear of gaining weight despite being underweight. Another factor in diagnosis is amenorrhoea, the absence of menstruation for at least three consecutive menstrual cycles. 90% of sufferers are female. Sufferers have a preoccupation with thinness, dieting and exercise.

**You need to be able to describe and evaluate two explanations of anorexia nervosa**

**The genetic explanation of anorexia nervosa**

The genetic explanation of anorexia says that genes can predispose someone to develop schizophrenia and that is why it can run in families. There is an increased risk of developing anorexia if you have a parent, sibling or twin with anorexia. Genes may lead to biochemical imbalances in the brain such as low levels of serotonin, which is associated with anorexia. Genes may also cause structural changes in the hypothalamus, which is involved in the regulation of eating. Genetic abnormalities might also lead to damage to neural pathways (nerve cells carrying messages) in the brain. Eating behaviour that is controlled by these neural pathways may then be abnormal.

**Evaluation:**

Studies- Kortegaard et al. (2001) found a slightly higher concordance for anorexia nervosa in MZ twins compared to DZ twins. Holland (1984) found a higher concordance rate for eating disorders in MZ twins (55%) than DZ twins.
However, MZ twins often share a more similar environment than DZ twins so it is difficult to separate out the effects of genes from environment. The fact that MZ twins do not have a 100% concordance rate for anorexia, suggests that environment plays a significant role in the development of the disorder. Twin studies are correlational so it is difficult to establish cause and effect.

Explanation-The genetic explanation for anorexia nervosa is reductionist as it does not take into account psychological, social and cultural factors.

**Social learning theory as an explanation for anorexia nervosa**

Pressure from media images may contribute to the development of anorexia nervosa. Social learning theory can explain this in terms of young people paying attention to the fact that many celebrity role models are extremely thin and retaining this information. Young people have the ability to reproduce being thin if they diet excessively and will do it if they are motivated to do so. They can see that their thin role models are famous and rich and they may think that in order to be successful like their role models they have to be thin too.

They may also think that being excessively thin is necessary to be accepted. This provides the motivation to diet excessively.

**Evaluation:**

Studies-Lai (2000) found that the rate of anorexia increased for chinese residents in Hong Kong as the culture slowly became more westernised. This supports the idea that western thin role models lead to anorexia. Crisp et al. (1976) found that dancers and fashion models were more likely to develop anorexia nervosa, which also supports SLT. Mumford et al. (1991) found that Arab and Asian women were more likely to develop eating disorders if they moved to the West. Fearn (1999) found that after the introduction of Western TV channels to the island of Fiji, eating disorders previously unknown on the island began to appear.

Explanation- Social learning theory does not explain why anorexia usually develops in adolescence. Anorexia nervosa may be related to fears about growing up and family issues rather than media images. Another limitation of social learning theory as an explanation of anorexia nervosa is that everyone sees pictures of slim people, but not everyone develops eating disorders.

**You need to be able to describe and evaluate two treatments for anorexia nervosa**

**Free Association as a treatment for anorexia nervosa**

The aim of the therapy is to uncover unconscious conflicts that are disturbing the anorexic so that they can work through them at a conscious level. During the therapy, the client/patient lies on a couch facing away from the therapist. Clients are given a term such as 'family' and asked to talk about it freely. If the client runs out of things to say, the therapist can give them a key word such as 'mother' or 'weight' to encourage them to talk more. If the client talks about anything unusual, the therapist might explore this further as this can be a key to unconscious conflicts. The therapist's job is to interpret what the client says. They then explain their interpretations to the client and help them come to terms with their unconscious conflicts.

**Evaluation:**

Directive-The therapist has a lot of power in free association as they interpret what the client/patient says. If the client disagrees, then this is called repression. Therefore, the therapy is directive.

Effectiveness-Free association has not been found to be particularly effective for anorexia. It is may not be helpful for anorexics to talk at length about their weight issues and obsessions.

Side effects-The client may become dependent on the therapist.

Expense-Free association forms part of the therapy psychoanalysis and can go on for a long time.

Reasons-Free association addresses the underlying causes of anorexia as it looks at childhood experiences and unconscious motivations for the disorder.

Types of people-Free association has been found to work better with people who are good at expressing their thoughts and feelings (i.e. YAVIS clients-young, attractive, verbal, intelligent and successful clients).

**Rational Emotive Therapy (RET) as a treatment for anorexia nervosa**

Rational emotive therapy (RET) is based on the idea that negative, irrational thoughts can lead to abnormal (maladaptive) behaviour. It aims to replace a person's irrational thoughts with more realistic ones. It works on an ABC model, where A stands for an activating event, B for the beliefs about A and C for the consequences. For example, with an anorexic, the activating event (A) might have been that they saw their friends make fun of a girl at school for being fat. The beliefs (B) about A might have been that they thought they needed to be thin in order to be accepted and liked. The consequences (C) might be that they have started dieting excessively. During therapy, an anorexic would be questioned about their beliefs so that any irrational thoughts can be identified. The therapist then tries to change the person's beliefs so that they have a more realistic view of the world. For example, they might be asked to identify people who are not thin but well-liked. They may also be set homework, where they have to practice thinking and behaving in a more rational way.

**Evaluation:**

Directive-RET is directive as the therapist has a lot of power over their client, they argue with them about their beliefs and tell them how to change their thinking.

Effectiveness-RET focuses on changing present irrational thoughts rather than taking into account childhood experiences so it can work quickly to change behaviour.
Brandsma et al. (1978) found that RET works well on people who are perfectionist and many anorexics have such tendencies. Silverman et al. (1992) did 89 outcomes studies of RET and found that it was more effective or equal to other types of therapy for a wide range disorders.

Side effects-None

Expense-RET requires a trained professional to deliver the treatment so it can be expensive. However, it is less expensive than psychoanalysis (free association) as it can be delivered relatively quickly.

Reason-RET does not deal with the underlying causes of anorexia. It just tries to change negative, irrational thoughts. It may be better to treats anorexics with a mixture of RET and family systems therapy as it does not take into account family relationships, which may contribute to the anorexia.

Types of people-RET can be used with most anorexics.

**You need to be able to describe and evaluate one treatment/therapy in the social approach-Family Systems Therapy**

Family systems therapy is a type of psychotherapy that involves all members of the family. It views a child's behaviour as being affected by their role and position within the family. A therapist or a team of therapists will discuss family issues that might have led to their child developing the mental health issue. The aim of the therapy is to try and change the way the family interacts and communicates. The family attends a therapy session for one hour a week for several months. During therapy, family interactions are analysed and suggestions given about how to improve communication within the family. Family systems therapy views the family as a whole so that individual's mental disorder is seen as being related to the way the family 'system' works. Children and adolescents often benefit from family therapy that includes the extended family as there can be problems passed down from generation to generation. Individuals within the family are encouraged to maintain their own sense of self whilst still remaining connected to the family. This is called differentiation. Another concept within family systems therapy is the idea that emotional relationships in families are often triangular. Whenever two members in the family system have problems with each other, they will "triangle in" a third member as a way of stabilizing their own relationship. Common family triangles include a child and his or her parents; two children and one parent; a parent, a child, and a grandparent.

**Evaluation:**

Directive-The therapist has a lot of power in family systems therapy as they suggest different ways of communicating within the family.

Effectiveness-Family systems therapy has been found to particularly effective with anorexic teenagers.

Side effects-There can be greater family tension in the middle of the therapy.

Expense-Family systems therapy is expensive as it requires a trained therapist and sessions can go on for several months.

Reasons-It is good at uncovering some of the underlying issues behind a mental disorder. For example, it can change dysfunctional family relationships that may be the cause of the mental disorder. However, it ignores individual psychological and biological factors that may have caused the mental disorder.

Types of people-Family systems therapy does not take into account differences in family units. It is more focused on the 'nuclear' family type and does not take into account different family units such as extended families. Not all family members may be willing to come to therapy.

**You need to be able to describe and evaluate one treatment/therapy in the cognitive approach-Ellis' Rational Emotive Therapy (RET)**

Rational Emotive Therapy (RET) operates within the ABC framework: A is the activating event, a fact or event or behaviour or attitude of another person; B is the beliefs we hold about A and C is the cognitive, emotional or behavioural consequence of A. Ellis believed that humans control their emotions through the beliefs held at B and he believed that we are capable of learning to control and modify our belief systems and the consequences. RET involves challenging people's dysfunctional beliefs and replacing them with more realistic ones. Another word for this is cognitive restructuring. It may also involves setting patients homework tasks in order to practise rational thinking. For example, someone with depression might be asked to go out with friends to challenge their belief that life is not enjoyable.

**Evaluation:**

Directive-RET is directive as the therapist has a lot of power over their client, they argue with them about their beliefs and tell them how to change their thinking.

Effectiveness-RET focuses on changing present irrational thoughts rather than taking into account childhood experiences so it can work quickly to change behaviour compared to longer-term therapies such as psychoanalysis.
Silverman et al. (1992) did 89 outcomes studies of RET and found that it was more effective or equal to other types of therapy for a wide range disorders. Engels et al. (1993) looked at 31 outcome studies and found that RET was more effective for treating anxiety based disorders than systematic desensitisation or combination therapies. However, these studies tended to look at patients who had been treated by experts in RET and so it may not as effective when it delivered by professionals who are not so familiar with the therapy.

Side effects-None

Expense-RET requires a trained professional to deliver the treatment so it can be expensive. However, it is less expensive than psychoanalysis (free association is part of psychoanalysis) as it can be delivered relatively quickly.

Reasons-RET does not deal with the underlying causes of a mental disorrder. It just tries to change negative, irrational thoughts.

Types of people-RET can be used on a wide range of people.

**You need to be able to describe and evaluate one treatment/therapy in the psychodynamic approach-free association**

One treatment in the psychodynamic approach is free association (part of psychoanalysis). The aim of the therapy is to uncover unconscious conflicts that are disturbing the individual and to give them some insight into their problems. During the therapy, patients are asked to talk about anything that they want to whilst lying on a couch facing away from the therapist. If the person is not sure what to talk about the therapist offers key words such as 'family' or "love' to encourage the person to talk freely. Often the therapist will direct their clients/patients to recall early childhood experiences and relationships. The therapist's job is to interpret what the patient says. They then explain their interpretations to the patient and help the patient come to terms with their unconscious conflicts.

**Evaluation:**

Directive-The therapist has a lot of power in free association as they interpret what the client/patient says. If the client disagrees, then this is called transference or repression. Therefore, the therapy is directive.

Effectiveness-Eysenck (1952) looked at a number of outcome studies and claimed that psychoanalysis was no better than no treatment at all. However he judged the recovery of the psychoanalysis group unfairly. Bergin and Garfield reanalysed the data and found that people who don't undergo therapy have a 30-43% recovery rate but those with therapy have an 83% success rate. This suggests that free association can be an effective therapy.

Side effects-Free association may reinforce obsessive thoughts. Clients/patients can become very dependent on their therapist as the treatment goes on for a long time.

Expense-Free association forms part of the therapy psychoanalysis and can go on for a long time (on average 2 years).

Reasons-Free association addresses the underlying causes of a mental disorder as it looks at childhood experiences and unconscious motivations for the disorder.

Types of people-Free association has been found to work better with people who are good at expressing their thoughts and feelings (i.e. YAVIS clients-young, attractive, verbal, intelligent and successful clients). It is better for people with mild depression and anxiety. It is not so useful with severe depression, severe anxiety, anorexia and schizophrenia.

**You need to be able to describe and evaluate one treatment/therapy in the biological approach-Drug Therapy**

Drug therapy works by changing the brain's chemistry. The four main types of drugs used to treat mental disorder are antianxiety drugs for anxiety, anti-depressant drugs for depression, anti-bipolar drugs for bipolar disorder and anti-psychotic drugs for schizophrenia. Anti-psychotic drugs such a clozapine can be used for schizophrenia. They work by fitting into the dopamine receptors in the brain, blocking the effects of dopamine as high levels of dopamine are related to schizophrenia. Prozac and Seroxat are anti-depressant drugs called SSRIs-they work by increasing the levels of serotonin in the brain as low levels of serotonin are related to depression. However, they do have side effects and have been related to suicide attempts. Two anti-anxiety drugs are Valium and Librium, which act as tranquillisers and reduce anxiety.

**Evaluation:**

Directive-Patients usually have control over whether they take their drugs or not unless they are in a psychiatric hospital. Therefore, drug therapy can be seen as non-directive.

Effectiveness-Drugs can work quickly to reduce the symptoms of schizophrenia or severe depression although they cannot cure the mental disorder. Drugs can help people feel mentally more stable so that they can access talking therapies such as CBT. Anti-psychotic drugs allow schizophrenics to live in the community without having to be admitted to a psychiatric hospital.

Side effects-Drugs can be addictive and a people often need higher and higher doses as they develop a tolerance to the drugs. Many drugs have side effects. For example, anti-psychotic drugs have many nasty side effects such as constipation, weight gain and in rare cases neuroleptic malignant syndrome (fever, muscle stiffness and loss of consciousness). Many schizophrenics stop taking anti-psychotics due to the side effects.

Expense-Drug therapy can be expensive over the long-term but in the short-term they are not as expensive as therapists.

Reasons- Drug therapies have also been criticised for not addressing the underlying cause of a mental disorder such as anxiety or depression and only treating the symptoms. GPs may see drugs as a quick and easy way of helping someone with a mental disorder but talking therapies are more effective long-term.

Types of people-Drug therapy may not work well on everyone with mental disorder. For example, anti-psychotics do not help all schizophrenics and drugs may not be the best treatments for anorexics.

**You need to be able to describe and evaluate one treatment/therapy in the learning approach-Token economy programmes**

Token economy programmes (TEPs) use operant conditioning to change behaviour for the better. Tokens are given for adaptive behaviour e.g. anorexics reaching a certain weight. The tokens are secondary reinforcers and they can then be exchanged for primary reinforcers, something the person naturally desires e.g. a trip to Alton Towers. TEPS can also be used with schizophrenics in institutions to get them to perform more self-care tasks. For example, tokens can be given for brushing teeth and these tokens could then be exchanged for primary reinforcers such as chocolate. It is important that the target behaviours and rewards are agreed upon in advance.

**Evaluation:**

Directive-TEPs are directive as the doctors or nurses in the mental health unit decide when tokens are given out and for what behaviours.

Effectiveness- TEPs can quickly change behaviour. TEPs are good at getting sufferers of anorexia nervosa to a reasonable weight after which issues can be addressed and getting psychotic patients to behave in a cooperative way. Allyon and Azrin (1968) used a TEP to change the behaviour of 45 chronic schizophrenics who had been institutionalised for an average of 16 years. They were given tokens for making their beds or combing their hair. After the TEP, the schizophrenics were much better at looking after themselves.

Side effects-TEPs can lead to learned helplessness where the patients feel that they have no choice about taking part in the programme. TEPs may also stop people looking inside themselves for the problem.

Expense-TEPs are usually quite cheap to deliver as nurses and assistants working in the mental health unit need little training to deliver the programme.

Reasons-TEPs may only change behaviour in the short-term and they do not address underlying issues. For example, a person may be anorexic due to family issues and giving tokens does not deal with these issues.

Types of people-TEPs may work well with anorexics and schizophrenics in a mental health unit but they may be viewed as patronising by a person with anxiety or depression living in the community.

**You need to be able to compare treatments from each approach**

You can compare the treatments in terms of DESERT.

Directive-How much power does the therapist have? A treatment is directive if the therapist has more power than the patient in terms of how the treatment progresses. A treatment is non-directive if the therapist and patient work together to decide how the treatment progresses.

Effectiveness-How effective are the treatments? What do studies show?

Side effects-Do the treatments have any side effects?

Expense-How expensive are the treatments?

Reasons-Do the treatments address the underlying causes of the mental disorder?

Types of people-Can the treatments only be used on certain types of people?

Exam tip: When comparing, use phrases such as:

'Both treatments are......'
'They are different because ...........'
'X treatment focuses on......... whereas Y treatment focuses on......'
'They are similar because they both......'
'Both treatments have studies to support their effectiveness. For example.......'

When comparing treatments, it is also useful to consider whether they are nomothetic/idiographic, reductionist/holistic and whether they place the blame for the disorder on the individual.

**Nomothetic/Idiographic**: A treatment is nomothetic if it treats all people as the same. In contrast, a treatment is idiographic if it views everyone as an individual with different requirements.

Token Economy Programmes (learning approach) are nomothetic because they are based on the idea that everyone can be treated the same and that behaviour can be changed through the principles of operant conditioning.

Drug Therapy (biological approach) is nomothetic because it is based on the assumption that all people with the same mental disorder can be treated with the same drugs.

Rational Emotive Therapy (cognitive approach) is nomothetic because it suggests that all people can be treated through changing their faulty beliefs.

Family Systems Therapy (social approach) is idiographic because it believes that every family is different and should be treated differently.

Free Association (psychodynamic approach) is idiographic because it treats everyone as individuals with different childhood experiences and unconscious conflicts.

**Reductionist/Holistic:** A treatment is reductionist if it does not take into account all the different factors that could have led to the mental disorder. In contrast, a treatment is holistic if it considers all the factors that could have led to the mental disorder.

Token Economy Programmes (learning approach) are reductionist as they do not take into account social or biological factors in the development of mental disorder. TEPs view mental disorder as learnt behaviour that can be changed through simple behaviour modification.

Drug Therapy (biological approach) is reductionist as it only considers biological factors in mental disorder not social or psychological factors.

Rational Emotive Therapy (cognitive approach) is reductionist as it views the causes of mental disorder as being related to distorted beliefs only and does not take into account biological or social factors.

Family Systems Therapy (social approach) is reductionist as it focuses on the relationships within the family only rather than individual psychological or biological factors.

Free association (psychodynamic approach) is reductionist as it views mental disorder as being entirely related to childhood experiences and unconscious conflicts rather than taking into account social and biological factors.

**Does the therapy place blame on the individual for the disorder?** A treatment places blame on the individual if it views the causes of the disorder as being within the individual's control.

Token Economy Programmes (learning approach) do place blame on the individual for the mental disorder. The individual must change their maladaptive behaviour.

Drug Therapy (biological approach) does not place any blame on the individual for their mental disorder as the individual is not viewed as being able to control their genes or the chemical imbalances in their brain.

Rational Emotive Therapy (cognitive approach) does blame the individual for their faulty beliefs.

Family Systems Therapy (social approach) does not blame the individual as it views mental disorder as being caused by dysfunctional relationships in the whole family unit.

Free association (psychodynamic approach) views childhood experiences as being important in the development of mental disorder. Therefore, the parents may be blamed for the mental disorder rather than the individual.

**You need to be able to describe and evaluate Rosenhan (1973) On being sane in insane places**

Aim: To see whether the sane can be distinguished from the insane using the DSM classification system. Rosenhan wanted to see whether clinicians would be able to tell the difference between a patient suffering from a real mental disorder and a healthy 'pseudopatient.'

Procedure: Rosenhan and seven volunteers arrived at a range of hospitals reporting a single symptom, hearing voices saying 'empty', 'hollow' and 'thud.' They gave real information about themselves such as details about their families and childhood. However, they gave false names and those in the medical profession gave a false occupation. As soon as the eight pseudopatients were in hospital, they started behaving normally.

Results: All the pseudopatients were admitted and none were detected as being sane. It was an average of 19 days before any of them were released. Even when they were released all but one were given the diagnosis of schizophrenia in remission. In no case did any of the doctors and nurses notice that there was nothing wrong with them.

Conclusion: Rosenhan concluded that staff in psychiatric hospitals were unable to distinguish those who were sane from those who were insane and that DSM is not a valid measurement of mental illness.

**Evaluation:**

Generalisability-The study was carried out in 1973 so the findings of the study may not apply to the present day. The DSM had been revised many times since 1973 to improve its validity. Furthermore, doctor-patient relationships have changed.
The pseudo-patients had insisted on being admitted to the hospital themselves so the psychiatrists may have been more cautious about releasing them. Not all people diagnosed with schizophrenia ask to be admitted to a hospital so the treatment of the pseudo-patients may not be representative of how other patients would be treated.
The psychiatrists would have also been careful about releasing an individual who had only recently been admitted too fast. However, a wide range of hospitals were used so the results can be generalised to other psychiatric hospitals at the time.

Reliability-The study was conducted in the field so extraneous variables were hard to control and so the study would be difficult to repeat.

Application to real life-The study highlighted problems with DSM and how psychiatric patients are treated in hospital.

Ecological validity-The study had ecological validity as it was carried out the doctors' and nurses' normal working environment (psychiatric hospitals) so they would have behaved naturally.

Experimental validity-The doctors and nurses in the psychiatric hospital were unaware the patients were fake so they would not have displayed any demand characteristics. Therefore, the study has good experimental validity. However, the fact that the pseudopatients were released with the diagnosis of 'schizophrenia in remission' shows that the psychiatrists did recognise something different about them as this is a rare diagnosis for real patients.

Ethics-There are a number of ethical issues with the study. The hospital staff were deceived about the pseudopatients' symptoms and they did not know they were in a study so they were unable to give consent. However, Rosenhan did protect the anonymity of the staff and hospitals afterwards.

**You need to be able to describe and evaluate one study on anorexia nervosa.**

**Holland et al. (1988)**

Aim: To see whether anorexia nervosa may have a genetic basis by comparing the incidence of anorexia nervosa in identical (MZ) and non-identical (DZ) twins.

Procedure: Participants were 30 female twin pairs (16 MZ and 14 DZ pairs), four male twin pairs and one set of male triplets. The twins and triplets were selected because one of the twins (and one of the triplets) had been diagnosed as suffering from anorexia nervosa. Concordance rates were found between the twin and triplets for anorexia nervosa. They also analysed data from the Eating Disorder Questionnaire (EDI) and data about weight loss, length of amenorrhoea and other characteristics related to anorexia nervosa. They also collected information about the twins' family background.

Results: A higher concordance rate for anorexia nervosa was found in the MZ female twins (56%) compared to female DZ twins (5%). Nearly 5% of other female first degree relatives also had a history of anorexia nervosa. None of the male co-twins had anorexia nervosa but this may be due to the small sample of males.

Conclusion: They concluded that there is a genetic basis for anorexia nervosa. However the fact that the concordance rate was not 100% for the MZ twins suggests that the environment still has a role to play in the development of the disorder.

**Evaluation:**

Generalisability-The small sample size makes the study hard to generalise to the wider population.

Reliability-Participants may not have been entirely truthful on the Eating Disorders Questionnaire so if the study was repeated it may be difficult to get the same results. The independent variable (whether the twins were MZ or DZ twins) was not manipulated by the researchers so it is hard to establish whether genes are the cause of anorexia nervosa.

Application to real life-The study suggests that females with a family history of anorexia nervosa, should be given greater support.

Validity- MZ twins often share a more similar environment than DZ twins as well as greater genetic similarity so it is difficult to separate out the effects of genes from the environment. This questions the validity of Holland et al.'s findings. Wade (1998) investigated genetic and environmental risk facts in a large sample of female twins and found that environmental influences were more important than genetics in terms of their attitudes towards food and weight.

Ethics-The study collected data on vulnerable adults with anorexia so it is possible that the questioning may have caused participants psychological distress.


**You need to be able to describe and evaluate one study on schizophrenia.**

**Heston (1966)**

Aim: To see whether there is a genetic basis for schizophrenia.

Procedure: Heston identified 47 adults who had been adopted at birth because their biological mothers had schizophrenia. They had all been separated from their mothers in the first few days of life. He compared these to a group of 50 adults who had been adopted whose biological mothers did not have schizophrenia and who were believed to be mentally healthy. A number of methods were used to compare the adoptees. He measured psycho-social adjustment, he carried out personal interviews and he gave them a

Minnesota Multiphasic Personality Inventory (MMPI), which is a personality test in mental health. He also got three psychiatrists to independently rate the children and he compared their school, police, veteran and hospital records.

Results: Heston found that 10 % (5/47) of the children of schizophrenic mothers became schizophrenic as adults, compared to none of the control group of adoptees.

Conclusion: There is a genetic basis for schizophrenia. Even though none of the adults were raised by schizophrenic parents, those who had biological mothers with schizophrenia were more likely to develop the disorder.

**Evaluation:**

Generalisability-Not all mothers with schizophrenia have their children adopted. Therefore, the sample of adoptees in this study may not be representative of all children who mothers have schizophrenia. There may have been something different about the schizophrenic mothers that led to them giving up their babies for adoption.

Reliability-This study would be hard to replicate as there was no control over the variables. The researchers were not able to control the environment of the adoptees.

Application to real life-This study helps us to understand the role of genes in the development of schizophrenia.

Validity-A problem with adoption studies is selective placement. When children are adopted, they are often placed in a family that is as similar as possible to their biological family. Therefore, if the behaviour of the adoptive family is similar to the the biological family, this might lead to an increased incidence of schizophrenia in these adoptees rather than their genes. It can be difficult to separate out the effects of nature (inherited characteristics) and nurture (learnt characteristics).

Validity-Rich qualitative data was collected from the interviews with the adoptees.

Ethics-There were issues with confidentiality and breach of privacy as the participants school, police, veteran and hospital records were examined. There was also a risk of psychological harm with the study especially as some of the adoptees were vulnerable and did have mental health issues.

**You need to be able to describe one key issue in clinical psychology-understanding schizophrenia**

Schizophrenia is a psychotic disorder, which affects about 1% of the population. Many of the symptoms of schizophrenia cause distress to the sufferers and their families. Therefore, it is important that psychiatrists and clinical psychologists develop effective treatments for schizophrenia. Understanding the causes of schizophrenia can aid clinicians and help families deal with the disorder better. However, there are different types of schizophrenia so there may be different causes.

A biological explanation for schizophrenia is that genes can predispose someone to develop schizophrenia. The Heston study showed that 10% of adoptees who had a mother with schizophrenia went onto develop it themselves compared to none in a control group. This suggests a genetic basis for schizophrenia. Gottesman's study found a 0.48 concordance rate for schizophrenia in MZ twins compared to only 0.17 concordance in DZ twins so it supports the idea that schizophrenia has a genetic basis.

Another biological explanation for schizophrenia is that high levels of the chemical dopamine in the brain can lead to schizophrenia. Donnelly et al. (1996) found that schizophrenic patients produce more homovanillic acid (a metabolite/waste product of dopamine) in their urine. Anti-psychotic drugs work by blocking the effects of dopamine in the brain. Such drugs have enabled schizophrenics to live in the community rather than being institutionalised. However, anti-psychotic drugs do not work on all schizophrenics and they can have serious side effects. Many schizophrenics stop taking the drugs due to the side effects. There is also the criticism that anti-psychotic drugs just sedate schizophrenics rather than really curing them, which is why other treatments such as cognitive behavioural therapy are so important.

A cognitive explanation for schizophrenia is that schizophrenics have problems with processing information. Frith and Done (1986) found that schizophrenic patients with negative symptoms did worse on verbal fluency tasks (such as name as many fruits as you can). This supports the idea that schizophrenics have difficulties in information processing. Another study that shows that people with schizophrenia have problems with information processing is Bentall et al. (1991). They got schizophrenic and non-schizophrenic participants to come up with words or read words from a list. One week later they got the participants back. They found that schizophrenic participants with hallucinations found it very difficult to remember whether they had come up with words themselves, read them or whether the words were new. Non-schizophrenic participants were much better at this, which indicates that schizophrenics have trouble distinguishing between their own thoughts and other people's thoughts.

Cognitive behavioural therapy involves questioning and changing a schizophrenic's maladaptive thoughts/distorted beliefs. For example, the therapist might question the schizophrenic's beliefs about how powerful the voices are that they hear in their head. They might also change their faulty interpretations of the world such as the belief that everyone is out to get them. The behavioural part of the therapy involves changing their behaviour, for example, getting them to ignore the voices they hear in their head or to ignore ideas that their thoughts are being put in their head by someone else.

A psychodynamic explanation for schizophrenia is that growing up in a family with disturbed communication patterns can lead to schizophrenia. Lidz et al. (1965) found that 90% of schizophrenic patients had seriously disturbed families. Schofield and Balian (1959) found that schizophrenic patients were more likely to have mothers who were cold and domineering.

A social explanation of schizophrenia is social deprivation. Castle found that most schizophrenics were born in deprived areas. Deprivation and poor social status may make them vulnerable to developing schizophrenia.

The stress-diathesis model of schizophrenia suggests that some people have a genetic predisposition to schizophrenia, which can then be triggered by social factors.

**You need to be able to describe a practical you did in Clinical Psychology**

**Example practical: Designing a leaflet to help the public understand schizophrenia better.**

Aim: To design a leaflet to inform schizophrenics and their family and friends about the symptoms of schizophrenia and treatments for schizophrenia.

Procedure: The term 'schizophrenia charities' was put into the google search bar in order to find out as much information on the symptoms and treatments for schizophrenia as possible. Information on schizophrenia was also sourced from textbooks. Key information was picked out to share with the target audience in the leaflet. It was then written in an accessible way so that people without a medical or psychological background could understand it. Colour and pictures relating to schizophrenia were added to the leaflet to draw attention to it.

Evaluation: The leaflet could have included more information on different treatments for schizophrenia but space was limited. The tone of the leaflet was suitable for the target audience.

**You need to be able to describe what is meant by primary and secondary data and be able to evaluate the use of it in research**

Primary data is data that is gathered first hand e.g when an experiment, observation, questionnaire is carried out and data collected.

Evaluation: Primary data can be tested for reliability e.g if you gather data from a laboratory experiment; you can repeat the experiment again to see whether the data can be replicated. You can then see whether the data is reliable. Primary data is also up-to-date as it is data that is collected in the present rather taken from previous research. However, primary data takes more time and money to collect.

Secondary data is data that is gathered from a secondary source e.g. data gathered from books, journals, records etc. that already exist.

**Evaluation:**

It takes less time and money to gather secondary data as you don't have to carry out any studies yourself, you can just look the data up in books, journals and records. However, secondary data can be out-of-date as it involves using data from past studies and records.

**You need to be able to describe and evaluate two research methods used in the study of schizophrenia, including one study for each of the two research methods.**

**Adoption Studies as an example of a research method for studying schizophrenia- Heston**

Adoption studies compare an adopted child to their biological parents and adoptive parents. If a child has a higher chance of developing schizophrenia due to their biological parents having schizophrenia despite no incidence of schizophrenia in the adoptive family, this suggests a role for genes in the development of schizophrenia. Adoption studies might also use a control group of adoptive children whose biological parents did not have schizophrenia to make comparisons. This helps determine the role of genes in the development of schizophrenia as an adopted child lives in a different environment to their biological parents. Sometimes adopted children are followed into adulthood to see whether they are more similar to the biological or adoptive parents.

Heston(1966) compared adopted children whose mothers had schizophrenia with a control group of adopted children whose mothers did not have schizophrenia. He found that 10% of the children whose mothers had schizophrenia went onto develop it themselves compared to none in the control group.

**Evaluation:**

Adoption studies enable us to compare the influences of genes versus environment in the development of schizophrenia as adopted children live in a different environment to their biological parents. However, most people are not adopted so adoptees are not representative of the wide population. For example, the mothers in Heston's study may have had a more severe form of schizophrenia that led to them putting their babies up for adoption. This could have affected the incidence of schizophrenia amongst the adoptees. Adopted children are also selectively placed in families similar to their biological families and so their environment may be very similar to the biological family. This makes it difficult to separate out the effects of nature versus nurture on the development of schizophrenia.

**Interviews as an example of a research method for studying schizophrenia- Goldstein**

An interview involves the researcher asking the respondent questions so an interview can be used to ask schizophrenics and their families about their symptoms and experiences. It may form the basis of a case study or as a follow-up to other research methods. Structured interviews produce quantitative data. All participants are asked the same questions in the same order. They are very similar to questionnaire except questions are read out. An unstructured interview involves an informal or in-depth conversation. Little is planned in advance (perhaps the first couple of questions) and they allows the interviewee to explain answers and introduce new issues. Unstructured interviews obtains rich, qualitative data. A semi-structured interview involves some prepared questions but also some opportunities for interviewees to expand on answers

Goldstein's study (1988) used interviews to investigate the differences in how males and females experience schizophrenia. She used trained interviewers to gather data about the symptoms of the patients and to find out about past experiences, age, gender, ethnicity, class, marital status, level of education and level of social functioning.

**Evaluation:**

Unstructured interviews tend to be valid because they allow the interviewer to explore issues that the respondent brings up, so there will be a focus on what the interviewee wants to reveal. Interviews gather qualitative data as well which means that the data is detailed and in-depth. Detailed interview data can be analysed by looking for themes but this process can be subjective. The interviewers may affect the data by the way the ask questions e.g in the Goldstein study the way the interviewers asked questions about the patients' symptoms may have affected answers. The patients may have given socially desirable answers or not wanted to admit to certain symptoms. At another time, the patients might have reported different symptoms so there is an issue with the reliability of interviews. Certain characteristics about the interviewer such as their dress or manner can also affect replies.

**Student answer to exemplar exam question in Clinical Psychology:**

**Describe one treatment for schizophrenia from the Biological Approach. Evaluate this treatment using research evidence.** (12 marks)

Note: The question asks for one treatment only and how it can be used to treat one mental disorder only.

Student answer:

Drug therapy can be used by the psychiatrist to treat schizophrenia. Anti-psychotic drugs are used with schizophrenics to block the effects of dopamine. The neurotransmitter dopamine is involved in cognitive functions such as attention and problem-solving. Dopamine in the frontal lobes of the brain, controls the flow of information from other areas of the brain. Therefore, by reducing the availability of dopamine in the brain, anti-psychotic drugs can reduce symptoms related to information processing such as thought disorders. It is thought that both typical and atypical anti-psychotics work by inhibiting dopamine at the receptor level. Typical anti-psychotics such as chlorpromazine could reduce the symptoms of schizophrenia but cause severe side effects. Atypical antipsychotics (newer drugs) reduce the symptoms of schizophrenia but with fewer side effects. Clozapine is an example of a new generation anti-psychotic drug.

Anti-psychotic drugs can help schizophrenics to manage their symptoms and to live in the community. They tend to act quickly and can stabilise a patient so that they can access other treatments such as cognitive behavioural therapy. However, a problem with anti-psychotic drugs is that they can have unpleasant side effects, which can cause schizophrenics to stop taking the drugs. Patients can develop a tolerance to the drugs so that they need higher doses for the drugs to work. There is also the criticism that anti-psychotics only sedate patients rather than really cure them. Atypical anti-psychotic drugs have fewer side effects but are more expensive than typical anti-psychotic drugs. Anti-psychotic drugs do not work on all schizophrenics.
Level 4 answer: 10 out of 12 marks

**Commentary:**

This student describes how anti-psychotics can be used to treat schizophrenia well. However, there could also have been some discussion of practical considerations. For example, they could have discussed how psychiatrists prescribing anti-psychotic drugs need to carefully monitor how a patient is responding to them. The psychiatrist may then need to adjust the dosage or even try out a different type of anti-psychotic.

This student could also have used some studies to support their evaluation. Kane (1992) found that chlorpromazine was effective with 75% of schizophrenics. Emsley (2008) found that injecting risperidone could reduce both positive and negative symptoms of schizophrenia and led to high remission rates. The effectiveness of atypical anti-psychotics for schizophrenia in terms of number of re-hospitalisations is similar to that of typical anti-psychotics. Stargardt et al. (2008) found that atypical anti-psychotics were only cost-effective in severe cases as it was only in these cases that the atypical anti-psychotics reduced re-hospitalisations.

# Chapter 9-Issues and Debates

## You need to be able to define Key Terms in Issues and Debates

**Content analysis:** A content analysis involves changing qualitative data into quantitative data. This often means tallying how many times certain themes occur within a source such as newspaper article, magazine article, journal article, radio programme or television programme. The source may be coded or broken down into manageable categories, for example, by words, phrases, sentences or themes. The researcher then analyses the presence and meaning of these categories and draws conclusions. For example, a researcher might tally how often negative or positive comments about daycare occur within two newspaper articles and draw conclusions about how daycare is portrayed in the media.

**Ethnocentrism:** can occur if we interpret research findings or people's behaviour entirely through the lens of our own culture without taking into account cultural differences. This can lead to cultural bias. For example, ethnocentrism can occur if clinicians do not take into account cultural differences in the diagnoses of people with mental health issues.

**Social control:** occurs when psychology is used to control people often for the benefit of others. For example, if drugs are given to children with ADHD to make them calmer, this can be seen as a form of social control.

**Token Economy Programmes (TEPs):** are based on operant conditioning principles and aim to change behaviour through giving consequences. Desired behaviour is rewarded with tokens, which can then be exchanged for primary reinforcers. For example, a prisoner might be given tokens for cooperative behaviour and these tokens might be exchanged for a phone card.

**Practitioners**: work with people who have mental health issues. They include psychiatrists, doctors, clinical psychologists, nurses and therapists.

**Science**: A theory is considered scientific if it can be tested and is based on empirical evidence. In scientific research, a researcher will come up with a hypothesis (prediction), which can be tested. For example, Bandura's Bobo doll experiment wanted to test whether children would learn aggressive behaviour through observing a model.

**Nature**: refers to how our genes and biology affect our development. For example, the extent to which intelligence is based on our genes.

**Nurture**: refers to how our environment and experiences affect our development. For example, the extent to which intelligence is based on our family environment and education.

Exam tip: Remember to define and give an example.

**You need to know the assumptions of the learning, psychodynamic, social, cognitive, and biological approaches**

Cognitive approach assumptions: The way we process informations affects our behaviour and emotions.
Like a computer we are influenced by the ways in which our brains are hardwired and by the ways in which we have been programmed behave.

Social approach assumptions: Behaviour is influenced by the social setting we are in and the people around us. Culture and society affects our behaviour.

Learning approach assumptions:  Behaviour is influenced by our environment.
Animals differ from humans only in the complexity of their behaviour.
Behaviour is measurable- we can set up a stimulus and observe and measure the response- can be studied scientifically.

Psychodynamic approach assumptions: Our behaviour and feelings as adults are largely rooted in our early childhood experiences.
Our behaviour and feelings are strongly affected by our unconscious mind i.e. mental processes of which we are not consciously aware.

Biological approach assumptions: Behaviour is strongly influenced by genetics.
Behaviour is strongly influenced by the nervous system. Behaviour is influenced by hormones.

**You need to be able to describe and evaluate (including strengths and weaknesses) two contributions to society within each approach from Units 1 and 2.**

**Social approach contribution to society-understanding prejudice**

Social identity theory says that prejudice can arise from the mere existence of another group. Prejudice can be explained by our tendency to identify ourselves as part of a group and to classify other people as either within or outside that group. There are three stages to social identity theory: 1)Social Categorisation-This is when we categorise ourselves as being in a particular group often based on stereotypes. The group that we belong to is the in-group and any comparison group is the out-group.  For example, when someone classifies themselves as a football supporter of a certain team then they view all other football teams as the out-group.
2)Social Identification-This refers to when we identify with a particular group and adopt the behaviours of that group. We may also take on the group's values and norms. For example, a football supporter may adopt the behaviours of their club such as certain football chants and they may wear clothes that identify them as being part of the group such as wearing the club's scarf.
3)Social Comparison-This is when we compare our own group (the in-group) more favourably against other groups (out-groups) to boost our self-esteem. For example, football supporters may view fans of their team as much better than other football fans. This can lead to discrimination and sometimes even dehumanisation of the out-group. Football supporters of one football team may even end up fighting supporters of a different

football team.

Social identity theory is supported by a number of studies such as Tajfel et al.'s (1971) minimal groups study, which found that boys overwhelmingly chose to allocate points to boys who has been identified as in the same group as themselves. Poppe and Linssen found that Eastern Europeans favour their own country over other Eastern Europeans. However, social identity theory does not explain individual differences in prejudice. Studies show wide variations in the degree to which people discriminate against the out-group. Realistic conflict theory is another theory of prejudice. It argues that prejudice occurs due to competition over scarce resources. Sherif et al.'s study (1961) supports realistic conflict theory. The study involved putting boys in two groups at a summer camp. The boys quickly identified with their own group and became particularly hostile to the out-group during a tournament where only one group could win.

## Social approach contribution to society-understanding blind obedience

Agency theory can help us understand why the Nazis were so obedient to Hitler and why US soldiers abused prisoners at Abu Ghraib. Agency theory says that people will obey authority figures in order to maintain a stable society and that they are socialised to be obedient in childhood. In the agentic state, people will put aside their own free will even when it causes them moral strain. When on trial, the Nazis and the US soldiers said that they thought they were just obeying orders and did not assume responsibility for their actions. Milgram's study supports the idea of an agentic state as it found that people were willing to give electric shocks to an innocent person on the orders of an authority figure. Blass showed students a film clip of Milgram's study and found that the students attributed more responsibility for giving the electric shocks to Milgram (the authority figure) rather than the participants. This supports the idea that people expect others to obey authority figures. Hofling et al. found that nurses would obey a doctor to give an overdose of a drug Astroten even when it went against hospital regulations.
However, agency theory does not explain individual differences in obedience, for example, why some people did not obey Hitler in World War II.

## Cognitive approach contribution to society-understanding problems with eyewitness testimony (EWT)

EWT refers to the recalled memory of a witness to a crime or incident. Innocent people have been convicted on the basis of eyewitness testimony alone and have later been found innocent using DNA evidence. Cases like this call into question the reliability of eyewitness testimony. There is also the issue that juries tend to place too much trust in eyewitness testimony. The police can also distort witnesses' memories by the way they ask questions. Eyewitness Testimony can be considered unreliable because: a) Leading questions can influence eyewitness memory and produce errors in recall. Loftus and Palmer (1974) found that they could affect participants' recall by changing the way a question is worded. Participants were asked how fast a car was going when it 'hit', 'smashed', 'collided' or 'bumped'. Participants gave a higher estimate of speed if the word was 'smashed' rather than 'collided', they were also more likely to report seeing broken glass in the 'smashed' condition when asked back a week later. b) The weapon focus

effect: Studies show that when a weapon is used by a criminal, witnesses focus on the weapon rather than the criminal's face or their environment, probably because a weapon is a major threat. Loftus et al. (1987) showed half of their participants a film with a customer in a restaurant holding a cheque, and the other half were shown a film with a customer holding a gun. They found that participants had worse recall for the customer's face when they were holding a weapon.
c) Yarmey (2004) found that when participants had actually spoken to a female target, only 49% of them could identify her in a photo line-up when she was present and when she was not present 38% of them identified someone in the photo line-up who was completely different. d) Poor line-up procedures may lead to misidentification of a suspect. Simultaneous line-ups (where all the people are presented together in the line-up) may lead to witnesses using a relative judgement strategy (choosing a person who looks most like the perpetrator of the crime rather than really looking at the person's individual characteristics to see whether they match up). e) Meissner and Brigham (2001) found that people are less able to recognise people from a different ethnic background to them so this can lead to problems in eyewitness identification. f) Buckout (1974) highlighted that photo line-ups can be biased if the suspect's photo is physically different from the fillers. g) Busey and Loftus (2006) pointed out that lack of double-blind procedures can mislead witnesses. They gave the example of a police officer who knew who the suspect was in a line-up and when a witness identified the suspect, the police officer said sign here as if to confirm their identification was correct. h) Wells and Bradfield (1998) found that if participants were told that their identification of a criminal was correct, they became more confident. Therefore, by the time a case gets to court, a witness who has had their identification confirmed by a police officer, may be overly confident even if they are wrong. i) If there is a long period of time between recall and the incident, people are likely to forget details. j) Stereotypes can affect eyewitness memory. People's views on what type of person commits a crime can affect recall. People are less likely to believe that a man in a suit committed a crime compared to someone who is scruffily dressed. k) The memory conformity effect can affect witnesses' memory for events. For example, if witnesses discuss a crime incident together, their memory for events becomes more similar. Wright et al. (2000) placed people in pairs to investigate the memory conformity effect under controlled conditions. One of the pair saw pictures of a man entering with the thief; the other saw pictures without the man. They were then asked to recount the story together but fill out questionnaires separately. About half of the participants who had not seen the picture with the man agreed with their partner's account and said that there was a man entering with the thief.

On the other hand EWT can be considered reliable because a) Yuille and Cutshall (1986) examined the recall of witnesses to a real life gun shooting in Canada. 21 witnesses saw a man try to rob a gun shop and then shoot the shop owner. The shop owner shot back and killed the thief. After the witnesses had been interviewed by police, the researcher used the opportunity to ask them whether they would like to take part in their research into eyewitness testimony. 13 of the 21 witnesses agreed to take part in their research 5 months later. They found that even 5 months after the incident, witnesses had good recall of events and were not affected by the leading questions asked. This study suggests that eyewitness memory in real life is not as likely to be distorted as laboratory experiments suggest. b) Rinolo et al. (2003) questioned 20 survivors of the shipwrecked Titanic shipwreck and found that 15 of the 20 witnesses were able to recall details accurately many years later despite inaccurate media coverage. c) Cognitive interviews can improve eyewitness testimony: this involves getting the witness to freely describe events without the risk of leading questions. Eyewitnesses are asked to not leave out any detail even if they think it is unimportant and they may be asked to recall the incident in reverse order. Questions can be asked at the end in order for information to be un-altered. d) Flashbulb memory may lead witnesses to recall crime incidents very clearly as they are likely to have strong emotions related to the incident and may replay events in their mind.

Exam Tip: You may be asked to discuss problems of research into eyewitness testimony. You should then discuss problems with laboratory research and field research in relation to eyewitness testimony.

## Cognitive approach contribution to society-cognitive interviews

If police officers use leading questions during interviews with witnesses, this can lead to inaccuracies later. Therefore, the cognitive interview has been developed to improve witnesses' recall of events. During a cognitive interview, witnesses are asked to freely recall as much information as they can remember and to describe everything they could see, hear, smell or touch. Witnesses are also asked to recall events in different orders and from different perspectives. Open ended questions are used rather than leading ones e.g. What happened next? The cognitive interview is based on Tulving's encoding specificity principle, which suggests that recall is better if a person has the same cues at retrieval as they had when they encoded the information. By getting witnesses, to mentally reinstate the context of an incident using cues such as sight, sound, smell and touch, they should be able to recall the incident better.

Stein and Memon (2006) and Geiselman (1986) found that the cognitive interviews increases both the quality and quantity of information recalled by witnesses. Research has also shown that people questioned using cognitive interviews are less likely to be influenced by leading questions.

However, Milne (1997) found that the cognitive interview did not lead to better recall than normal interviewing techniques.

However, the effectiveness of cognitive interviews may be affected by the fact that police officers do not always use all the elements of the cognitive interview as it is very time-consuming.

## Psychodynamic approach contribution to society-Free association

The aim of the therapy is to uncover unconscious conflicts that are disturbing the individual and to give them some insight into their problems. During the therapy, patients are asked to talk about anything that they want to whilst lying on a couch facing away from the therapist. If the person is not sure what to talk about the therapist offers key words such as 'family' or ''love' to encourage the person to talk freely. Often the therapist will direct their clients/patients to recall early childhood experiences and relationships. The therapist's job is to interpret what the patient says. They then explain their interpretations to the patient and help the patient come to terms with their unconscious conflicts.

Evaluation:

The therapist has a lot of power in free association as they interpret what the client/patient says. If the client disagrees, then this is called transference or repression. Therefore, the therapy is directive. Eysenck (1952) looked at a number of outcome studies and claimed that psychoanalysis was no better than no treatment at all. However he judged the recovery of the psychoanalysis group unfairly. Bergin and Garfield reanalysed the data and found that people who don't undergo therapy have a 30-43% recovery rate but those with therapy have an 83% success rate. This suggests that free association can be an effective therapy. A problem with free association is that it may reinforce obsessive thoughts. Clients/patients can become very dependent on their therapist as the treatment goes on for a long time (on average 2 years). A strength of free association is that it addresses the underlying causes of a mental disorder as it looks at childhood experiences and unconscious motivations for the disorder. Free association has been found to work better with people who are good at expressing their thoughts and feelings (i.e. YAVIS clients-young, attractive, verbal, intelligent and successful clients). It is better for people with mild depression and anxiety. It is not so useful with severe depression, severe anxiety, anorexia and schizophrenia.

**Psychodynamic approach contribution to society-understanding of the significance of dreaming**

Freud proposed that dreams fulfil our wishes. He called dreams 'the royal road to the unconscious'. At night, the mechanisms which suppress the urges of the id relax and the id's desires are expressed through the content of dreams. He distinguished between the manifest content of dreams (what we actually dream about) and the latent (hidden) content of dreams. The manifest content of the dream is symbolic for the latent content. The ego does dream work to protect us from guilty or painful feelings (the true meaning of our dreams is disguised). For example, dreaming of being naked could be symbolic for feeling vulnerable. The latent (hidden) content of dreams can be established through dream analysis.

Evaluation:

Freud's wish fulfilment theory of dreaming has face validity as people do dream about recent events and things that are playing on their mind and some dreams are even recurrent. Therefore, the idea that dreams can symbolise unconscious desires is credible. However, Freud's theory that dreams are meaningful is based on case studies, which are not generalisable. There are biological theories of dreaming that are supported by greater empirical evidence. One biological theory of dreaming says that dreams are an interpretation of random firing of neurones in the brain. Dreams do not always make sense so this theory can explain this. Another biological theory of dreaming suggests that dreaming is a way of getting rid of unwanted connections made between nerve cells in the day and removing waste information.

**The biological approach contribution to society-understanding of autism**

Understanding that autism has a biological basis takes the blame away from the parents and helps professionals to meet the needs of people with autism better. One biological theory is that autism is related to high levels of testosterone in the womb and that this leads to an extreme male brain. This theory is supported by the fact that autistic children tend to be particularly good at male-orientated tasks and autism occurs four times more frequently in boys. Auyeung et al. (2009) found that pregnant women who had high levels of testosterone in the amniotic fluid were more likely to have children who had autistic traits at age eight, such as a lack of sociability and poor verbal skills. Baron-Cohen et al. (2003) found that autistic children achieve low scores for empathy and high scores for systemising on questionnaires, which is more of a male trait.

Autism has also been related to genes. Jorde et al. (1991) found that children who have a sibling with autism are 25 times more likely to develop it themselves than a child in the general population. Bailey et al. (1995) found a 60% concordance rate for autism in MZ twins compared to a 0% concordance for DZ twins. This suggests that there is a genetic basis for autism. DNA studies have been carried out to identify genes, which are related to autism. Schellenberg et al. (2006) found that chromosomes 4 and 7 are linked to autism.

**The biological approach contribution to society-Drug therapy**

The four main types of drugs used to treat mental disorders are: anti-anxiety drugs, anti-depressant drugs, anti-bipolar drugs and anti-psychotic drugs. Drugs work by changing the brain's chemistry. For example, anti-psychotics work by blocking dopamine receptors so the effects of dopamine (a neurotransmitter) are reduced. In this way, anti-psychotics help with the symptoms of schizophrenia such as hallucinations. Prozac and Seroxat are anti-depressant drugs and they work by increasing the levels of serotonin (a neurotransmitter) in the brain as low levels of serotonin are related to depression. Two anti-anxiety drugs are Valium and Librium, which act as tranquillisers and reduce anxiety.

Evaluation:

Drug therapy can work quickly to reduce the symptoms of schizophrenia or severe depression although they cannot cure the mental disorder. However, they can help people feel mentally more stable so that they can access talking therapies such as CBT. Anti-psychotic drugs allow schizophrenics to live in the community without having to be admitted to a psychiatric hospital. On the other hand, drugs can be addictive and people often need higher and higher doses as they develop a tolerance to the drugs. Many drugs have side effects. For example, anti-psychotic drugs can cause the following side effects: constipation, weight gain and in rare cases neuroleptic malignant syndrome (fever, muscle stiffness and loss of consciousness). Many schizophrenics stop taking anti-psychotics due to the side effects. Drug therapy can be expensive over the long-term but in the short-term they are not as expensive as therapists. Drug therapy has also been criticised for not addressing the underlying cause of a mental disorder and only treating the symptoms. GPs may see drugs as a quick and easy way of helping someone with a mental disorder but talking therapies are more effective long-term.

# The learning approach contribution to society-Aversion therapy

Aversion therapy uses classical conditioning to get rid of addictions or unwanted behaviours. Patients' unwanted addictions are paired with a drug that makes them sick or an electric shock. Aversion therapy can be used with alcoholics. Alcohol is paired with an emetic drug (a drug which causes nausea and vomiting). Over time the alcoholic associates alcohol with being sick and does not want to drink alcohol anymore. Other drinks such as soft drinks are given without the drug so that the person is not conditioned to feel sick to all drinks. Aversion therapy can also be used with paedophiles. Paedophiles can give themselves a self-administered electric shock every time they look at a child or a picture of a child.

Evaluation:

Aversion therapy can help alcoholics when used alongside another treatment. However, its effects may not be permanent. The association between alcohol and vomiting may fade over time if the person drinks alcohol without taking the emetic drug.
There are also ethical issues with aversion therapy as it can be distressing and the patient may feel a lack of control. Aversion therapy is not usually carried out without a patient's permission but some patients may feel they can't decline the therapy. Aversion therapy has been used on homosexual males in the past when homosexuality was illegal. Therefore, a criticism of aversion therapy is that it can be used as a form of social control rather than a treatment.

# The learning approach contribution to society token economy programmes (TEPs)

TEPs use operant conditioning to change behaviour for the better. Tokens act as secondary reinforcers and are given for desired behaviour. For example, in psychiatric institutions e.g. anorexics may be given tokens for making certain weight gains. Tokens may be given in prisons and schools for cooperative behaviour. These tokens can then be exchanged for primary reinforcers-something the person finds naturally rewarding such as a trip to Alton Towers for school children or more time in the exercise yard for prisoners.

Evaluation:

TEPs can quickly change behaviour. They are good at getting sufferers of anorexia nervosa to a reasonable weight after which the issues can be addressed or schizophrenics to behave in a cooperative way in psychiatric institutions. TEPs can also improve behaviour in schools particularly with younger children and control aggressive behaviour in prisons. The drawback to TEPs is that they often fail to transfer to life outside the institution and they may only change behaviour in the short-term. There are also ethical issues with TEPs as the people giving out the tokens may show favouritism or abuse their power. Therefore, TEPs should be carefully supervised to ensure that tokens are given fairly and consistently.

**You need to be able to describe and evaluate one contribution to society from two of the Unit 3 applications (Criminological, Child, Health) and one contribution from Clinical Psychology**

**Criminological Psychology: The reliability of eyewitness memory (see contribution from the cognitive approach earlier).**

**The Child Psychology contribution to society-understanding of the effects of daycare**

Research on daycare helps to inform the government about how long maternity leave should be and whether it is a good idea for mothers to go back to work quickly after having children. It also helps the government to understand what daycare provision they should offer in the early years. For example, many preschools now offer 15 hours of free childcare once children reach 3-years-old. Parents also want to know whether putting their children into daycare has any negative effects. Research suggests that too many hours of daycare when a child is very young is not a good idea and as a result maternity leave has increased. Research also shows that preschools, which take children from 2-years-old benefit children socially and cognitively especially those from deprived backgrounds. Good quality daycare is extremely important to prevent any negative effects. A study that supports the use of day care is Sylva et al.'s (2004) EPPE study. It was a longitudinal study into the effectiveness of pre-school care for over 3000 children in the UK. It compared children's cognitive and social development between the ages of 3 and 7 for those attending nurseries, playgroups or pre-school classes with those cared for at home. It used SATs results and reports from pre-school staff, parents and schoolteachers to assess development. It found positive effects for daycare in terms of social and cognitive development. Another study that supports the use of day care is Andersson (1996). They followed 126 Swedish children who had been in daycare in early childhood and assessed their cognitive and social development at 13-years-old. They found that these children had better academic scores and social skills compared to a control group of children who had been cared for entirely by their mothers.

However, a study that looks at the disadvantages of daycare is Belsky and Rovine (1998). This study analysed attachment types using the strange situation when the children were aged between 12-months-old with their mothers and when the children were 13-months-old with their fathers. They found that the children who had spent long periods of time in daycare, were more likely to be insecurely attached. Another study that looks at the negative effects of day care is Baydar and Brooks-Gunn (1991). They questioned 1000 mothers over the telephone about their use of daycare and their children's behaviour and academic progress. They found that children whose mothers had returned to work in their first year had a higher incidence of behaviour difficulties and poor cognitive development. A US study of more than 17,000 children found that there is a relationship between number of hours in non-parental care and behaviour (Early Childhood Longitudinal Study, Ritter & Turner, 2003). This research suggests that mothers should not go back to work too early or for long hours. However, many mothers find caring for a baby or toddler tiring and stressful. They may not want to stay at home looking after their child. Obviously, if a mother is very stressed and unhappy this will affect the baby and in such situations it would be better for the mother to return to work. Brown and Harris (1978) found that women who don't work and have several young children to care for are more likely to be depressed. There is no sense in a mother staying at home if she is depressed and unhappy. The child is more likely to become securely attached if the mother is happy but around less. Ultimately, it is hard for a mother to meet her child's needs and at the same time meet her own needs but a mother must be happy for her child to be happy. The Institute of Education in London studied 17,000 children born to American and British mothers in the 1990s, 1970s and 1980s (Joshi, 2002). They did not find any major impact on children from mothers returning to work in the preschool years and the increased income from mothers working would have improved the children's standard of living. However, children whose mothers returned to work after their first year and who worked only part-time were slightly less anxious than children whose mothers had gone back to work full-time before they turned one. Harr (1999) measured emotional adjustment and academic attainment in 628 children and found very few differences between children of mothers who did not work and those who worked full-time. However, once children reached school age, those children whose mother worked part-time were better adjusted than those of full-time employed mothers. Interestingly, children's emotional adjustment and academic progress were positively associated with mothers' satisfaction with their parent/worker status. On the other hand, parents need to be careful about choosing childcare. Good quality childcare is important and too many hours in childcare can have detrimental effects. Russell (1999) analysed the results of 101 studies of childcare and found that overall research showed negative rather than positive effects.

## The Clinical Psychology contribution to society token economy programmes as a treatment for mental disorders

Helping people recover from mental disorder benefits society. Token economy programmes (TEPs) uses operant conditioning to change behaviour for the better. The tokens are secondary reinforcers and are given for adaptive behaviour e.g. anorexics eating a good meal or schizophrenics carrying out more personal care tasks. The tokens can then be exchanged for primary reinforcers; something a person finds naturally rewarding e.g. a trip to Alton Towers for an anorexic or chocolate for a schizophrenic.

Evaluation:

TEPs are directive as the doctors or nurses in the mental health unit decide when tokens are given out and for what behaviours. However, TEPs can quickly change behaviour. TEPs are good at getting sufferers of anorexia nervosa to a reasonable weight after which the issues can be addressed and getting psychotic patients to behave in a cooperative way. Allyon and Azrin (1968) used a TEP to change the behaviour of 45 chronic schizophrenics who had been institutionalised for an average of 16 years. They were given tokens for making their beds or combing their hair. After the TEP, the schizophrenics were much better at looking after themselves. TEPs are also quite cheap to run as nurses and assistants working in the mental health unit need little training to deliver the programme. However, TEPs can lead to learned helplessness where the patients feel that they have no choice about taking part in the programme. TEPs may also stop people looking inside themselves for the problem. TEPs may only change behaviour in the short-term as they do not address underlying issues. For example, a person may be anorexic due to family issues and giving tokens does not deal with these issues. Furthermore, TEPs may work well with anorexics and schizophrenics in a mental health unit but they may be viewed as patronising by a person with anxiety or depression living in the community.

Note: Any treatment in clinical psychology can be seen as a contribution to society.

## You need to be able to discuss the nature-nurture debate

Exam tip: If you get a simple question such as 'discuss the nature-nurture debate', then half your essay should be on which approaches and studies support the nature side of the argument and half your essay should be on which approaches and studies support the nurture side of the argument. However, the questions can vary quite a lot. You may be asked to discuss particular approaches and why they are nature or nurture.

The nature side of the argument says that we are born to think, feel and behave a certain way.
The nurture side of the argument says that our environment affects the way we think, feel and behave.

## You need to know how each approach supports the nature-nurture debate

**Exam tip**: If you only have to use two approaches to discuss the nature-nurture debate, then use the biological approach and the learning approach as the biological approach is mostly nature and the learning approach is mostly nurture.

The biological approach mainly supports the nature side of the debate. It says that we are born with certain genes and a nervous system that affect the way we think, feel and behave. However, the biological approach accepts that our environment, for example, our diet can affect our development. The learning approach mainly supports the nurture side of the debate. It says that most of our behaviour is learnt from our environment through operant conditioning, classical conditioning and social learning theory. However, it accepts that we are born with some natural behaviours such as automatic reflexes.

You may need to refer to other approaches when discussing the nature-nurture debate.

The social approach supports the nature and nurture side of the debate. It supports the nature side of the debate because it says we are born with the desire to be social animals. On the other hand, it supports the nurture side of the debate because it says that society and our interactions with other people in our environment affect our behaviour.

The cognitive approach supports the nature and nurture side of the debate. It supports the nature side of the debate because it says that we born with the ability to process information in a certain way using certain brain structures. On the other hand, it supports the nurture side of the debate because it says that we encode information from our environment.

The psychodynamic approach supports the nature and nurture side of debate. It supports the nature side of the debate because it says we are born with certain instincts. On the other hand, it supports the nurture side of the debate because it says our experiences in childhood, our environment, affect us later in life.

**You need to be able to describe studies that either support nature or nurture**

Heston's adoption study and Gottesman's twin study support the nature approach as they showed a genetic link for schizophrenia.

Bandura's Bobo doll Study (1961) supports the nurture approach as it showed how children will imitate aggressive behaviour learnt from their environment.

**Possible nature-nurture essay**

The nature-nurture debate refers to the controversy over whether we are born to think, feel and behave in a certain way or whether we learn it from our environment. The nature side of the argument says that our behaviour is determined from birth. The biological approach is the main supporter of nature side of the debate. It focuses on how our genes, nervous system, brain structure and hormones affect our behaviour. It used research methods such as twin and adoption studies, DNA studies and brain scans to study the effects of genes and brain structure on behaviour. The biological approach promotes treatments such as drug therapy, electroconvulsive therapy and brain surgery because it believes that behaviour is changed only through physical means. Twin and adoption studies have been carried out to demonstrate a genetic basis for behaviour. For example, Holland et al. (1988) carried out a twin study to look for a genetic link for anorexia nervosa. They found a higher concordance rate for MZ female twins (56%) compared to female DZ twins (5%) and concluded that anorexia nervosa does have a genetic basis. Heston (1966) conducted an adoption study to see if there is a genetic basis for schizophrenia. They found that 10% of the adopted children whose mother had schizophrenia developed it themselves compared to none of the control group. This suggests that schizophrenia is inherited to a certain extent. However, it is difficult to separate out the effects of nature and nurture in both twin and adoption studies. MZ twins share a more similar environment than DZ twins and this may be why they have higher concordance rates for mental disorders. A problem with adoption studies is that children are often selectively placed into adoptive families who are similar to their biological family, so it is difficult to distinguish between genetic and environmental factors in the children's development.

The nurture side of the debate suggests that we learn all our behaviour from our environment. The learning approach mainly supports the nurture side of the debate as it says that we learn behaviour through classical conditioning, operant conditioning and social learning. The learning approach has used experiments to show how children can learn behaviours from their environment. For example, Watson and Rayner classically conditioned little Albert to be afraid of a white rat he was originally unafraid of. Bandura, Ross and Ross (1961) found that children would copy aggressive behaviour shown by an adult role model to a plastic bobo doll. Such studies support the idea that we learn behaviour from our environment.

However, behaviour is likely to be a mixture of both nature and nurture. For example, a child may be born with a genetic predisposition to have a high IQ but they will only develop a high IQ if they are exposed to a stimulating environment and have a good education. Similarly, a person may be born with a genetic predisposition to develop anorexia nervosa but if they grow up with few stressors and in a culture such as Egypt where being fuller-figured is considered beautiful, they are less likely to develop anorexia nervosa.

**You need to be able to discuss the question of whether psychology should be called a science**

Note: If you get a question on whether psychology is a science, you will need to be able to define what scientific means and be able to discuss which approaches, research methods and studies are and are not scientific. AO1: is/ should be scientific. AO2: isn't/ shouldn't be scientific.

Scientific knowledge is built from testing theories and collecting empirical data. A researcher may come up with a hypothesis (prediction) based on a theory. The hypothesis is then tested to see whether it is supported by empirical evidence. A key concept in science is falsifiability, which refers to whether a theory can actually be tested or not. Laboratory experiments enable hypotheses to be tested under controlled conditions. In a laboratory experiment, an independent variable in manipulated and a dependent variable in measured. The extraneous variables are controlled in order to establish a cause and effect relationship. Laboratory experiments collect quantitative data, which is objective and can be statistically analysed. Science is based on the idea of objectivity and being able to replicate findings.

Note: You might want to use the terms 'nomothetic' and 'idiographic' when discussing whether an approach is scientific or not.

The term 'nomothetic' refers to looking at people as a group. Nomothetic approaches believe that all people respond/learn in a similar way, they come up with general laws about behaviour and are considered more scientific. The learning approach is nomothetic as it says we all learn behaviours from our environment, through classical conditioning, operant conditioning and social learning.

The term 'idiographic' refers to looking at people as unique individuals. Idiographic approaches view each person as having individual characteristics that make them different to other people. They are considered less scientific. The psychodynamic approach is idiographic as it views everyone as unique with different thoughts, emotions, childhood experiences and unconscious conflicts.

**You need to know which approaches are scientific and which approaches are not scientific**

The learning approach is a scientific approach as it tries to measures responses to certain stimuli in controlled environments. For example, Skinner measured how often a rat would press a lever when given rewards. The learning approach focuses on objective, empirical evidence from laboratory experiments.

The biological approach is a scientific approach. It focuses on how our genes, hormones, brain structure and the nervous system affect our behaviour. The biological approach uses scientific methods such as laboratory experiments and brain scans to gather empirical evidence.

The cognitive approach is scientific in some ways and not scientific in others. It uses scientific methods such as experiments to test memory and how people process information. However, it also has concepts such as schemas, which cannot be scientifically proven.

The social approach is scientific in some ways and not scientific in others. It uses scientific methods such as experiments to test obedience and prejudice. However, it also uses unscientific methods such as interviews to find out about people's opinions and feelings. Qualitative data from interviews are open to interpretation and can be biased.

The psychodynamic approach is not scientific. It is concerned with the unobservable aspects of human behaviour and it has concepts (such as the id, ego and superego) that are very difficult to investigate and which are not falsifiable. It uses case studies and clinical interviews which are open to interpretation and can be biased.

**You need to be able to describe a study that is scientific**

**Loftus and Palmer's** (1974) study on eyewitness testimony aimed to be scientific. They showed all participants the same 7 film clips of traffic accidents under controlled conditions. They investigated leading questions by changing only one verb in the question 'How fast were the cars going when they hit each other?' The verb hit' was replaced by 'smashed', 'collided' 'bumped' and 'contacted' in the five conditions. They also carefully measured a dependent variable, participants' speed estimates. Therefore, they were able to establish a cause and effect relationship between the verb in the question and participants' speed estimates.

**Milgram's** study of obedience also aimed to be scientific. It investigated participants' obedience to an authority figure using a laboratory experiment, with good controls. All participants were asked to give increasingly severe electric shocks to Mr. Wallace up to 450V. They all heard the same standardised instructions and were given the same verbal prods such as 'you must continue' throughout the experiment.

**You need to be able to describe a non- scientific study**

**The Little Hans case study** is not scientific as it did not manipulate or measure any variables and there were no controls. Case studies are also open to interpretation and Freud may have been influenced by the father's comments about Little Hans. Little Hans' father already knew about the Oedipus complex and may have interpreted Little Hans' behaviour in a biased way.

# Possible essay on whether psychology is a science

There is a debate over whether psychology is a science. This may be because there are different approaches within psychology. Some approaches such as the learning approach are more scientific and use well, controlled laboratory experiments to collect objective, quantitative data. In contrast, other approaches in psychology such as the psychodynamic approach are less scientific as they use cases studies and interviews, which are open to interpretation.

The learning approach and the biological approach are more scientific as they tend to collect data from controlled experiments. They use theories to develop hypotheses, which are then tested to see whether they are supported or not by empirical evidence. These approaches aim to build a body of scientific knowledge from the data collected. The biological approach uses laboratory experiments and brains scans to understand more about how the brain works. It also uses twin studies and adoption studies to establish genetic links for mental disorders and developmental disorders. However, twin and adoption studies are correlational and cannot separate out the influence of genes from the environment. The learning approach uses laboratory experiments to see how we learn behaviour through association, consequences and observation. For example, Pavlov measured how much a dog with salivate to the sound of a bell when it had associated the bell with food. Bandura, Ross and Ross (1961) rated how aggressive children were to a Bobo doll after the children had observed a role model. However, even controlled experiments in psychology can be problematic as they are subject to experimenter bias and demand characteristics. For example, the children in the Bandura, Ross and Ross' study may have thought they were supposed to be aggressive to the Bobo doll.

The cognitive and the social approach are scientific in some ways but not others. The cognitive approach uses controlled laboratory experiments to investigate memory and forgetting. However, the operationalisation of the variables in experiments may lead to problems with validity. For example, learning and recalling a list of words may not be a valid way of testing memory. The cognitive approach also has concepts that are less scientific such as schema, which are difficult to test. The social approach uses laboratory experiments to investigate obedience and prejudice, which are scientific. However, it also uses interviews and field studies to gather data, which can be subject to bias and are less scientific.

The psychodynamic approach is not scientific. It comes up with theories such as the concepts of the id, ego and superego that are difficult to test and which are not falsifiable. The psychodynamic approach is also idiographic as it views each person as a unique individual rather than coming up with general laws of behaviour. It uses case studies and clinical interviews as research methods, which are open to interpretation.

**You need to be able to name and describe at least five ethical guidelines that apply to humans**

**Distress:** Participants should be protected from psychological or physical harm. The risk of harm should be no greater than that found in everyday life.

**Informed Consent:** Participants should be provided with enough information about the aim of the study and the procedure so that they can make an informed choice about whether to take part or not.

**Deception:** Participants should not be deceived about the aim of the study or the procedure. If deception is unavoidable, then permission should be sought from the British Psychological Society.

**Debriefing:** Participants should be fully informed of the purpose and expected outcomes of the study after they have taken part.

**Right to withdraw:** Participants should be told that they are free to leave the study at any time and they have the right to remove their results at the end, regardless of any payment they have received.

**Confidentiality:** Participants' should be guaranteed anonymity and their data should be stored securely.

**You need to be able to describe and evaluate two studies that relate to ethical issues.**

**Milgram(1963)** (see more information on study under laboratory experiments.) Baumrind criticised Milgram's obedience study for the stress and emotional conflict experienced by participants. Although at the beginning of the experiment participants were told they could withdraw, many felt they couldn't withdraw because of the verbal prods to continue. He deceived participants, as he told them the experiment was about memory when it was actually about obedience. As participants were deceived he did not get their informed consent. However, he did use presumptive consent, by asking other people before the experiment how they would feel about taking part and what their responses would be. Most people predicted that only 3% of people would obey. However, presumptive consent is not the same as consent from the actual participants. Milgram did thoroughly debrief all participants, and all were followed up by psychiatrists a year later. He made sure that all participants saw Mr Wallace after the experiment, so that they could see he was okay.

**Hofling et al. (1966)**

Aim: To see whether nurses would obey a doctor when doing so would go against hospital regulations and potentially harm patients.

Procedure: Boxes of harmless capsules labelled Astroten were places in 22 wards of two hospitals. The labels on the boxes said that the maximum daily dose was 10mg. A researcher calling himself a doctor, telephoned nurses on duty in each ward and instructed them to give a patient 20 mg of the drug Astroten without written authorisation. In a third hospital, 22 other nurses were given the scenario of a doctor giving orders over the telephone and asked whether they would obey the doctor in these circumstances.

Results: When nurses were given the scenario, 21 of the 22 nurses said that they would not obey the doctor's instructions. However, in the experimental situation, 21 of the 22 nurses asked to give an overdose of Astroten, did obey the doctor's orders.
Conclusion: Most nurses believe that they will not obey a doctor unquestioningly. However, most nurses are obedient to doctors when given orders.

Evaluation of ethics: The nurses did not know they were taking part in the study so they did not give informed consent and they were deceived. Another issue is that the nurses may have been distracted by the fake doctor's orders when they should have been attending to other patients.  However, the study has important implications. It suggests that nurses should be encouraged to question doctors if they don't agree with what they are being asked to do or if they are concerned.

## You need to be able to analyse the costs versus benefits of different studies.

When psychologists carry out research they have two considerations in mind: the benefit to the society and psychological understanding and the costs in terms of possible harm to the participants. This is called an ethical dilemma.

## Milgram's study of obedience and ethics

Milgram's study has benefits for society and psychological understanding. It helped us to understand obedience and why the Nazis were so obedient to Hitler in WWII. It also suggests that soldiers, police officers and other professionals who may be vulnerable to blind obedience should be trained to question authority figures when they feel they are being asked to do something wrong. If people are trained to question authority when necessary, then we can protect against atrocities such as the torture of Iraqi prisoners by US soldiers in Abu Ghraib. However, Milgram's study did have costs to the participants. Participants were deceived about the true aim of the study and did not give informed consent. They thought the study was on the effects of punishment on learning when it was actually on obedience. Participants were also caused distress. It is possible the study could have cause psychological harm in the long-term. However, participants were debriefed thoroughly. They were also followed up by psychiatrists a year later and no long-term harm was found.

## Zimbardo's study of social roles in a prison environment and ethics

One of the benefits of Zimbardo's study is that it helps us to understand why people can lose their identity so quickly and take on different social roles. It also makes us aware of how people in positions of authority can abuse their power. The study suggests that those who are in positions of authority should be regulated. The military funded Zimbardo's study and its findings could have helped them regulate the military hierarchy better. However, it is possible that the findings from Zimbardo's study could have been misused by the military to exert excessive control over their personnel. There were costs to the participants in the study. Many of the participants were caused distress and they found it difficult to withdraw from the study. One participant even had a nervous breakdown. However, the participants said afterwards that they had learnt something valuable from the study.

**You need to be able to describe and evaluate animal studies**

Animal studies involve studying animal behaviour either in a laboratory or in the field. In an experiment, an independent variable is manipulated and a dependent variable is measured. For example, Skinner measured how many times a rat would press a lever when it received a reward. In a field study, animal behaviour may be observed after changing something in the environment such as the animal's habitat. Often animal behaviour is recorded on video so that the animal's behaviour is not affected by human presence. Sometimes mechanical devices are used with animals to see how they respond. For example, Skinner used a mechanical device called a Skinner's box and Thorndike used a puzzle box. Thorndike's experiment involved placing a kitten in a box with an escape latch. Through trial and error the kitten would find the escape latch and when it got out of the box it receive food as a reward.

Advantages: Animals are easier to use than humans because of ethical issues. Animals are also smaller on average, which makes certain experiments easier to run. For example, Skinner needed a small animal for his Skinner's box. Some animals such as rats breed quickly, which means that means that you can see how selective breeding affects behaviour. For example, if you breed rats that are good at finding their way around mazes together, then you can see whether their offspring are particularly good at mazes. Field studies on animals have ecological validity because they are done in the animals' natural setting.

Disadvantages: Humans are more complex than animals and so it is difficult to generalise results from animal studies to humans. There can be ethical issues with carrying out studies on animals.

**Describe 5 ethical guidelines for non- human (animal) research**

**Caging and Stress:** Experimenters should avoid or minimise stress and suffering for all living animals. The cages the animals are kept in during the experiment should be large enough for the animals to be comfortable.

**Number or animals used:** Researchers should use as few animals as possible.

**Wild Animals:** Endangered species should not be used, unless the research has direct benefits for that species e.g. conservation.

**Qualified Experimenters:** The researchers conducting the experiment should have the necessary qualifications. They should also have a licence from the Home office for that particular experiment.

**Look for alternatives:** Alternatives to using animals must always be sought, such as using humans or computers.

**It is useful to know at least one study using animals that has ethical issues.**

**Harlow and Zimmerman's (1959)** study has ethical issues. They took baby monkeys and raised them in a laboratory. They gave the baby monkeys a wire monkey with a bottle to feed from and a cloth monkey to get comfort from and hold onto. All the monkeys formed strong attachments with the cloth monkey and mainly used the wire monkey for food. Harlow and Zimmerman concluded that comfort is more important than food for an attachment to form. When the monkeys were placed back with other monkeys, their behaviour was abnormal and they were not accepted by the group. They had problems with mating and were poor parents to their own offspring. This study has serious ethical issues as the baby monkeys were caused a lot of distress and were psychologically damaged for the rest of their lives.

**Rechstaffen et al. (1983)** aimed to see the effects of sleep deprivation on rats. In this laboratory experiment, researchers placed rats on a disc above a bucket of water. When the rats fell asleep the disc would rotate and in order to not fall into the water, the rats had to stay awake and walk on the disc. The rats eventually died after severe sleep deprivation. It is questionable whether there is any clear benefit to this research and it certainly caused the rats to suffer distress and die.

**Pavlov** looked at how you can classically condition dogs to salivate to the sound of a bell. This study did not have any serious ethical issues.

**You need to be able to describe the Bateson's cube.**

Bateson's cube has 3 edges labelled; quality of research, animal suffering and certainty of medical benefit. These are on a scale high to low. When a research proposal falls into the opaque region, experiment should not be conducted i.e. when quality of research is low, animal suffering is high and certainty of benefit is low.

**You need to be able to discuss reasons for doing research on animals.**

It could be argued that animals should be used in research to ease human suffering and that we should have more sympathy for our own species than other species. Another argument is that animals do not have the same feelings or experience the same pain as humans. Therefore, we should use animals in preference to humans for research. There are also strict laws and codes of conduct that protect animals used in research which minimises animal suffering. Less invasive methods are used where possible to study animal behaviour.

**You need to be able to discuss reasons for not doing research on animals**

A problem with using animals in research is that it is difficult to generalise the finding to humans as we are more complex. The human brain is different to animals, for example, we have consciousness and can imagine what others are thinking. Research shows that animals can suffer distress, pain and anxiety. Therefore, we should not use animals on moral grounds.

**You need to be able to describe and evaluate issues of ethnocentrism and cultural bias in psychological research**

**Ethnocentrism**: can occur if we interpret research findings or people's behaviour entirely through the lens of our own culture without taking into account cultural differences. This can lead to cultural bias. For example, ethnocentrism can occur if clinicians do not take into account cultural differences in diagnoses of people with mental health issues. When people view the values, culture and behaviours of their own group as better than other groups, this is an example of ethnocentrism.

For example, researchers may not take into account the beliefs, customs or language of people from a different culture when conducting research and interpreting findings. The vast majority of psychological research has been carried out in the USA by white, middle class, males which can create bias in the interpretation of findings. If the findings of studies conducted in the USA are generalized to all cultures, this can be seen as ethnocentric. For example, views about the signs and symptoms of mental disorders in DSM may be ethnocentric. However, DSM-5 tries to overcome cultural issues in diagnosis by describing how people from different cultures talk about mental health issues differently.

**Cultural bias** occurs when people from one culture make assumptions about the behaviour of those from another culture based on their own cultural norms and practices. Most psychological research has been carried out in Europe and the USA so it has a Western bias.

**Cross-cultural research**

Cross-cultural research refers to researchers repeating studies in different countries/cultures to see if a theory is universal and can explain human behavior across all cultures. Cross-cultural research on obedience has been carried out. For example, Milgram's study has been repeated in other countries with similar results. This suggests that people have similar obedience levels in other countries. Meeus and Raaijmaker's study looked at obedience in Holland with administrative psychological violence rather than physical violence and found high levels of obedience even though Dutch culture is more liberal than American culture.

There has also been cross-cultural research on attachment types using the Strange Situation. Ainsworth's classification of different attachment types has been criticised for being culturally biased. However, research has found that type B (secure) attachments are the most common across all cultures. This suggests that the strange situation procedure is a useful tool for assessing attachment type across all cultures. Van Ijzendoorn amd Kroonenberg (1988) compared the results of 32 cross-cultural studies and found that there were differences in the proportions of different attachment types in different cultures. However, type B (secure) attachments were the most common type of attachment in all the studies from different cultures, with the exception of one study from Germany. Interestingly, there were more differences in attachment types within a culture compared to between cultures.

How can cultural bias be reduced?

1) By taking into account a culture's customs and norms before interpreting the results of studies. For example, it is important to take Japanese culture into account before deciding that more children in Japan have insecure resistant attachments. Miyake et al. (1985) found that Japanese infants had a higher proportion of resistant attachments but this may be due to Japanese mothers rarely leaving their children with anyone else and encouraging dependency.

2) Ethnographic fieldwork can reduce cultural bias. This is where researchers immerse themselves in the culture and customs of a country or tribe so that they understand better the reasons for their behaviour. However, total immersion in another culture is not always achievable.

3) Back translation. It is useful to translate the interviews in other languages more than one time using different translators to make sure the people's views are fully understood.

4) Taking into account other culture's beliefs when making a diagnosis of mental disorder e.g. hearing voices after bereavement is considered normal in Indian culture rather than a sign of schizophrenia.

5) Acknowledge how our own cultural background affects the interpretation of data.

6) Use an emic approach. This assumes that all cultures are different and findings are only significant within the culture they were found.

**Evaluation:**

It may not be possible to truly understand another culture. We are always affected by our own beliefs and culture. There are also problems with translation. We can never be certain we are talking about the same thing (a problem of equivalence). There are strengths of an etic approach, which assumes that human behaviour is common and applies findings universally.

**You need to be able to describe issues related to the use of psychological knowledge as a means of social control and assess ethical and practical implications of such control. Issues should include: use of drug therapy; token economy programmes; classical conditioning and the influence of the practitioner in treatment.**

Psychology has been used to get people to conform to the rules and norms of society. This is called social control.

Psychological therapies can be used to control people so that they conform to society's norms. When therapies are used to control people rather than to help them then this can be seen as social control. If therapies are being used to control people then this raises ethical issues. Furthermore, if professionals delivering therapies have too much power then this is an ethical issue to. Sometimes people who are a danger to themselves or others due to mental health reasons are forcibly brought to a psychiatric institution under the Mental Health Act. Society needs to be careful that the rights of the individual are not infringed in these circumstances. However, it could be argued that we need social control so that people can live in society safely without fear of harm.

Drug therapy can be viewed as a form of social control when they are given to people with mental health problems. For example, schizophrenics are given anti-psychotic drugs to control their symptoms. However, some schizophrenics and their families suggest that the drugs only sedate them rather than help them. There are also many side effects to taking anti-psychotic drugs. Another problem with drug therapy is that it does not deal with the underlying causes of mental disorder, it just suppresses the symptoms. It could be argued that schizophrenics are given drugs so they live and behave by society's rules and expectations rather than to treat their illness. Another example of social control is when drugs such as Ritalin are used to treat children with ADHD. Some argue that as increasing numbers of younger and younger children are being diagnosed with ADHD, it is not a problem with the children but with society. It has been said that Ritalin just slows children down so that parents and teachers can cope with behaviour that might actually be quite normal in young children. Perhaps behaviour management techniques should be taught to parents and teachers so that they can control children's behaviour without the use of drugs. There are also issues over whether the practitioner has too much power in drug therapy because drugs are invasive. One of the practical issues with drug therapy is that patients may stop taking their drugs due to nasty side effects. Drug therapy is more effective when used alongside counselling or other talking therapies.

Token Economy Programmes (TEPs) are used in mental health institutions, schools and prisons to control behaviour and they can be viewed as a form of social control. In mental health institutions, patients are rewarded for more adaptive behaviour. For example, anorexic patients are given tokens if they eat well or gain a certain amount of weight each week and these tokens can be exchanged for leisure time or outings. However, if a TEP is the only therapy used it only serves to control their behaviour rather than change it. TEPs may only change behaviour in the short term and learnt behaviour does not transfer easily to the outside world especially if the underlying causes of the disorder have not been dealt with. Token economy programmes are also used with prisoners. Tokens (secondary reinforcers) are given for cooperative and non-aggressive behaviour. Once the prisoners have a certain number of tokens, they can exchange them for something they actually wants such as a phone card (a primary reinforcer). However, there are ethical issues with TEPs as staff implementing a token economy programme have a lot of power. It is important that staff do not favour or ignore certain individuals if the programme is to work (the practitioner may have too much influence and power). Therefore, prison staff need to be trained to give tokens fairly and consistently even when there are shift changes. Another practical issue with TEPs is that they can be time-consuming to deliver effectively as prison staff need to agree on desired behaviours with individual prisoners in advance. Prisoners should also know exactly what they will receive tokens for and how many tokens they need to get before they can exchange them for a reward. An issue with TEPs are that they are unlikely to stop recidivism as they only change behaviour in the short-term.

Aversion Therapy uses classical conditioning to get rid of unwanted behaviours. It works by the association of an unpleasant stimulus with the unwanted behaviour. A paedophile can be conditioned to respond to children with fear rather than sexual arousal by pairing thoughts about children with painful electric shocks. Many people may see this as an acceptable form of social control as it is performed with the offender's consent and counselling. However, in the past when homosexuality was illegal, aversion therapy was used on homosexual men as an alternative to a prison sentence. This shows how aversion therapy has ethical issues and is open to abuse. Even nowadays, people may only consent to aversion therapy because they feel under pressure to have the treatment and during the treatment they may feel out of control (the practitioner may have too much influence). There are practical issues with aversion therapy as the association has to be made very clear. For example, in the treatment for alcoholism it would be important for the person to drink water and soft drinks without the drug, or they may become conditioned not to drink at all.

Psychoanalysis can also be seen as a form of social control. The therapy involves the therapist trying to uncover unconscious thoughts and desires through techniques such as free association and dream analysis. The therapist can be seen to have too much power as the individual is told to accept the therapist's interpretation whether or not they agree. This leads to a power imbalance. The therapy has also been criticised for making patients dependent on the therapist as the therapy goes on for a long time (on average 2 years).

**You need to be able to describe and explain using concepts, theories and research the key issues studied in Units 1, 2, 3, and 4.**

**Unit 1-Social Approach- A key issue in the social approach is understanding football violence.**

Rival football fans can end up fighting, shouting and throwing objects at each other on the streets after a football match. The violence is sometimes organised and orchestrated by a leader. The police often have to act to stop the violence and can be attacked themselves. When football matches have occurred between countries where there is a history of violence, certain individuals are prevented from attending the matches because they are viewed as ring leaders. If the causes of football violence are understood better, it may help the police and others to work out ways to reduce the violence, which is why it is a key issue.

Social identity theory can be used to explain why football fans become violent to rival football fans. Fans may categorise themselves as belonging to an in group (followers of a particular football team) and categorise fans of rival football teams as being the out-group. They identify strongly with their in-group by wearing scarves and strips that reflect their group membership. The fans compare themselves more favourably against rival football fans and deride the out-group in order to boost their self-esteem. Fans may focus on the fact the other team cheats more and this feeling of superiority allows them to dehumanise opposition fans. In some people, this may spill over into football violence/hooliganism.

Realistic conflict theory explains how competition over resources can lead to conflict between groups. This theory explain how football fans can become prejudiced towards each other as their football teams are in competition with each other to win the football match-only one team can win so this means there is competition over resources. Football fans identify themselves as being in one group, the in-group. Other rival football teams/fans are the out-group. During a football match there is competition between groups and so hostility occurs.

Sherif et al.'s study can be applied to why football violence occurs between rival football fans. They found that when two groups of boys were put in competition with each other at a summer camp, the boys quickly became hostile to the other group. However, Sherif's study only used boys so it may not explain the prejudice of female football supporters.

Levine et al. (2005) carried out an experiment on football supporters. Fans were invited to a secluded part of the university campus where they watched a stranger fall and apparently injure themselves. In one condition the person having the accident wore their team colours whilst in another condition they wore neutral colours, or those of a rival football club. Football fans were much more likely to help someone wearing their team colours.

Agency theory can also explain football violence. Fans may be obeying orders from ring leaders whom they view as authority figures. However, they may feel uncomfortable about obeying the orders and experience moral strain. Denial can be used as a coping mechanism so that they don't feel guilty for their actions.

One way football violence can be reduced is for the police to target ringleaders. If the instigators of the violence are removed, then there is no authority figure for the fans to follow and so conflict may stop.

**Unit 1-Cognitive Approach- A key issue in the cognitive approach is the (un)reliability of eyewitness testimony (see contributions to society)**

**Unit 2-Learning Approach-A key issue in the learning approach is whether impossibly' thin role models in the media lead to anorexia nervosa**

Social learning theory suggests anorexia nervosa may be due to role models in the media. Young people may feel they have to get to around the same weight as thin celebrities in order to be accepted. Teenagers pay attention to the fact that many celebrity role models are extremely thin. They retain this information. They have the ability to reproduce being thin if they diet excessively and will do it if they are motivated to do so (ARRM). They can see that their role models are famous and rich and this may motivate them to be thin too. Teenagers may think that being thin is what is needed to be accepted.

There are a number of studies which support social learning theory as an explanation of anorexia nervosa. Lai (2000) found that the rate of anorexia increased for chinese residents in Hong Kong as the culture slowly became more westernised. Crisp et al. (1976) found that dancers and fashion models were more likely to develop anorexia nervosa. Mumford et al. (1991) found that Arab and Asian women were more likely to develop eating disorders if they moved to the West.
However social learning theory does not explain why the disorder usually develops in adolescence or why everyone sees the pictures of slim people but only a few develop

anorexia nervosa. There are psychodynamic explanations for anorexia nervosa such as fear of growing up and family issues.

**Unit 2-Biological Approach-A key issue in the biological approach Is whether autism an extreme male brain condition.**

Baron-Cohen et al. (2005) suggests that autism is an extreme male brain condition. He also linked the cause of autism with high levels of testosterone in the womb.
Research supports the idea that autism is an extreme male brain condition. Male brains are heavier than female brains and those with autism have an even heavier brain than a normal male brain. Male brains also grow more quickly, as does the brain of someone with autism. On average males are better at spatial tasks such as map reading, mathematical reasoning and systemising and autistic children tend to focus on such skills. On average, females are better at language tasks and interpreting emotions, which autistic children have more difficulty with. Auyeung et al. (2009) found that pregnant women who had high levels of testosterone (a male hormone) in the amniotic fluid were more likely to have children who had autistic traits at age eight, such as a lack of sociability and poor verbal skills. Baron-Cohen et al. (2003) found that autistic children scored higher on systemising, a male trait, than the general population.

However, autistic people do not have greater brain lateralisation than normal people, which contradicts the idea of autistic people having an extreme male brain. Autism may have a genetic basis. Jorde et al. (1991) found that children who have a sibling with autism are 25 times more likely to develop it themselves than a child in the general population. Bailey et al. (1995) found a 60% concordance rate for autism in MZ twins compared to a 0% concordance for DZ twins. This suggests that there is a genetic basis for autism. DNA studies have been carried out to identify genes, which are related to autism. Schellenberg et al. (2006) found that chromosomes 4 and 7 are linked to autism. There may also be environmental causes of autism. Difficulties at birth and exposure to rubella in the womb have been linked to autism.

**Unit 2-Psychodynamic approach-A key issue in the psychodynamic approach is whether dreams are meaningful**

There is a debate about whether dreams are meaningful. Freud proposed the major function of dreams is wish-fulfilment. At night, the mechanisms which suppress the urges of the id relax and the id's desires are expressed through the content of dreams. However, the ego does dream work to protect us from guilty or painful feelings (the true meaning of our dreams is disguised). Freud distinguished between the manifest content of dreams-what we actually dream about and the latent (hidden) content of dreams. The manifest content of the dream is symbolic for the latent content. For example, dreaming of flying might be symbolic for a desire for sexual intercourse. The latent content of dreams may be established through dream analysis.

Freud was probably correct to say that the content of our dreams reflects things that are on our minds and the idea that dreams can symbolise unconscious desires is credible. Dreams about recent events are common and some dreams are recurrent. However, since symbols in dreams are supposed to represent unconscious thoughts it is impossible to scientifically study them or validate their meaning. There are biological theories of dreaming that are supported by empirical evidence and have more credibility. Dreams do not always make sense. One biological theory of dreaming says that dreams are an interpretation of random firing of neurones in the brain. Another biological theory of dreaming suggests that dreaming is a way of getting rid of unwanted connections made between nerve cells in the day and removing waste information. Deary & Tate (1987) found junior doctors deprived of sleep performed less well on memory tasks than junior doctors not on duty. This study shows that dreaming is important for improving thinking but not necessarily meaningful.

**Unit 3-A key issue in the criminological psychology is the (un)reliability of eyewitness testimony (see contributions to society).**

**Unit 3-A key issue in child psychology is the effects of daycare (see contributions to society).**

**Unit 4-A key issue in clinical psychology is understanding schizophrenia**

Schizophrenia is a psychotic disorder, which affects about 1% of the population. Many of the symptoms of schizophrenia cause distress to the sufferers and their families. Therefore, it is important that psychiatrists and clinical psychologists develop effective treatments for schizophrenia. Understanding the causes of schizophrenia can aid clinicians and help families deal with the disorder better. However, there are different types of schizophrenia so there may be different causes.

A biological explanation for schizophrenia is that genes can predispose someone to develop schizophrenia. The Heston study showed that 10% of adoptees who had a mother with schizophrenia went onto develop it themselves compared to none in a control group. This suggests a genetic basis for schizophrenia. Gottesman's study found a 0.48 concordance rate for schizophrenia in MZ twins compared to a 0.17 concordance rate in DZ twins, supporting a genetic link for schizophrenia.

Another biological explanation for schizophrenia is that high levels of the chemical dopamine in the brain can lead to schizophrenia. Donnelly et al. (1996) found that schizophrenic patients produce more homovanillic acid (a metabolite/waste product of dopamine) in their urine. Anti-psychotic drugs work by blocking the effects of dopamine in the brain. Such drugs have enabled schizophrenics to live in the community rather than being institutionalised. However, anti-psychotic drugs do not work on all schizophrenics and they can have serious side effects. Many schizophrenics stop taking the drugs due to the side effects. There is also the criticism that anti-psychotic drugs just sedate schizophrenics rather than really curing them, which is why other treatments such as cognitive behavioural therapy are so important.

A cognitive explanation for schizophrenia is that schizophrenics have problems with processing information in the brain. Frith and Done (1986) found that schizophrenic patients with negative symptoms did worse on verbal fluency tasks (such as name as many fruits as you can). This supports the idea that schizophrenics have difficulties in information processing. Another study that shows that people with schizophrenia have problems with information processing is Bentall et al. (1991). They got schizophrenic and non-schizophrenic participants to come up with words or read words from a list. One week later they got the participants back. They found that schizophrenic patients with hallucinations found it very difficult to remember whether they had come up with words themselves, read them or whether the words were new. Non-schizophrenic patients were much better at this, which indicates that schizophrenics have distinguishing between their own thoughts and other people's thoughts.

Cognitive behavioural therapy involves questioning and changing a schizophrenic's maladaptive thoughts/distorted beliefs. For example, the therapist might question the schizophrenic's beliefs about how powerful the voices are that they hear in their head. They might also change their faulty interpretations of the world such as the belief that everyone is out to get them. The behavioural part of the therapy involves changing their behaviour, for example, getting them to ignore the voices they hear in their head or to ignore ideas that their thoughts are being put in their head by someone else.

A psychodynamic explanation for schizophrenia is that growing up in a family with disturbed communication patterns can lead to schizophrenia. Lidz et al. (1965) found that 90% of schizophrenic patients had seriously disturbed families. Schofield and Balian (1959) found that schizophrenic patients were more likely to have mothers who were cold and domineering.

A social explanation of schizophrenia is social deprivation. Castle found that most schizophrenics were born in deprived areas. Deprivation and poor social status may make them vulnerable to developing schizophrenia.

The stress-diathesis model of schizophrenia suggests that some people have a genetic predisposition to schizophrenia, which can then be triggered by social factors.

**To be able to describe and evaluate nine research methods with one study for each method.**

### Method 1: Laboratory Experiments

Laboratory experiments involve manipulating an independent variable and measuring a dependent variable. Extraneous variables are controlled so that a cause and effect relationship can be established.

### Evaluation:

Laboratory experiments have standardised procedures, which are easy to replicate so that reliability can be tested. Data from laboratory experiments is quantitative and objective. Therefore, such data is considered scientific. However, laboratory experiments lack ecological validity because they take place in artificial environments and often involve artificial tasks.

**Milgram (1963)**

Aim: The aim of the experiment was to investigate what level of obedience would be shown when participants were told by an authority figure to administer electric shocks to another person.

Procedure: A volunteer sample of 40 males aged between 20 and 50 years of age, were recruited from a newspaper advertisement. Participants were told that the study was about the effects of punishment on learning and that they would be paid $4.50 for taking part. When participants arrived at Yale University, they were asked to draw lots for who would have the role of teacher or learner in the experiment. The draw was set up so that the participant was always the teacher and Mr. Wallace (the confederate) was always the learner. Participants were then shown an electric shock generator, which had 30 switches from 15V to 450V. They were then asked to give increasing levels of electric shocks to the learner if he got any words incorrect on a word pair task. Unbeknown to the participants the electric shocks were fake. At certain voltages, Mr. Wallace pretended to show signs of pain. At 315V, Mr. Wallace became silent. Whenever the participants said they wanted to stop giving the electric shocks, they were given verbal prods to continue.

Results: 100% (40/40) of the participants obeyed up to 300 volts and 65% (26/40) of the participants were fully obedient and gave all the shocks to 450V. During the study many participants showed distress at having to give the electric shocks.

Conclusion:
People will obey authority figures even when it means causing harm to an innocent person. Milgram suggested the high levels of obedience in the study may have been due to the fact that the experiment took place at the prestigious Yale University. The participants may also have felt they should continue with the study because they had volunteered and were offered payment for their participation.

**Evaluation:**

Generalisability- All of Milgram's participants were volunteers who are likely to be more obedient than other participant so in the sample is not generalisable in this respect.
It could also be argued that Milgram's study is not generalisable as it was only carried out on American males who are not representative of the wider population. However, when Milgram tested females in exactly the same way, he found identical levels of obedience. Studies testing obedience across the world have found similar levels of obedience.

Reliability-Milgram's study was reliable because it had a standardised procedure, which makes it easy to repeat and get the same results. A script was followed and all participants heard the same recordings from Mr. Wallace. They were also give the same verbal prods such as 'You must continue' when they said they wanted to stop. This makes the study easily replicable.

Application to real life-The study can be applied to real life as it shows how under pressure people will obey an authority figure. The study has been used to explain why the Nazis were so obedient to Hitler even when it harmed innocent people. It can also explain why people are so obedient to their bosses at work even when it might cause harm to others such as firing colleagues.

Ecological validity-Some psychologists have suggested that Milgram's study lacks ecological validity or mundane realism as it involved an artificial situation. People are not usually asked to give electric shocks to another person for wrong answers on a word pair task. However, Milgram argued that the study does reflect how people behave in the real world as people do recognise and follow the orders of authority figures.

Experimental validity-The study has experimental validity as the participants believed the shocks were real. The fact that participants showed signs of distress such as nervous laughter shows that their belief in the experimental situation was genuine. In fact, Milgram took great care to make sure his study had experimental validity. He rigged a draw with the participant and Mr. Wallace so that participants thought they had randomly been allocated the role of teacher. He also gave a sample 45V shock so that participants believed the shocks they were giving were real.

Ethics-One of the main criticisms of Milgram's study was the effects it had on participants. Participants did not give informed consent and were deceived. They were told that the aim of the study was to investigate the effects of punishment on learning when it was actually about obedience. They also thought they were giving real electric shocks when they were fake. Furthermore, participants were not protected from psychological harm as many experienced distress and may have felt bad about themselves after the experiment for being so obedient. They were also given verbal prods to continue throughout the experiment. However, Milgram did give participants the right to withdraw at the beginning of the experiment. He also thoroughly debriefed his participants and they were followed up a year later by psychiatrists. 84% of participants said they were glad or very glad to have taken part in the experiment.

## Method 2: Field experiments

Field experiments are carried out in participants' natural environment. An independent variable is manipulated and a dependent variable is measured. Field experiments often involve a clear procedure and researchers try to control extraneous variables as much as possible so that the study can be tested for reliability.

## Evaluation:

Field experiments have greater ecological validity than laboratory experiments as they take place in participants' natural environment. They also have carefully controlled and planned procedures so the study can be repeated. This means that they can be as reliable as laboratory experiments. However, as field experiments take place in the participants' natural environment, not all the extraneous variables can be controlled and the findings might not be reliable despite the researchers' efforts. Field experiments may lack validity as the independent and dependent variables are carefully operationalised.

**Yarmey (2004)** carried out field experiment to investigate eyewitness memory using photo identification. The study had a number of different independent variables.

Aims: 1) To investigate eyewitness testimony in the field 2) To see how good participants would be at identifying a woman they had spoken to for approximately 15 seconds in a photo line-up 3) To see if a disguise of a baseball cap and dark sunglasses would affect eyewitnesses' recall 4) To see whether being told you are going to be a witness to an incident affects recall 5) To see if a time gap before identification affects recall.

Procedure: 590 participants (men and women) were approached by a woman (the target) in public places and asked for directions or for help finding a piece of lost jewellery. They spoke to her for approximately 15 seconds. The target was seen originally either with or without a baseball cap and dark sunglasses. Witnesses were either prepared or not prepared at the time of the encounter for a subsequent memory test. After 2 minutes, a female researcher approached the participants and asked them to take part in the study immediately or 4 hours later. Half of the witnesses were given retrieval instructions prior to the memory tests. The first memory test involved a questionnaire about the physical characteristics and clothing of target and the second memory test asked participants to identify the target from a set of six photographs. Half the witnesses were shown a set of photos with the target amongst them (target present condition) and the other half were shown a set of photos without a photo of the target (target absent condition). A separate group of 379 introductory psychology students were asked to predict how well the eyewitnesses would be able to recall the target and identify her from a set of photographs.

Results: Witness preparation helped participants recall the clothing of the target but did not help them recall physical characteristics. Witness preparation, target disguise, whether they had to recall immediately or after 4 hours, gender of the witnesses, and retrieval instructions had no significant effects on identification of the target woman.When the target was in the photo line-up, correct identification occurred 49% of the time, when she was not present 62% correctly said the target was not there. In contrast, students given the written scenario thought the target would be less likely to be identified correctly if the target was absent from the photo-line-up.

Conclusion: As witnesses only make a correct identification 50% of the time when the target is present, jurors should question the reliability of eyewitness accounts.

**Evaluation:**

Generalisability -The range of ages of the participants and the large sample size makes the study generalisable. However, the witness's recall focused on a situation where the participants met and spoke to the target, which is not the case for all eyewitness incidents. Therefore the findings can only be applied to similar situations.

Reliablity- The control over the conditions means that the study is replicable and reliable. All participants were approached by a target asking for directions or help finding a piece of jewellery in a public place. Timings were controlled carefully, for example, a female researcher approached the participants 2 minutes after the encounter with the target asking them to take part in the study. However, there might have been some situational variables that could have affected results such as how busy the participant was, which makes the study harder to replicate.

Application to real life-The study suggests that we should be careful about witness testimony as the participants were only able to identify the target about 49% of the time when she was present in the photo line-up. When the target was not in the photo line-up, participants wrongly identified someone else as being the target 38% of the time. If real witnesses wrongly identify a person in a photo line-up, it could lead to innocent people being convicted of a crime.

Validity- The study was carried out in a natural environment of a public place and the target just approached participants so the study has ecological validity to a certain extent. However, the participants may have lacked the emotional involvement of real witnesses to a crime incident and so their memory may not have been as good. There were no real consequences for the participants to recall the target correctly whereas real life witnesses are aware that their testimony might put an innocent person in jail.

Evidence-Haber and Haber's (2001) meta-analysis supports Yarmey's study. They analysed 48 studies on eyewitness identification in a line up where the person to be identified (the target was present) They found that in 51% of the cases the target was correctly identified by the witness, which is similar to Yarmey's findings.

**Method 3: Natural Experiments**

Natural experiments are carried out in real-life settings. The independent variable occurs naturally but a dependent variable is still measured. It is difficult to establish cause and effect due to lack of control over the independent variable.

**Evaluation:**

Natural experiments are not reliable as the extraneous variables cannot be controlled due to the natural environment. However, natural experiments have good ecological validity as the participants are in a real-life setting.

**Charlton et al. (2000)**

Aim: To investigate the effects of television on children's behaviour.

Procedure: They video-recorded and observed children's behaviour in the playground of two schools before TV was introduced to the island of St. Helena and 5 years after the introduction of TV. Behaviour was categorised as either prosocial (positive behaviour such as sharing, displaying affection) or anti-social (negative behaviour such as kicking, verbal abuse) and tallied. They used a number of observers to establish inter-rater reliability. Only behaviours that were agreed upon were included in the results. They then compared the children's behaviour before and after the introduction of TV.

Results: There was no increase in aggressive behaviour after the introduction of TV. In fact, the children showed more prosocial behaviour after the introduction of TV.

Conclusion: TV does not lead to children becoming more aggressive.

**Evaluation:**

Generalisability-St. Helena is a remote island in the Atlantic ocean with a strong sense of community, where children are closely supervised. Therefore, it is difficult to generalise the results other cultures.

Reliability-The study used a number of observers to ensure inter-rater reliability. However, the study would be difficult to repeat as the children were in their natural environment and it was a unique situation.

Application to real life- The study suggests that TV does not lead to more aggressive behaviour so we should not be overly worried about children watching too much TV.

Validity- The study has ecological validity as the children were observed in their natural environment-a playground at a school.

Ethics-The researchers gained permission from the schools and parents before observing the children's behaviour.

**Method 4: Questionnaires**

Questionnaires involve written questions to find out about people's views and opinions. They are able to collect data from lots of people as everyone is asked the same questions and can answer them in their own time. Questionnaires can be sent by post, filled in on the internet, given face-to-face or left in a public place for people to pick up. The questions can either be closed or open. Closed questions may involve a Likert type scale or yes/no questions. Open questions ask people explain what they think about a certain topic in their own words. If closed questions are used then quantitative data can be obtained. If open questions are used then qualitative data can be obtained.

**Evaluation:**

Questionnaires allow data to be gathered from large samples without too much cost. If closed questions are used, the quantitative data can be statistically analysed. It is also easy to compare the data from closed questionnaires as everyone answers the same questions. Questionnaires with closed questions can be easy to replicate. Questionnaires with open questions can collect rich, qualitative data. However, a problem with questionnaires is that people may give socially desirable answers because they want the researchers to think well of them. Participants may also misunderstand the questions and interpret the questions differently. Questions asked beforehand could affect later answers. Questionnaires with closed questions can limit participants' responses, which affects validity. Questionnaires with open questions are open to interpretation.

**Funk et al. (2004)**

Aim: To see if there is children who are exposed to real life and media violence are less empathic and more aggressive.

Procedure: The sample consisted of 150 children from religious private primary schools and one public daycare centre in a MidWestern city of the USA. The children were asked to complete four questionnaires in different orders to avoid order effects. One of the questionnaires asked about the children's family background and about their media use and preferences. This included questions about the number of hours they spent playing computer games, watching television, watching films on DVD or at the cinema and using the internet. Children chose from six time range categories: no time; 1–2 h; 3–6 h; 7–10 h; 11–14 h; more than 15 h. The children had to categorise the type of television programmes and films they watched into categories such as cartoons, sport, fighting and destruction. A second questionnaire asked about their exposure to real life violence in different settings. This was a 34-item questionnaire including such statements as "I have seen someone carry a gun," and "I have been attacked with a knife." The children were asked to rate the items on a scale (0=Never, 1=Sometimes, 2=A lot) and Impact (0=Not at all upsetting, 1=Somewhat upsetting, 2=Very upsetting). A total score was calculated for frequency of exposure. A third questionnaire measured the children's attitudes to violence. Children were asked to read statement such as 'Parents should tell their kids to fight if they have to,' and 'People with guns or knives are cool' and rate the items on a scale (1=No, 2=Maybe, 3=Probably, 4=Yes). The fourth questionnaire measured children's empathy and included statements such as 'When I see a kid who is upset it really bothers me,' and 'If two kids are fighting, someone should stop it.' The children had to rate these statements on a scale as well (1=No, 2=Maybe, 3=Probably, 4=Yes).

Results: Exposure to video game and film violence was associated with lower empathy and stronger pro-violence attitudes. The study did not find a strong relationship between exposure to real-life violence and desensitisation to violence but this may be because the children in the sample had modest exposure to real-life violence. No relationship was found between television violence and aggression but this may be because only 5% of television choices fell within the one category with violence. The boys reported only watching television for an average of 5.6 hours and girls reported only watching television for 2.9 hours, which is much less than reported averages.

Conclusion: Children's exposure to violent computer games and violent films should be limited.

**Evaluation:**

Generalisability- The majority of the children were attending religious private schools and so the sample was better educated and had higher socioeconomic status than the general population. The mothers of the children had a higher level of education than average and this may have made them monitor their children's television viewing more carefully. Therefore, the sample is not representative of the wider population.

Reliability-The study used structured questionnaires with scales and categories. Such questionnaires are easy to replicate and so the study is reliable.

Application to real life-The study suggests that we should be particularly careful about exposing children to computer game violence as it can lead to pro-violence attitudes and lower empathy.

Validity-The structured questionnaires may have limited the children's responses. For example, the children were asked to categorise the television programmes they watched into categories such as cartoons, sport, fighting and destruction. Some of the children may have simply categorised the programmes they watched as cartoons even when they were cartoons including lots of fighting and destruction. Furthermore, the children may not have accurately reported their own media use. They may have under-estimated the amount of time they watched television and they may have been so desensitised to television violence that they did not categorise their programmes as being violent.

Ethics-The study involved children so parental consent would need to have been obtained.

## Method 5: Observations

There are structured laboratory observations and naturalistic observations. Structured laboratory observations involve careful controls and a set-up situation that can be repeated. There is often more than one observer and observations tend to be carried out through a one-way mirror to avoid the researchers' presence affecting participants' behaviour. Naturalistic observations involve observing participants in their natural environment. For example, observing children's behaviour in a playground.

Observations can be overt or covert. Covert observations involve observing a person or group of people without their knowledge. Overt observations involve observing a person or group of people with their knowledge.

Observations can also be participant or non-participant. A participant observation involves the researcher interacting with the person or group of people that they are observing. A non-participant observation involves the researcher observing behaviour from a distance without having any influence or getting involved.

An observation can be carried out by counting the frequency of certain behaviours during a fixed period of time.
Event sampling-when you record every time an event such as a kick occurs
Time sampling-when you record what is happening every set amount of time e.g. every 5 minutes.
Point sampling- The behaviour of just one individual in the group at a time is recorded.
Inter-observer reliability-Comparing the ratings of a number of observers as an individual observer may be biased.This would increase the reliability of the data collected if all the observers agree.

## Evaluation:

Researchers may find it difficult to record all the behaviours shown, although event sampling, time sampling and point sampling can help. Video recordings can be used to record participants' behaviour and played back later so that all actions can be noted. It may also be difficult to analyse or interpret all the data collected. Observers often have to be specially trained so that they can record behaviours quickly and to avoid bias.

Participant observations allow researchers to experience the same environment as their participants. However, the researcher's involvement can affect the behaviour of participants. In contrast, non-participant observations allow researchers to observe participants' behaviour more objectively as they are not directly involved in the action. However, if participants are aware they are being observed, they may still change their behaviour.

Covert observations enable researchers to observe participants behave naturally as the participants do not know they are being observed. However, there are ethical issues with observing participants without their consent. They do not have the right to withdraw, they have not given informed consent and there also issues of confidentiality especially if their behaviour has been video-recorded. The British Psychological Society advises that it is only suitable to conduct a covert observation in a place where people might reasonably be expected to be observed by other people such as a shopping centre or other public place. Overt observations do not have as many ethical issues as covert observations. However, when participants know they are being observed they may change their behaviour so that it appears socially desirable. Therefore, overt observations can be less valid.

**Ainsworth & Bell (1978)** carried out a controlled observation called 'The strange situation' to measure attachment type.

Aim: To measure attachment type by observing how 12- to 18-month-old children respond to their parents after being left with a stranger.

Procedure: The observation involved recording children's behaviour through a one-way mirror during eight 3 minute episodes. Each parent-child pair were observed at different times. Episode 1 involved the parent and child being introduced to the experimental room. During episode 2, the parent and child were left alone and the parent was told to let the child explore the room. Episode 3 involved a stranger entering the room and talking to the parent for a short time whilst approaching the child. The parent was then asked to leave quietly. During episode 4, the child was left alone with the stranger who tried to interact with them. Episode 5 involved the parent coming back and trying to comfort their child, before leaving again. During episode 6, the child was left alone in the room completely. The stranger then came back into the room in Episode 7 and tried to approach the child. The final part of the observation, episode 8, involved the parent entering the room, greeting their child and picking them up. The stranger then left quietly.

Observers behind a one-way mirror rated the child's separation anxiety (how distressed the child was at being left by their parent). Children with secure attachments will become distressed at being left alone by a stranger but they will not be inconsolable. The observers also looked at the child's willingness to explore and proximity to their parent. A securely attached child will feel confident to move further away from their parent and explore. The third aspect of behaviour that was observed was stranger anxiety. Children who are more securely attached show greater stranger anxiety. The fourth type of behaviour observed was how the children behaved on being reunited with their parent. Securely attached children show happiness and relief at being reunited with their parent whereas insecurely attached children will ignore or show anger on reunion with their parent.

Results: 70% of the children had a Secure Attachment (type B). They did show distress at being parted from their parent but they were easily consoled when their parent returned. 15% of the children had an insecure/avoidant attachment (type A). They showed indifference to their parent when they left, and did not show any stranger anxiety. They also avoided contact with their parent when they were reunited. The parent tended to ignore their child when they were playing. 15% of the children had an insecure/resistant attachment (type C). These children became very distressed when their parent left and were inconsolable. When they were reunited with their parents they showed their anger by seeking comfort from their parents and then rejecting it. The parent tended to be over-sensitive or angry and rejecting.

Conclusions: Secure attachments (type B) are the most common.

**Evaluation:**

Generalisability-This study was conducted in the USA and so the findings may not be generalisable to other cultures. However, the strange situation has been used to assess attachment type in other cultures and secure attachments (type B) have been found to be the most common.

Reliability- The observation had a standardised procedure, which makes it easy to repeat and so the study is reliable. Waters (1978) found 90% reliability when infants were tested and retested using the strange situation between the ages of 12 and 18 months.

Application to real life-Parents with insecurely attached children can be given training to help them be more sensitive to their children.

Validity- The study lacks ecological validity because it was an artificial situation. The children's behaviour may have been more affected by how well they adjusted to the unfamiliar setting rather than their parent leaving.  Children who are used to being left in daycare are less likely to be affected by their parents leaving the room so the strange situation may be measuring how familiar the children are with being left rather than attachment type. This calls into question the validity of the strange situation for measuring attachment. Children's temperament rather than attachment type may also affect their behaviour during the observation. Children who are born with a more irritable temperament may be inconsolable after being left by their parent but this may not be because they are insecurely attached. However, Sroufe et al. (1999) found that children who had been assessed as securely attached using the Strange Situation at 12-months-old, were more popular, more empathic and had greater self-confidence and leadership skills in adolescence. This study suggests the strange situation is a valid way of measuring attachment type as it can predict future behaviour. One problem with this study is that it does not take into account children who have atypical attachments. It is now recognised

229

that some children have disorganised attachments (type D), which are related to abusive parenting.

Ethics-The study did not protect the children from psychological harm as many of the children became very distressed. However, it could be argued, that the children were only left for short periods of time as might happen in everyday life.

## Method 6: Interviews

An interview involves the researcher asking the respondent questions. It may form the basis of a case study or as a follow-up to other research methods. Structured interviews produce quantitative data. All participants are asked the same questions in the same order. They are very similar to questionnaire except questions are read out. An unstructured interview involves an informal or in-depth conversation. Little is planned in advance (perhaps the first couple of questions) and they allows the interviewee to explain answers and introduce new issues. Unstructured interviews obtains rich, qualitative data. A semi-structured interview involves some prepared questions but also some opportunities for interviewees to expand on answers

## Evaluation:

Unstructured interviews tend to be valid because they allow the interviewer to explore issues that the interviewee wishes to discuss. However, interpretation of participants' responses can be subjective and participants may give socially desirable answers. Certain characteristics about the interviewer such as their dress or manner can also affect replies. Structured interviews are more replicable, and therefore, more reliable.

## Goldstein (1988) Gender differences in the course of schizophrenia

Goldstein's study (1988) used interviews to look at differences in how males and females experience schizophrenia. She used trained interviewers to gather data about the symptoms of the patients and to find out about past experiences, age, gender, ethnicity, class, marital status, level of education and level of social functioning.

Aim: To see if there are gender differences in the course of schizophrenia i.e. if women with have fewer re-hospitalisations and shorter hospital stays than men.

Procedure: Goldstein used 90 patients to investigate gender differences in the course of schizophrenia. She used trained interviewers to gather data about the symptoms of the patients. The interviewers also asked the patients how well they were functioning in everyday life by considering marital status, occupational status, peer relationships, isolation and interests. The course and severity of the illness was measured by looking at the number of times the patients had been in hospital and how long the hospital admissions had been over a 10 year period.

Results: Women had a significantly lower number of re-hospitalisations than men and had shorter stays in hospital over the 10 year period. Premorbid functioning (what a person is like cognitively, socially and emotionally at or before the onset of the disease in terms of isolation, peer relationships and interests) affected number of re-hospitalisations. Social functioning, such as marital and occupational status, affected the lengths of stays in hospital.

Conclusion: Men tend have a worse experience of schizophrenia than women. This may be due to their poorer premorbid functioning (how well someone functions before diagnosis).

## Evaluation:

Generalisability- All the schizophrenics in the study returned to their families after hospitalisation so the findings may not generalise to schizophrenics who don't return to their families.

Reliability-The study collected data on number of hospital stays and lengths of stays from the New York State Department of Health. This part of the study is easy to replicate. Angermeyer et al. (1987) replicated the study and found the same results, so it is reliable.

Application to real life-The study found that men have a more severe course of schizophrenia than women, which suggests that men may need greater support.

Validity-This longitudinal study looked at the schizophrenics' hospitalisations and lengths of stays over a long period of time, which would have given a good indication of the severity of their schizophrenia. The study did not suffer from erosion of the sample so it avoided bias. Therefore, the study has validity. The interviews gathered rich, detailed data about the schizophrenics' premorbid history and social functioning, which also makes the study more valid. However, the way the interviewers asked questions might have affected the symptoms reported and participants may have been unwilling to discuss all their symptoms.

Ethics-The participants were schizophrenics who are vulnerable, so Goldstein would have needed to make sure that no distress was caused by their interviews and diagnoses.

## Method 7: Content Analysis

A content analysis involves changing qualitative data into quantitative data. This often means tallying how many times certain themes occur within a source such as newspaper article, magazine article, journal article, radio programme or television programme. The source may be coded or broken down into manageable categories, for example, by words, phrases, sentences or themes. The researcher then analyses the presence and meaning of these categories and draws conclusions. For example, a researcher might tally how often negative or positive comments about daycare occur within two newspaper articles and draw conclusions about how daycare is portrayed in the media.

## Evaluation:

As the data comes from secondary sources such as newspaper articles or television programmes, it does not change. Therefore, other researchers can check whether any conclusions are correct or not. The quantitative tallying of themes allows the data to be statistically analysed. There unlikely to be any ethical issues with a content analysis, as it only involves analysing existing sources. However, the categorising and tallying of themes in a content analysis can be subjective.

## Dietz (1998)

Aim: To examine the portrayal of women and the use of violent themes in a sample of 33 popular Nintendo and Sega Genesis computer games.

Procedure: The seventeen most popular Nintendo computer games and the sixteen most popular Sega Genesis games were selected for the content analysis. Dietz used the following categories to examine the portrayal of women in the games: no female characters at all, female characters portrayed as sex objects or prizes (based upon physical appearance such as wearing revealing clothing or body shape, or characterizations including women leaving with the male winner), females as the victim (based upon women who had been kidnapped or assaulted as part of the plot), females as the hero (based upon whether or not there were female characters who were or could be the action character and winner of the game ) and females in feminine roles (based upon appearance, such as wearing pink, long dresses and characterisation, such as playing supportive roles to men). A coding sheet was used for each game to record how often each category occurred along with detailed descriptions of the roles played by the female characters and their physical appearance. Each computer game was also analysed for the use of violence using a coding sheet. The categories were: no violence or aggression; socially acceptable aggression, defined as the use of aggression in controlled environments and in situations in which society expects aggression (for example, sports games); violence directed at women; and violence directed at others. Detailed descriptions about the object of the game and the use of violence were recorded.

Results: There were no female characters in 41% of the games with characters. 15% of the games portrayed women as heroes or action characters. 21% of the games portrayed women as the victim.  28% of the games portrayed women as sex objects and 21% depicted violence directed at women. Nearly 80% of the games included aggression or violence as part of the strategy or object.

Conclusion: Computer games portray women in a negative and gender-stereotyped way. This can impact on young people's view of men and women's roles within society. Girls may feel that their appearance is their most important attribute and that they need protection. Boys may feel that their role is to protect or possess women through the use of violence.

## Evaluation:

Generalisability-Dietz chose thirty-three of the most popular computer games for the content analysis so that they were representative of what most young people like to play.

Reliability-The counting of how often certain categories occurred within the computer games makes the study easy to replicate and reliable.

Application to real life-The study suggests that children should not be over-exposed to violent and gender-stereotyped role models in computer games.

Validity-Boys play computer games more frequently and for longer periods of time than girls so the portrayal of more males as heroes in the most popular computer games may reflect boys' preferences. Computer games aimed at girls may have a different emphasis and portray women in a more positive light. There may have been subjective interpretation of the content of the computer games and categorisation, which makes the study less valid.

Ethics-You don't need to comment on ethical issues for this study as there are none. The content analysis involved analysing existing computer games.

## Method 8: Case Studies

A case study is an in-depth study of one person or one group of people. A number of different techniques are used to gather data. For example, the researcher may observe, interview and carry out a number of experiments on the same person. Triangulation is used to pool data together from the different types of research method and to draw conclusions.

## Evaluation:

Case studies are not generalisable as they are carried out on only one person or one group of people who are often unique and not representative of the wider population. It is also difficult to replicate case studies because they involve unique individuals and the interpretation of the observations and interviews is subject to bias. Therefore it is hard to establish reliability in case studies. However, triangulation is used to draw conclusions about the same concept so this improves the reliability of the findings. An advantage of case studies is that they gather rich, detailed information about the individuals using a number of different techniques, so this increases their validity. There can be ethical issues with case studies. Often they involve studying unique individuals who are more vulnerable than normal. Therefore, researchers have to be careful to protect them from psychological distress.

## Freud (1909) Little Hans

Aim: To report the findings of how a young boy overcame his phobia of horses.

Procedure: Freud gave advice to Little Hans' father based on the father's reports of the boy's behaviour. It is thought that Freud only met the boy once.
When Little Hans was 3-years-old, he developed an active interest in his 'widdler' (penis), and also those of other people. When Little Hans was 5-years-old, he developed a phobia of horses after seeing a horse die in the street. Little Hans' father knew about Freud's theories and wrote to him asking him for advice. The father gave Freud detailed information about the conversations he had had with Little Hans. Freud interpreted Little Hans phobia as being related to his worries about losing his mother and his mother's

threat that she would cut off his penis if he didn't stop playing with it. Freud also thought that Little Hans who enjoyed getting into bed with his mother, had a repressed desire for her. Freud then met Little Hans and asked him about what he didn't like about horses. Little Hans' comments led Freud to believe that Hans' phobia of horses related to the Oedipus complex. Little Hans' fantasy about being married to his mother and having his own children was also interpreted as being related to the Oedipus complex. In another fantasy, Little Hans described how a plumber came and gave him a bigger penis.

Conclusion: Freud believed that Little Hans' behaviour provided support for the Oedipus complex. He believed that Little Hans desired his mother and this made him fear his father. Little Hans' phobia of horses was symbolic of his fear of his father.

**Evaluation:**

Generalisability-This was a unique case study of one boy who is not representative of the wider population. It is also difficult to generalise the findings to boys growing up in single-parent families. Furthermore, it is difficult to apply the findings to girls who don't have a penis (although Freud said they develop penis envy).

Reliability-The study is hard to replicate as it was a unique situation and involved subjective interpretation of the conversations between Little Hans and his father.

Application to real life-The study involved getting Little Hans to talk as much possible about his fears to his father. Psychoanalysis has developed from the idea of getting people to talk freely about their problems to uncover unconscious conflicts.

Validity-Freud was able to gather lots of in-depth qualitative data from Little Hans' father who reported on the many conversations he had with Little Hans. This makes the study more valid. However, Little Hans' father was a supporter of Freud's theories and may have interpreted Little Hans' behaviour in a biased way. It is thought Freud only met Little Hans once and his interpretation of Little Hans' behaviour is subjective. There are other explanations for Little Hans' behaviour other than the Oedipus complex. He saw a horse die in the street and so he may have associated his fear of the situation with all horses (classical conditioning).

Ethics-Little Hans may have been embarrassed by the case study when he was older so he may not have been protected from psychological distress.

**Method 9: Correlational Techniques**

Correlational studies look for a relationship between two variables. For example, it may look for a relationship between number of hours of violent TV watched and levels of aggression. An example of a positive correlation is: the more hours of violent TV watched, the more aggressive people become. An example of a negative correlation is: the more hours of violent computer games played, the less helpful people are.
Adoption and twin studies are types of correlational study. For example, a twin study might see how strong the relationship is between one twin's IQ and the other twin's IQ.

**Evaluation:**

studies can demonstrate a relationship between two variables, which was not noticed before. They can also be used to look for relationships between variables that cannot be investigated by other means. For example, researchers can look to see whether there is a relationship between parents having low expectations of their children and the children's later academic performance. Manipulating such variables would be unethical. However, correlational studies cannot establish cause and effect relationships. A third factor may affect both variables under investigation. For example, although a correlational study might show a relationship between the number of hours of violent TV watched and levels of aggression, we cannot be certain that the violent TV programmes led to the aggression. It may be that children who watch violent TV programmes are naturally more aggressive and so seek such programmes out.

**Sheehan (1983)**

This study looked at 226 children aged 5- to 10-years-old to see whether there were correlations between watching violence on TV, the amount of TV the children watched and aggressive behaviour. They measured the children's for sex-typed behaviour, aggressive fantasies, identification with TV characters and peer-rated aggression. They found that there was a relationship between watching violence on TV, intensity of TV viewing and aggressive behaviour. The correlation was stronger for boys than girls.

**Evaluation:**

Generalisability- This study was part of a cross cultural investigation of TV viewing and its effects in six different countries, which makes the study more generalisable.

Reliability-The study may be difficult to replicate as some of the measures of sex-typed behaviour and peer-rated aggression are subjective.

Application to real life-The study suggests that children should not spend too much time watching violent TV as it can lead to later aggression.

Validity-The study was correlational so cannot establish a cause and effect relationship between watching violent TV and aggressive behaviour. Children who are naturally more aggressive may choose to watch violent TV or they may come from a violent family which leads them to watch more violent TV.

Ethics-The study involved children so consent needed to be gained from the children and parents. Getting a child's peers to rate their aggression may have caused psychological harm.

**You need to be able to define quantitative and qualitative and give general strengths and weaknesses of both (including issues of reliability and validity.)**

Quantitative data is numerical data. Quantitative research e.g. laboratory experiments tend to use large samples of people or animals so that results can be generalised to the wider population. Statistical tests can be done on quantitative data to see how far the results are likely to be due to chance. If a quantitative research is repeated, often the same data will be found. This shows that quantitative data is reliable. However, the careful operationalising of variables in quantitative research means that real life events and interactions are not being measured (lack of validity).

Qualitative data is descriptive and often takes into account people's views and opinions. It can be gathered in natural situations so it is valid. However, qualitative data is harder to replicate and can lack reliability.

**You need to know which research methods produce quantitative data and to be able to describe them.**

Experiments, questionnaires with closed questions and structured interviews are good sources of quantitative data.
Questionnaires with closed questions consist of a list of pre-set questions that a participant answers usually involving yes/no or applying a scale.
Experiments are controlled studies often carries out in controlled conditions. An IV is manipulated and then a DV measured as a result. Objectivity is aimed for, hence the controls.
Structured interviews have set questions and there is an interviewer who asks questions.

**You need to know which research methods produce qualitative data.**

Case studies, unstructured interviews, clinical interviews and questionnaires with open questions produce qualitative data.
Case studies aim for an in-depth study of one individual or group. They gather information from many sources using more than one means of gathering data.
Unstructured interviews may begin with an aim and an idea of what questions are to be answered. They do not have set questions. The interviewer can explore areas that come up.
Clinical interviews involve an analyst listening to a client and using techniques such as free association and dream analysis. The aim is to uncover unconscious thoughts.
Questionnaires with open questions have preset questions but participants are able to express their views and opinions freely. There is no scale.

**You need to be able to compare research methods.**

If you are asked to compare research methods, you should consider the following:

Does the research method collect quantitative or qualitative data? If the research method collects quantitative data then it can be statistically analysed and is more objective. If the research method collects qualitative data it is usually more detailed and richer. However, the data is likely to be subjective.

Does the research method use primary or secondary data?

Does the research method give reliable data? Are studies using this research method easy to repeat?

Does the research method give valid data? Do studies using this research method collect rich, detailed in-depth data? Are studies using this research method carried out in participants' natural environment?

Does the research method require more than one researcher to carry out the study? For example, observations require more than one observer to establish inter-observer reliability.

How do the research methods gather data? Is any counting involved? Is any description involved?

**Exam tip:** When comparing, do not just describe each research method in turn. Instead, describe how the research methods are similar or different.

**Student answer to exemplar exam question in Issues and Debates:**

**A researcher wants to investigate how students feel about the way universities recruit applicants. The researcher decided to conduct a survey.**

**a) Explain how the researcher might design and carry out the survey.** (6 marks)

Student answer:

The researcher could carry out a structured questionnaire with closed questions and a Likert scale to find out about students' opinions on the application procedure for university. Once the researcher has come up with their questions, they could test their questions on a few participants to see whether they make sense in a pilot study. They can then use any feedback from participants to adjust their questions. The questionnaire could then be set up on a website such as Survey Monkey so that participants can complete it in online in their own time. The researcher could then approach schools and ask them whether they would pass on the website address for their online questionnaire to students applying for university. The schools could be told that they will be given a copy of the research findings, which they may find useful. However, participants would need to know that their anonymity would be protected; otherwise they may be worried about being honest. Once a certain time period has elapsed such as 2 months the questionnaire could be closed.

**Commentary:**

This student has applied their understanding of questionnaires to the scenario well. However, they could have discussed how they decided on which questions to ask. It would have been necessary to conduct some preliminary research to decide what concerns students have about the university application process. There should also have been some discussion about sample size; a few hundred responses are required for the sample to be representative. Another point that could have been covered is how the data would be analysed. Quantitative data from a structured questionnaire using a Likert scale can be analysed statistically.

**b) The researcher recruits her sample by sending leaflets round to school sixth forms asking students to take part. Explain the strengths and weaknesses of recruiting a sample in this way.** (4 marks)

Student answer:

The sample was a volunteer sample. Participants who have volunteered for a study are less likely to drop out as they have agreed to take part in the study. However, they are also unlikely to be representative of the wider population as only certain people will volunteer to take part. Volunteers are often more helpful than the wider population and this can lead to demand characteristics.

**Commentary:**

This student could have expanded their point about why volunteers are unrepresentative of the wider population. Volunteers often have more time, are more willing to please and are more helpful than the wider population. An advantage of volunteer samples is that it can be quick and cheap to recruit volunteers as the researchers do not have to be careful about how they select participants unlike a quota sample.

**Note:** In the Issues and Debates section of Unit 4, you may be given a scenario and asked to design a study using your knowledge of research methods. This is one example.

5824330R00134

Printed in Great Britain
by Amazon.co.uk, Ltd.,
Marston Gate.